Clarence Larkin

The Book of Daniel

THE BOOK OF DANIEL

REV. CLARENCE LARKIN

Author of the Great Book on

"DISPENSATIONAL TRUTH"

And Other Biblical Works

Published by the

REV. CLARENCE LARKIN ESTATE

P. O. Box 334

Glenside, Pa. 19038, U.S.A.

Printed in U.S.A.

THIS BOOK IS

DEDICATED

TO THE

LORD JESUS CHRIST

WHO BY HIS SPIRIT

ENABLED THE AUTHOR TO WRITE IT

FOR THE INFORMATION AND

EDIFICATION OF THE

REDEEMED

TABLE OF CONTENTS

Page

Introduction 1

The Prophetic Word 5

The Book of Daniel 10

EXPOSITION OF THE BOOK

First Division—Historical. Chapters 1 to 6.

Chapter 1. The Beginning of Gentile Dominion 19

Chapter 2. Nebuchadnezzar's Dream 28

Chapter 3. The Golden Image 56

Chapter 4. The Tree Dream 69

Chapter 5. The Fall of Babylon 78

Chapter 6. The Lions' Den 106

Second Division—Prophetical. Chapters 7 to 12.

Chapter 7. The Four Wild Beasts 117

Chapter 8. The Ram and the He-Goat 155

Chapter 9. The Seventy Weeks 169

Chapter 10. The Scripture of Truth—

Part I—The Relation of Supernatural Beings to the Earth. Chap. 10:1 to 11:1 219

Part II—The Pre-written History of the Kings of the North and South. Chap. 11:2-35 228

Part III—The "Time of the End." Chap. 11:36 to 12:13 246

CHARTS

Book of Daniel .... Facing Page 5

Prophetic Days of Scripture 98

Daniel and Revelation Compared .... Facing Page 117

Daniel's Seventieth Week .... Facing Page 169

The Seventy Weeks of Scripture 203

Introduction

This exposition of the book of Daniel is the closing and crowning work by Rev. Clarence Larkin, a servant of God, whose life was wholly devoted to the study, teaching, and preaching of God's precious word. During the more than forty years of his quiet, but blessed ministry as a pastor and teacher, he made a very faithful use of his time and opportunity to thoroughly study the whole counsel of God as embodied in the Scriptures, not only for his own heart, but in order to help others as fully as possible to know their Lord and Saviour.

Calling to his aid the best books on the exposition of the Bible by the ablest scholars and teachers of this and other days, and depending upon the Holy Spirit for needed illumination, the author obeyed the conviction that it was the will of God to pass on to the Church of Christ the results of the years of his enrichment in the knowledge of God and of His word. At the sacrifice of time, pleasure, strength, and financial profit, he gave himself to prepare, not only this book on "Daniel," but also a book on "Revelation," "Second Coming of Christ," "Rightly Dividing the Word," and "Dispensational Truth," without doubt the best book of Bible charts that is printed.

Suffering in body, yet strong in the power of the Holy Spirit, Rev. Larkin pressed on till this book of Daniel was completed, then His loving Saviour and Lord said "Come home and rest with Me."

Through this consecrated servant, the Lord has given to His Church a wealth of wisdom concerning

His redemptive counsels, in such form that every believer may be greatly aided in the study to show themselves approved unto God, workmen who need not be ashamed, rightly dividing the word of truth.

The writer of this note thanks God for the great blessing to his own life and ministry through his intimate acquaintance with Rev. Larkin, and with his teaching, and heartily commends this volume now dedicated to the Lord and to all of His blood-bought ones.

Our prayer is that every reader may be greatly blessed, like Daniel, in being given "understanding" of the counsels of God concerning the present and future evil times, and the glories of Christ which are yet to be manifest.

Yours in His Service,

W. W. RUGH,

Founder of the Bible Institute of Pennsylvania

The Book of Daniel

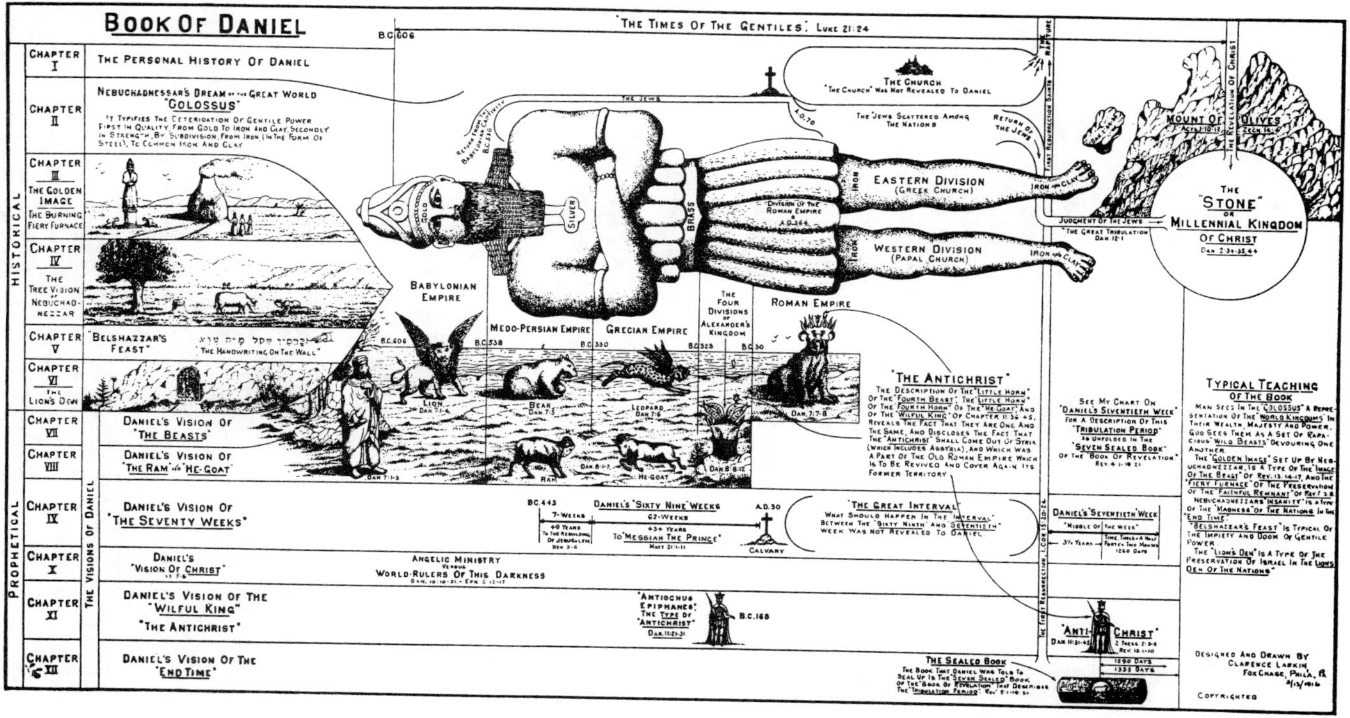
BOOK OF DANIEL
"THE TIMES OF THE GENTILES." LUKE 21:24
B.C. 606
HISTORICAL
CHAPTER I
THE PERSONAL HISTORY OF DANIEL
CHAPTER II
NEBUCHADNESSAR'S DREAM OF THE GREAT WORLD "COLOSSUS"
IT TYPIFIES THE DETERIORATION OF GENTILE POWER FIRST IN QUALITY, FROM GOLD TO IRON AND CLAY, SECONDLY IN STRENGTH, BY SUBDIVISION, FROM IRON, (IN THE FORM OF STEEL), TO COMMON IRON AND CLAY
CHAPTER III
THE GOLDEN IMAGE
THE BURNING FIERY FURNACE
CHAPTER IV
THE TREE VISION OF NEBUCHADNEZZAR
CHAPTER V
"BELSHAZZAR'S FEAST"
"THE HANDWRITING ON THE WALL"
CHAPTER VI
THE LION'S DEN
PROPHETICAL
THE VISIONS OF DANIEL
CHAPTER VII
DANIEL'S VISION OF "THE BEASTS"
CHAPTER VIII
DANIEL'S VISION OF "THE RAM" AND "HE-GOAT"
CHAPTER IX
DANIEL'S VISION OF "THE SEVENTY WEEKS"
CHAPTER X
DANIEL'S "VISION OF CHRIST"
CHAPTER XI
DANIEL'S VISION OF THE "WILFUL KING" "THE ANTICHRIST"
CHAPTER XII
DANIEL'S VISION OF THE "END TIME"
GOLD
SILVER
BRASS
IRON
IRON AND CLAY
RETURN FROM THE BABYLONIAN CAPTIVITY B.C. 536
THE JEWS
A.D. 70
DIVISION OF THE ROMAN EMPIRE A.D. 364
EASTERN DIVISION (GREEK CHURCH)
WESTERN DIVISION (PAPAL CHURCH)
THE CHURCH
"THE CHURCH" WAS NOT REVEALED TO DANIEL
THE JEWS SCATTERED AMONG THE NATIONS
RETURN OF THE JEWS
THE RAPTURE
FIRST RESURRECTION SAINTS
THE FIRST RESURRECTION, 1 COR 15:20-24
THE REVELATION OF CHRIST
MOUNT OF OLIVES
JUDGMENT OF THE JEWS
"THE GREAT TRIBULATION" DAN. 12:1
THE "STONE" OR MILLENNIAL KINGDOM OF CHRIST
DAN. 2:34-35, 44
BABYLONIAN EMPIRE
B.C. 606
MEDO-PERSIAN EMPIRE
B.C. 538
GRECIAN EMPIRE
B.C. 330
THE FOUR DIVISIONS OF ALEXANDER'S KINGDOM
B.C. 323
ROMAN EMPIRE
B.C. 30
LION
BEAR DAN. 7:5
LEOPARD DAN. 7:6
DAN. 7:7-8
RAM
DAN. 8:1-7
HE-GOAT
DAN. 8:8-12
DAN. 7:1-3
"THE ANTICHRIST"
THE DESCRIPTION OF THE "LITTLE HORN" OF THE "FOURTH BEAST", THE "LITTLE HORN" OF THE "FOURTH HORN" OF THE "HE-GOAT", AND OF THE "WILFUL KING" OF CHAPTER 11:36-45, REVEALS THE FACT THAT THEY ARE ONE AND THE SAME, AND DISCLOSES THE FACT THAT THE "ANTICHRIST" SHALL COME OUT OF SYRIA (WHICH INCLUDES ASSYRIA), AND WHICH WAS A PART OF THE OLD ROMAN EMPIRE WHICH IS TO BE REVIVED AND COVER AGAIN ITS FORMER TERRITORY
SEE MY CHART ON "DANIEL'S SEVENTIETH WEEK" FOR A DESCRIPTION OF THIS "TRIBULATION PERIOD" AS UNFOLDED IN THE "SEVEN SEALED BOOK" OF THE "BOOK OF REVELATION"
B.C. 445
DANIEL'S "SIXTY NINE" WEEKS
7-WEEKS
62-WEEKS
49 YEARS
434 YEARS
TO "MESSIAH THE PRINCE"
A.D. 30
CALVARY
"THE GREAT INTERVAL"
WHAT SHOULD HAPPEN IN THE "INTERVAL" BETWEEN THE "SIXTY NINTH" AND "SEVENTIETH" WEEK WAS NOT REVEALED TO DANIEL.
DANIEL'S "SEVENTIETH" WEEK
"MIDDLE OF THE WEEK"
3½ YEARS
1260 DAYS
ANGELIC MINISTRY VERSUS WORLD-RULERS OF THIS DARKNESS
"ANTIOCHUS EPIPHANES" THE TYPE OF "ANTICHRIST"
B.C. 168
"ANTI-CHRIST"
1290 DAYS
1335 DAYS
THE SEALED BOOK
THE BOOK THAT DANIEL WAS TOLD TO SEAL UP IS THE "SEVEN SEALED" BOOK OF THE "BOOK OF REVELATION" THAT DESCRIBES THE "TRIBULATION PERIOD".
TYPICAL TEACHING OF THE BOOK
MAN SEES IN THE "COLOSSUS" A REPRESENTATION OF THE "WORLD KINGDOMS" IN THEIR WEALTH, MAJESTY AND POWER. GOD SEES THEM AS A SET OF RAPACIOUS "WILD BEASTS" DEVOURING ONE ANOTHER.
THE "GOLDEN IMAGE" SET UP BY NEBUCHADNEZZAR, IS A TYPE OF THE "IMAGE OF THE BEAST" OF REV. 13:14-17, AND THE "FIERY FURNACE" OF THE PRESERVATION OF THE "FAITHFUL REMNANT" OF REV. 7:3-8.
NEBUCHADNEZZAR'S "INSANITY" IS A TYPE OF THE "MADNESS" OF THE NATIONS IN THE "END TIME".
"BELSHAZZAR'S FEAST" IS TYPICAL OF THE IMPIETY AND DOOM OF GENTILE POWER.
THE "LION'S DEN" IS A TYPE OF THE PRESERVATION OF ISRAEL IN THE LIONS DEN OF THE NATIONS.
DESIGNED AND DRAWN BY CLARENCE LARKIN, FOX CHASE, PHILA, PA.
COPYRIGHTED

I

The Prophetic Word

The Bible is unlike all other religious books in that it bases its "**Authenticity,**" "**Authority,**" and "**Inspiration**" on **PROPHECY.** All other religious books contain no predictions as to the future. If its authors had attempted to foretell future events, their unfulfilment would long ago have discredited their writings. Prophecy is—

HISTORY WRITTEN IN ADVANCE,

and proves the foreknowledge of God. This the Prophet Daniel opened to the heathen king, Nebuchadnezzar, in his interpretation of the king's "Dream"—

> "The Great God hath made known to the king what shall come to pass **HEREAFTER**: and the 'Dream' is **certain,** and the interpretation thereof **SURE.**" Dan. 2:45.

Prophecy is twofold, "**descriptive**" and "**predictive.**" The prophets were both "**forth-tellers**" and "**fore-tellers.**" They had both "**insight**" and "**foresight.**" Their prophetic utterances were not the deductions of reason, but were imparted to them by the Holy Spirit—

> "For the '**Prophecy**' came not in old time by the '**will of man**': but Holy Men of God spake as they were **MOVED BY THE HOLY GHOST.**" 2 Pet. 1:21.

The importance of the study of the "Prophetic Scriptures" is seen when we recall that two-thirds of the Scriptures are prophetic, either in type, symbol, or direct statement, and that more than one-half of them are as yet unfulfilled; and as those that have been fulfilled were **literally fulfilled,** as the promises in reference to the "First Coming" of Christ, so those as yet unfulfilled, will be as literally fulfilled. If then we would know the **"MIND OF GOD"** as to the future we must study the "Prophetic Scriptures," or remain in that class that the Apostle Peter speaks of as being—**"WILLINGLY IGNORANT,"** so as to claim **"ignorance"** as an excuse for conduct. 2 Pet. 3:3-8. We are living in a **"Dark World,"** and we need the **"SURE WORD OF PROPHECY"** to **LIGHT** us over the stormy "Sea of Time." 2 Pet. 1:19. When men see that God **has a "Plan and Purpose in the Ages"** they will take heart and not be discouraged by the things that are taking place on the earth in these days.

But we must not forget that—"No prophecy of the Scriptures is of any **private interpretation."** 2 Pet. 1:20. That is, no prophecy is to be interpreted by itself, but in harmony with the whole body of prediction on any given subject. It is not to be interpreted to suit the theory of any **"cult."** The **"Grasshopper Method"** of interpretation or exegesis must be avoided. There is no form of evil doctrine or practice that may not claim apparent Scriptural sanction and support from **isolated passages** taken out of their context, but no erroneous doctrine can ever find support in the Word of God when the whole united testimony of the Scriptures is weighed against it.

The prophecies are not to be **"allegorized"** or **"spiritualized."** God expounds prophecy by **literally fulfilling it in every detail.** For illustration, when God said to Abraham—

> "Know of a **surety** that thy seed shall be a stranger in a land that is not theirs, and shall **serve them**: and they shall **afflict them FOUR HUNDRED YEARS**: and also that nation, whom they shall serve will I **JUDGE** (by Plagues): and afterward shall they come out with **great substance,"** (see Ex. 12:35-36) Gen. 15:13-14,

did He mean that Abraham's seed should enter into some spiritual experience which would cause great mental disquietude and heart searching, out of which they would emerge richer in experience and spirituality, or did He mean exactly what the words literally imply? Let the history of their experience in Egypt, as recorded in the first twelve chapters of Exodus, answer. There was nothing allegorical in the whips of the Egyptian Taskmasters, nor spiritual in the double tale of bricks. The Divine law of prophetical interpretation is, that the prophecy will be **literally and in exact detail fulfilled.**

The requirements of a genuine prediction are five in number.

1. It must have been made known **PRIOR** to its fulfilment.

2. It must be beyond all **HUMAN FORESIGHT.**

3. It must give **DETAILS.**

4. **A SUFFICIENT TIME MUST ELAPSE BETWEEN ITS PUBLICATION AND FULFILMENT TO EXCLUDE THE PROPHET, OR ANY INTERESTED PARTY, FROM FULFILLING IT.**

5. There must be a **CLEAR AND DETAILED FULFILMENT OF THE PROPHECY IN EVERY PARTICULAR.**

For illustration, there were 16 detailed prophecies in reference to Christ's First Coming that were literally fulfilled during the last week of His life, as follows—

1. Sold for 30 pieces of silver. Zech. 11:12.
2. Betrayed by a friend. Psa. 41:9.
3. Forsaken by His Disciples. Zech. 13:7.
4. Accused by false witnesses. Psa. 35:11.
5. Dumb before His accusers. Isa. 53:7.
6. Spit upon and scourged. Isa. 53:5.
7. Hands and feet pierced. Psa. 22:16.
8. His garments divided by lot. Psa. 22:18.
9. Mocked by His enemies. Psa. 22:7-8.

10. Given gall and vinegar. Psa. 69:21.
11. Prayed for His murderers. Isa. 53:12.
12. Not a bone broken. Psa. 34:20.
13. Crucified with thieves. Isa. 53:12.
14. His forsaken cry. Psa. 22:1.
15. His side pierced. Zech 12:10.
16. Buried as a rich man. Isa. 53:9.

Now according to the law of "Compound Probabilities" there was one chance in 65,536 that all these prophecies would head up, or be fulfilled, in the same individual. And when we consider that these prophecies were made by different prophets during a period of 600 years, and half of them about 1000 years before Jesus was born, and notice how they dovetail together with such marvellous accuracy to describe the betrayal, trial, and crucifixion of Jesus, we cannot but admit that the men who foretold those incidents must have been indwelt by the "Spirit of God."

The student of Prophecy must learn to "Rightly Divide the Word." While all Scripture is profitable for **doctrine,** for **reproof,** for **correction,** for **instruction** (2 Tim. 3:16-17), and was written for our **learning,** it is not all addressed to us. Part of it is addressed to the **"JEWS,"** part to the **"GENTILES,"** and part to the **"CHURCH."** These three constitute the **"Three Classes"** into which humanity is divided. 1 Cor. 10:32. The "Jews" and "Gentiles" are distinct from each other, while the "Church" is composed of both, but as a **"NEW BODY."** Eph. 1:22-23; Col. 1:18; Gal. 3:27-28; Col. 3:10-11. The Church is not a subject of prophecy but of Revelation. The burden of prophecy is the Jews, Palestine, Jerusalem, and the Messiah. Therefore it is very important in studying the Scriptures not to give to the "Church" what belongs to the "Jews" or "Gentiles," and vice versa. The "Church" is not seen in the Old Testament. It treats only of the "Jews" and "Gentiles." The Old Testament chapter headings are misleading. They do not belong to the text but were put there by the publisher. For illustration, take the chapter headings of Isaiah 43 and 44, which read—"The Lord comforteth the **'Church'** with His promises." The very first verse of those chapters refutes the heading, distinctly saying that the chapter is addressed to **"ISRAEL,"** not the "Church." If we want to know about the "Church" we must confine ourselves to the New Testament, and there to the Acts and the Epistles. The entire history of God's chosen people "Israel" is given in the Scriptures. They are an earthly people. From their call in Abraham to the present time is history. Their regathering, repentance, and restoration to their own land, and their future earthly glory is the subject of prophecy. The prophetic history of the "Gentile Nations" is outlined in the Book of Daniel, the book we are about to study. This "Present Evil Age" and the manner of its ending is also the subject of prophecy. It behooves us therefore if we would know about the future events that are to come to pass on the earth that we should be students of prophecy. Men and women resort to fortune tellers, clairvoyants, and mediums to get information as to the future, when they have the "more sure word of prophecy." Because of the neglect of the study of Prophecy the Scriptures have fallen into disrepute, and scepticism and infidelity have become widespread, and an unscriptural optimism as to the world growing better is heard on every side. The neglect of the "Prophetic Word" leaves man ignorant of "God's Plan and Purpose as to the Ages," and makes him the easy prey of all the lying inventions and delusive "Cults" of the day. The only cure for the rationalism of the day is the study of Prophecy. The book we are about to study is a "Prophetic Foreview" of the "Gentile Nations" and their last great ruler—**THE ANTICHRIST.**

II

The Book of Daniel

No other book in the Bible has been attacked like the Book of Daniel. For 1600 years, beginning with Porphyry, a Syrian, in the Third Century, the book has been in the "Critic's Den" and fiercely assailed by sceptical writers. Porphyry claimed that instead of being written by Daniel about B. C. 533, it was a forgery written in the time of the Maccabees about B. C. 168, and after Antiochus Epiphanes, so clearly foretold in the book, had appeared, and was written to comfort and encourage the Jews in those trying times. Some modern critics claim that Daniel, if such a person ever lived, had nothing to do with the book at all, that a holy, pious, and gifted Jew, who lived after the time of Antiochus Epiphanes, (B. C. 165), wrote it, and that it is pure fiction. But how could a man who would write such a book and try to palm it off as real history be a holy and pious Jew? This shows to what an extremity those who do not want to accept the book, because it foretells the future, are driven.

There is no question but that the Book of Daniel existed long before the days of Antiochus Epiphanes, B. C. 175-165. How did it get into the Septuagint, the Greek translation of the Scriptures, that was completed in B. C. 285, or over 100 years before it is claimed that a pious Jew wrote it? Josephus, the Jewish Historian, gives us a history of the Jewish people from Abraham down to the destruction of Jerusalem. A. D. 70. Narrating incidents of the struggle with Antiochus Epiphanes, he says that these things came to pass **"according to the prophecy of Daniel which was given 408 years before."** Which means, according to Josephus, that the Book of Daniel was written about B. C. 573. Josephus also tells us that when Alexander the Great, who is foretold in Daniel's prophecies (Dan. 8:5-8) came in the course of his conquests to Jerusalem, B. C. 332, that Jaddua, the High Priest, showed him the reference to himself in the Book of Daniel, which so pleased him that he spared the city. According to this the Book of Daniel must have been written prior to B. C. 332. Again, Ezekiel was a contemporary of Daniel, and wrote in Babylon the book which bears his name. He was held in high esteem by his fellow exiles and was much consulted by them. If Daniel was in Babylon in high official position Ezekiel must have known it. But he need not necessarily have mentioned Daniel in his book. But he does. Three times his name is mentioned—

> "Though these three men, Noah, **DANIEL,** and Job, were in it, they should deliver but their own souls by their righteousness, saith the Lord God." Ezek. 14:14, 20; Ezek. 28:3.

Thus Ezekiel bears witness to the fact that such a man as Daniel existed, and that he was so noted for his righteousness as to be classed with Noah, and for his wisdom as to be classed with Job.

But the highest authority for the authenticity of the Book of Daniel is our Lord, who said in His Olivet Discourse—

> "When ye therefore shall see the 'Abomination of Desolation,' **spoken of by DANIEL THE PROPHET,** stand in the Holy Place, whoso readeth, let him understand." Matt. 24:15.

Whosoever therefore denies the Authenticity of the Book of Daniel impeaches the integrity and wisdom of the Lord Jesus Christ, for He, in the above quotation, affirms that there was such a Prophet as Daniel, and that He foretold that there was such a thing as the "Abomination of Desolation" to stand in the Holy Place of the Temple.

THE ARGUMENT OF SILENCE

It is claimed that no such person of influence and authority as Daniel ever lived at Babylon, because the name Daniel does not appear upon the monuments or among the historical records of Babylonia. The claim is premature because comparatively few such records have been unearthed or deciphered, and the absence of Daniel's name is no proof, for his Jewish name Daniel was changed to the heathen name Belteshazzar. Neither is it any proof because the name Belteshazzar does not appear, for the name might have been abbreviated and spelled differently, as was often the custom with lengthy names. The fact then of silence is no argument. For illustration, we read in Luke 2:41-50 that when Jesus was 12 years of age He went up to Jerusalem at the "Feast of the Passover." Did He not go up to any other Feast between that time and when He entered on His Public Ministry? We do not know. The Scriptures are silent. We know from John's Gospel that He went up to the Feasts regularly after His Baptism, is it not reasonable to suppose that He did before? The "Law" required every male to regularly attend the Feasts, and as Jesus scrupulously kept the Law, the inference is that He from His twelfth year went regularly to the Feasts, at least to the Passover Feast, which was a type of Himself. The silence then as to Daniel's name among the Babylonian records is no proof that he never existed.

It is a fact that we must not forget, that heathen monarchs, like Nebuchadnezzar, recorded on the monuments only the things that glorified themselves, and the great men of their Empires are not mentioned. What about the governors, judges, generals, priests, wise men, and the sculptors, architects, engineers, etc., who planned, and supervised the building of the magnificent walls, towers, bridges, tubes, temples and palaces of "Great Babylon?" Their names do not appear upon the records, why then Daniel's?

The Book of Daniel is discounted because it does not give a list of kings between Nebuchadnezzar and Belshazzar. But why should it? It would seem from the record that Daniel was deposed from his high office at the death of Nebuchadnezzar, and does not publicly appear until he is called on to pronounce the doom of Belshazzar. Why then should he record events, etc., not connected with the purpose of his book?

The presence of fifteen Persian and three Greek words in the Book of Daniel has led some to claim that the book could not have been written as early as B. C. 533. But the presence of these words is an argument for the early date. If the book had been written in the time of Antiochus Epiphanes, the author would not only have inserted a few Greek words, but he would have incorporated in it many Greek expressions and ideas. The Greek words are the names of musical instruments, probably imported by Nebuchadnezzar from Greece, or played by Greek musicians captured in war. The use of foreign words is confirmatory of Daniel's presence at the court of a country that was constantly being visited by emissaries from other lands.

Proofs of the Authenticity of the Book

Mention is made in chapter 1:3 of Ashpenaz, Master of the Eunuchs. The word in the original is **Rabsaris.** But until about twenty-five years ago the word was not found upon the monuments of Babylon, and its absence was used by the critics as proof that there was no such official at the court of Nebuchadnezzar, and therefore the Book of Daniel was not authentic. But the name has been discovered upon a conical brick preserved in the British Museum, thus proving that Daniel is right.*

We are told in chapter 1:2 that Nebuchadnezzar carried the vessels of the House of God (the Temple at Jerusalem) "into the land of Shinar, to the house of his god." From an inscription left by Nebuchadnezzar we find that it was his custom to thus place the choic-

*"Inspiration and Accuracy of the Holy Scriptures." John Urquhart. P. 358-359

est of his spoils in the house of his god. Could a writer, writing 400 years later, who knew nothing whatever of Nebuchadnezzar's custom, ascribe such conduct to him?

Again, the fact that at the Babylonian court there were a class of men called **"seers,"** who were classified as magicians, astrologers, and sorcerers, and over which Daniel was made head, is another proof of the historical character of the book, for a later fictional writer, picturing a vanished state of society after his imagination, would not be likely to give the proper classification.

THE GENTILE NATIONS

While the Book of Daniel treats of the "Times of the Gentiles," it does not give an outline of all the Gentile nations, but only of those which were successively to have sway over the territory of the "Prophetic Earth," or that part of the earth covered by the Old Roman Empire. Bible prophecy has nothing to say about the nations as such in their relation to one another, but only in their relation to Israel and the Holy Land.

> "When the Most High divided to the nations their inheritance, when He separated the sons of Adam (at Babel), He set the bounds of the people **ACCORDING TO THE NUMBER OF THE CHILDREN OF ISRAEL."** Deut. 32:8.

The key to all prophecy is the Jew. If the Jewish nation had not forsaken God and neglected His sabbaths, there would have been no "Times of the Gentiles." The "Times of the Gentiles" began when God transferred earthly rule from the Kings of Israel to the Gentile king Nebuchadnezzar, and they will continue until Israel again becomes the "Head of the Nations." Daniel is distinctly the Prophet of the "Times of the Gentiles." His vision sweeps the whole course of Gentile World Rule until the setting up of the Messianic or Millennial Kingdom of Christ. Daniel was not a Prophet in the same sense that Isaiah, Jeremiah, Ezekiel, and the Minor Prophets were prophets. Their mission was to go to the people and proclaim the Word of the Lord, while Daniel's mission was to record what was revealed to him through visions. While he did not have the "Prophetic Office," he had the "Prophetic Gift." The Book of Daniel is the Apocalypse of the Old Testament, as the Book of Revelation is the Apocalypse of the New Testament, and one cannot be understood without the other, and it is worthy of note that as Daniel is thrice called the man "greatly beloved," the Apostle John is called the "beloved disciple." To these two men was accorded the privilege of seeing in vision the whole "course of time" from B. C. 606, on down to the Second Coming of Christ.

THE DIVISIONS OF THE BOOK

The Book naturally divides itself into two grand divisions of six chapters each. The first division is mainly "Historical," and the second is "Prophetical." See Chart of the Book of Daniel. The Book is written in two languages. The first chapter, and the first three verses of the second are written in Hebrew, and so are chapters 8 to 12, but from the fourth verse of the second chapter to the end of the seventh the language is Aramaic, the ancient language of Syria, and substantially identical with Chaldaic, the language of ancient Babylonia, and the language at that time of trade and international intercourse. The use of the two languages is apparent. What concerns the Gentile Empires is written in their language, Aramaic, and what concerns the Jews is written in Hebrew. This is evidence that the Book was written at Babylon, and written by a Jew. As further evidence the Hebrew is the same in style as the Hebrew of Ezekiel, who was a captive at Babylon at the same time as Daniel.

DANIEL

Of Daniel himself we know more than of any of the other prophets. He was of the Tribe of Judah, and of noble, if not royal, blood. He was carried captive from Jerusalem in the third year of Jehoiakim, B. C. 606, in the first invasion of Judah by Nebuchadnezzar. He was probably twenty years of age when he was taken to Babylon, and in a short time he rose to a very high position in the Empire, which he held during the reign of Nebuchadnezzar. At his death Daniel went into retirement and is not heard of again until he was summoned to pronounce the doom of Belshazzar. He lived through the whole period of the "Seventy Years Captivity," and became the "Chief President" over the 120 Princes of the Kingdom, under Darius the Median, when he was at least ninety years old. He is the only spotless character in the Bible outside of the Lord Jesus Christ. There is not one flaw to be found in his character. He was a man "greatly beloved" of God. He associated with kings and politicians. He led a public life. He held office, yet his character was never impeached. He talked with angels. The Lord Himself appeared unto him, and he had visions of God. He was a great man of faith, and though his name is not mentioned in the great "Faith Chapter" of the New Testament, he is referred to in it as one who "stopped the mouths of lions." Heb. 11:33. He was the—

PROPHETIC STATESMAN

of his day. It was given to him to study the **"SIGNS OF THE TIMES,"** to know the outcome of all the world's boasted civilization, and to see that the nations of the earth should degenerate in political power until the clay of democracy, socialism, and anarchy should so weaken the nations that there would be no cohesion among them, and that the only salvation for a chaotic world would be the return of Christ, and the setting up of His Millennial Kingdom.

Exposition of the Book

First Division
Historical

Chapters 1-6

CHAPTER ONE

The Beginning of Gentile Dominion

THE CONQUEST OF JERUSALEM

"In the third year of the reign of Jehoiakim king of Judah came Nebuchadnezzar king of Babylon unto Jerusalem, and besieged it. And the Lord gave Jehoiakim king of Judah into his hand, with part of the vessels of the House of the Lord: which he carried into the land of Shinar to the house of his god; and he brought the vessels into the treasure house of his god." Daniel 1:1-2.

Jeremiah (25:8-11) places this captivity in the fourth year of Jehoiakim, Daniel in the third. This seeming discrepancy is explained by the fact that Nebuchadnezzar set out on his expedition near the close of the third year of Jehoiakim, from which point Daniel reckons, but did not accomplish the subjugation of Jerusalem till about the ninth month of the following year, and from this Jeremiah reckons.

After the "Confusion of Tongues," and the scattering of the descendants of Noah at Babel, the nations of the earth were held in an unseen leash by God, and no one was permitted to conquer and subdue all the rest. It was God's purpose to make the descendants of Abraham, the Hebrew Nation, the leading nation of the world, but their disobedience and idolatry prevented this. In B. C. 721, the "Ten Tribes" were carried into captivity to Assyria by King Sargon, and in B. C. 606, 115 years later, began the "Seventy Years' Captivity" in Babylon, as foretold by the Prophet Jeremiah (Jer. 25:11), of the remaining two Tribes, known as Judah.

While God had not, up to this time, permitted any one nation to be a world conqueror, yet there were certain great powers that were ambitious for that honor and were warring for supremacy. Among these nations was Babylon, that had already swallowed up Assyria. In B. C. 605, Pharaoh-necho, king of Egypt, marched against Babylon, and was overwhelmingly defeated by Nebuchadnezzar at the Battle of Carchemish on the west bank of the river Euphrates, as had been foretold by the Prophet Jeremiah. Jer. 46:1-26. The defeat of Pharaoh-necho by Nebuchadnezzar made Babylon the mistress of the world.

Nebuchadnezzar pursued Pharaoh-necho to Egypt, and having completely conquered Egypt, he marched against Jerusalem, and in the third year of the reign of Jehoiakim (B. C. 605) he besieged it. All resistance was speedily overcome, the city was taken, King Jehoiakim was loaded with fetters and ready to be carried a prisoner to Babylon (2 Chron. 36:5-8), when Nebuchadnezzar, hearing of the death of his father, released King Jehoiakim and restored him to his throne, and hastened home to Babylon to claim his father's throne. But he did not return empty handed. He plundered the Temple, and took away some of its golden vessels, and ordered Ashpenaz, the master of his eunuchs, to select from among the princes of royal and noble blood the most comely and intellectual of the Hebrew youths, and convey them to Babylon, that they might be instructed in the language and tongue of the Chaldeans.

Three years later Jehoiakim rebelled against Nebuchadnezzar, and the Lord sent neighboring bands of Chaldees, Syrians, Moabites and Ammonites to destroy Judah. 2 Kings 24:1-4. This continued for five years, when Jehoiakim died a disgraceful death (Jer. 22:17-19) and his son Jehoiachin reigned in his stead. But he only reigned three months, during which he did that which was evil in the sight of the Lord, when Nebuchadnezzar in B. C. 598 came the second time and besieged the city of Jerusalem and took it, and carried away Jehoiachin, and the princes, and all the mighty men of valor, even 10,000 captives, and 1000 craftsmen and smiths, leaving only the poorest sort of people behind. 2 Kings 24:8-16. This is commonly called—**"The Captivity,"** because of the number and character of those carried away, but the "Seventy Years Captivity" began in B. C. 606, because it ran out at the "Fall of Babylon," and the commencement of the reign of Cyrus, who issued the edict for the Jews to return to Jerusalem in B. C. 536.

Before departing with his captives, Nebuchadnezzar made the uncle of Jehoiachin king, and changed his name to Zedekiah. But he did that which was evil in the sight of the Lord, and rebelled against the king of Babylon, and in the ninth year of his reign, Nebuchadnezzar again besieged Jerusalem, and after two years took it (B. C. 587) and destroyed the Temple and the city, and from that time the Jewish Nation ceased to exist. 2 Kings 24:17-20; 25:1-21. This is called **"The Desolations,"** because of the desolate condition in which it left the city and the land for seventy years, as foretold by Jeremiah. Jer. 25:11. When Nebuchadnezzar became king in B. C. 606, the "Times of the Gentiles" began. His Kingdom was the first "World-wide Empire" the world had ever seen.

THE HEBREW CAPTIVES

"And the king spake unto Ashpenaz the master of his eunuchs, that he should bring certain of the children of Israel, and of the king's seed, and of the princes; children in whom was no blemish, but well favored, and skilful in all wisdom, and cunning in knowledge, and understanding science, and such as had ability in them to stand in the king's palace, and whom they might teach the learning and the tongue of the Chaldeans. . . . Now among these were of the Children of Judah, Daniel, Hananiah, Mishael, and Azariah: unto whom the 'Prince of the Eunuchs' gave names: for he gave unto Daniel the name of **'Belteshazzar;'** and to Hananiah, of **'Shadrach;'** and to

Mishael, of '**Meshach**;' and to Azariah, of '**Abed-nego.**'" Dan. 1:3-4, 6-7.

The Prophet Isaiah said to King Hezekiah—

"Hear the word of the Lord of Hosts: behold, the days come, that all that is in thine house, and that which thy fathers have laid up in store until this day, **shall be carried to Babylon**: nothing shall be left, saith the Lord. And of thy sons that shall issue from thee, which thou shalt beget, shall they take away: and they shall be **EUNUCHS** in the palace of the King of Babylon." Isa. 39:5-7.

We see from this Scripture that the four Hebrew captives, Daniel, Hananiah, Mishael, and Azariah, as they were of royal blood, were descendants of the good king Hezekiah, and that they were made **EUNUCHS**. This is confirmed by the fact that they were turned over to the "Prince of the Eunuchs," who changed their names, and who had supervision over them for three years. The name of Daniel (God is my Judge) was changed to "**Belteshazzar**" (Whom Bel favors); Hananiah (Beloved of the Lord) to "**Shadrach**" (Illumined by the Sun-God); Mishael (Who is as God) to "**Meshach**" (Who is like Venus); and Azariah (the Lord is my help) to "**Abed-nego**" (The servant of Nego). The purpose in changing their names was to wean them away from their land and religion, and get them to adopt the religion and habits of the heathen nation where their future was to be spent.

But changing a man's name does not change his character, and these young men had been too deeply rooted in the religion and faith of their own nation to adopt the practices of a heathen nation. There is a striking similarity between the experience of Joseph in Egypt and of Daniel in Babylon. Both were Hebrews. Both were prisoners in a strange and heathen land. Both were dreamers, and revealers of dreams. The moral character of each was severely tested. That of Joseph in the house of Potiphar (Gen. 39:1-23), and that of Daniel in the king's palace. These tests were especially severe on account of their age at the time. They were both about twenty. But both stood firm. Both were a great blessing to the homes where they dwelt, and both were raised to positions of great honor. The secret was their loyalty to their God.

The testing for Daniel and his companions was along the line of their religion. They were commanded to be fed with royal dainties and wine from the King's table.

> "And the king appointed them a daily provision of the king's meat, and of the wine which he drank: so nourishing them three years, that at the end thereof they might stand before the king." Vs. 5.

Now such fare, and from such a source, would be very attractive and appetizing for youths of a carnal nature, and they could have congratulated themselves that they had been selected for such an honor, and that they were to spend their lives in the midst of the comforts, luxuries, and pleasures of Babylon. There were many excuses they might have made to each other, such as that they were captives and must obey, or that they must comply with the customs of the country, for to disobey would cost them the favor of the king, and interfere with their advancement, and might even cost them their lives, which danger three of them actually did face when they were cast into the "Burning Fiery Furnace." They knew to refuse the food would make them appear singular, and expose them to criticism and ridicule, but they felt that for them there could be no compromise. For they knew that the meat from the King's table would at times be of a kind forbidden by the Law of their God, as swine's flesh (see Lev. 11:1-47); or it might be meat from which the blood had not been drawn (Lev. 17:10-14); or it might be meat that had first been offered to an idol, and to eat of which might be looked upon as approving the religious customs of Babylon

(1 Cor. 8:1-13), and cause them to be ceremonially defiled. There was therefore but one course to pursue, and in it Daniel was supported by his three companions, and so we read—

> "But Daniel **purposed in his HEART** that he would not defile himself with the portion of the king's meat, nor with the wine which he drank: therefore he requested of the 'Prince of the Eunuchs' that he might not defile himself." Vs. 8.

Daniel knew that he could only be defiled by his own act. Therefore he purposed in his heart not to **defile himself.** It was the crisis in his life, which was safely passed, otherwise we probably would never have heard of him again. We next read that God honored his loyalty by preparing in advance a way of deliverance.

> "Now God had brought Daniel into favor and tender love with the Prince of the Eunuchs. And the Prince of the Eunuchs said unto Daniel, I fear my lord the king, who hath appointed your meat and your drink: for why should he see your faces worse liking than the children which are of your sort? then shall ye make me endanger my head to the king." Vs. 9-10.

To this Daniel had a courteous reply. He did not assume a sanctimonious air, nor make a blatant display of his religious views. He made no assault on the Chaldean religion and the worship of idols, but in a frank and courteous manner made his request—

> "Then said Daniel to Melzar, whom the Prince of the Eunuchs had set over Daniel, Hananiah, Mishael, and Azariah, Prove thy servants, I beseech thee, ten days; and let them give us pulse to eat, and water to drink. Then let our countenances be looked upon before thee, and the countenances of the children that eat of the portion of

the king's meat: and as thou seest, deal with thy servants." Vs. 11-13.

This was a fair test. Daniel did not want to get the "Prince of the Eunuchs" into trouble and cause him to lose his head, and so he arranged the matter in this way satisfactorily with Melzar the Steward. Ten days was sufficient time to prove whether "pulse and water" would keep them in good condition.

"So he (Melzar the Steward) consented to them in this matter, and proved them ten days. And at the end of ten days **their countenances appeared fairer and fatter in flesh than all the children which did eat the portion of the king's meat.** Thus Melzar took away the portion of their meat, and the wine that they should drink; and gave them pulse." Vs. 14-16.

What was the outcome of the test?

"As for these four children, **GOD gave them knowledge and skill in all learning and wisdom:** and **Daniel had understanding in all visions and dreams."** Vs. 17.

Like Joseph and Moses, Daniel and his companions received their training in the palace of a king. They were chosen from among others to learn the language and literature of the Chaldeans, so as to act as wise men and councillors at court. There was nothing wrong in that. There is nothing in the Christian religion that forbids the acquisition of knowledge, or the study of the sciences, although it is a pathway beset with temptations that may lead to a loss of faith in God and His Word, but in Daniel's case there were no bad results. The fact that Daniel and his companions underwent a three-year course of instruction implies that there was a "Palace School" or "National University" for the instruction and training of youth of noble descent, and that such were fed from the

King's table, and therefore the school could not have been far away from the Palace, and that the special subject of study was the literature and language of a certain people called Chaldeans. Now we know from the clay libraries of Nineveh and Babylon that the Chaldeans were a learned people. They had made great advances in grammar, mathematics, astronomy, and the sciences. We must not forget that Babylon was located on the site of Babel, and that the people of Babel inherited all the skill and wisdom of the Antediluvians, who were the inventors of musical instruments, and skilled workers in iron. (Gen. 4:20-22.)

> "Now at the end of the days (three years) that the king had said he should bring them in, then the Prince of the Eunuchs brought them in before Nebuchadnezzar. And the king communed with them; and among them all was found none like Daniel, Hananiah, Mishael, and Azariah: therefore stood they before the king. And in **all matters of wisdom and understanding,** that the king inquired of them, he found them **TEN TIMES** better than all the magicians and astrologers that were in all his realm." Vs. 18-20.

There is a beautiful lesson for us in all this. Daniel and his companions had no hope of returning to their native land, at least not for seventy years, and they had every reason for falling in with the customs of the land. They did not act as they did because they foresaw that the end would be prosperity, they had every reason to expect the reverse, yet the outcome was that Daniel was made the "Chief of the Governors" over all the wise men of Babylon (Dan. 2:48), and the counsellor of Belshazzar, and "Prime Minister" under Darius. Let us like Daniel live

THE SEPARATED LIFE.

As Christians we find ourselves captives in the Babylonian life of wordliness and pleasure that surrounds us, and many of us instead of being transformed are conformed to this world. We have fallen in with the spirit of this "Present Evil Age," and are living a life of **"Compromise,"** the outcome of which is a life of powerlessness and spiritual barrenness, the result of which is we have no "dreams" or "visions" of the things that God is waiting to reveal to us out of His Holy Word. Let us dare to be a Daniel in these days of Babylonian worldliness.

CHAPTER TWO

Nebuchadnezzar's Dream

A TROUBLED KING

"And in the second year of the reign of Nebuchadnezzar, Nebuchadnezzar dreamed dreams, wherewith his spirit was troubled, and his sleep brake from him." Daniel 2:1.

As Nebuchadnezzar did not become king until after the death of his father, Nabopolassar, in B. C. 605, the second year of his reign would be B. C. 603, and as Daniel and his companions were carried captive in B. C. 606, and were in training for three years, the dream of Nebuchadnezzar did not occur until sometime after they had graduated from the "Palace School," or "National University." This accounts for why they were included among those who were to be slain (verses 13, 18), though for some reason they do not appear to have been informed as to the demand of the King. Verses 14-15.

But before we consider the "Dream" and its interpretation, it would be well to inquire as to why Nebuchadnezzar was chosen to receive the "Revelation" that it conveyed. The "Revelation" could have been made to Daniel or some other prophet. We often read of the **"Divine Right"** of kings. If there ever was a king who had a "Divine Right" to rule it was Nebuchadnezzar. He did not assume it, but was directly given it by God.

"Thus saith the Lord of Hosts, the God of Israel: thus shall ye say unto your masters: I have made the earth, the man and the beast that are upon the ground, by my great power and by my outstretched arm, and have given it unto **whom it seemed meet unto me.** And now have I given all these lands into the hand of **NEBUCHADNEZZAR** the King of Babylon, my servant; and the beasts of the field have I given him also to serve him. And **ALL NATIONS** shall serve him, and **HIS SON,** and **HIS SON'S SON,** until the very time of his land come: and then many nations and great kings shall serve themselves of him. And it shall come to pass, that the nation and kingdom which will not serve the same Nebuchadnezzar the King of Babylon, and that will not put their neck under the yoke of the King of Babylon, that nation will I punish, saith the Lord, with the sword, and with the famine, and with the pestilence, until I have consumed them by his hand." *Jer. 27:4-8.*

From this Scripture we see that Nebuchadnezzar was Divinely chosen for his work. Whether he knew it or not, we are not told. We do know, however, that he was greatly puffed up by his greatness. For we read that as he walked in his palace one day, he exclaimed—"Is not this great Babylon, that I have built for the house of the kingdom by the might of my power, and for the honor of my majesty?" Dan. 4:29-30. It seemed meet and proper therefore that he should have the "Dream," which, with its interpretation, would disclose to him that his greatness was not the result of his own ability apart from God, and that the glories of his Empire would soon pass away.

Thus it came to pass that early in his reign, as he lay one day on a sumptuous couch in his palace, thinking about the greatness of his kingdom and wondering what its future would be, he fell into a slumber. The impressions of his waking thoughts had not left him, and in his sleeping consciousness they began to visualize themselves until he saw in his dream a great Image, "whose brightness was excellent," and the "form thereof was terrible." The form was "terrible" doubtless because of the colossal size of the "Image," and its "brightness" was caused by a supernatural light that fell from the heavens and was reflected from the burnished metals that composed it. While the king, transfixed, looked in awe and astonishment upon the "Image," he saw a stone detach itself from a neighboring mountain and smite the "Image" upon its feet, and the "Image" collapsed, turned to powder, and was blown away, and to his amazement the "stone" grew larger and larger until it covered the whole plain on which the "Image" had stood.

We must distinguish between dreams and visions. Dreams occur in the transition stage between loss of "waking consciousness" and "sound sleep." Between the two there is what is called a state of "sleeping consciousness," during which we may dream but never know it. The dreams that we have and remember occur when we are waking, and if not of a vivid character they fade as we try to recall them. Visions occur in our wakeful moments when our mind is absorbed on some thought, so that we are unconscious as to what is going on about us. Visions are an ocular phenomenon and are seen when the eyelids are closed. The vision appears on the inside of the eyelid and is sufficiently luminous to be seen by the eye, and if the eyelid is not moved the vision will remain indefinitely and can be studied in detail. The writer speaks from his own experience as to this. For several days during a severe illness visions would appear in his waking moments whenever he closed his eyes.

Dreamers naturally dream of things with which they are familiar. A dreamer of fifty years ago would not dream of automobiles or airships, and a dreamer of today would not be likely to dream of the class of vehicles used one hundred years ago. In the time of Nebuchadnezzar gigantic statues were common. We find them today among the ruins of Egypt. Now Nebuchadnezzar had just returned from Egypt, having conquered it. What more natural then than having seen the gigantic statues of Egypt, erected by the Kings of Egypt to commemorate their memory, Nebuchadnezzar before he fell asleep had been thinking of such a method of preserving his own memory. But the difference was that the "Image" that Nebuchadnezzar saw was of **metal,** while the images of Egypt were of **stone.** The metallic character of the "Image," and its being composed of more than one kind of metal, was to the King significant, and as all Orientals lay much stress on dreams, and as it was God's method in Old Testament times of conveying to heathen kings, such as Pharaoh, what He purposed to do, naturally Nebuchadnezzar wished to know what his dream meant. But so awesome and frightful was it, that the King awoke in terror, troubled and perplexed, and before he could collect himself the dream had faded from his memory.

"Then the king commanded to call the **'Magicians,'** and the **'Astrologers,'** and the **'Sorcerers,'** and the **'Chaldeans,'** for to shew the king his dreams. So they came and stood before the king. And the king said unto them, I have dreamed a dream, and my spirit was troubled to know the dream." Verses 2-3.

The "Magicians" were such as practiced magic. That is, they practiced all the superstitious rites and ceremonies of fortune tellers, etc. "Astrologers" were men who pretended to foretell future events by the study of the stars. It was much in vogue among the Eastern nations of antiquity. "Sorcerers" were such as pretended to hold communication with the dead. They used potions, and claimed to possess supernatural power or knowledge gained in any manner, but especially through the aid of evil spirits, of which modern spiritualism is an example. The "Chaldeans" here mentioned were a sect of philosophers who made the sciences their special study. It was to this class that Daniel and his companions belonged.

"Then spake the Chaldeans to the king in Syriac, O king, live forever: tell thy servants the dream, and we will show the interpretation. The king answered and said to the Chaldeans, The thing is gone from me: if ye will not make known unto me the dream, with the interpretation thereof, ye shall be cut in pieces, and your houses shall be made a dunghill. But if ye shew the dream, and the interpretation thereof, ye shall receive of me gifts and rewards and great honor: therefore shew me the dream, and the interpretation thereof. They answered again and said, Let the king tell his servants the dream, and we will shew the interpretation of it. The king answered and said, I know of certainty that ye would gain the time, because ye see the thing is gone from me. But if ye will not make known unto me the dream, there is but one decree for you: for ye have prepared lying and corrupt words to speak before me, till the time be changed: **therefore tell me the dream, and I shall know that ye can shew me the interpretation thereof."** Verses 4-9.

The ancient fortune tellers and interpreters of dreams were adepts in the art of drawing out sufficient information to form a basis for some shrewd prognostication, and the framing of their answer in such an ambiguous manner that it would appear correct whichever way the event would go. The Chaldeans therefore figured that if the king would tell them the dream, they could agree on some interpretation that would seem plausible, and thus save their reputation. But this was inconsistent with their claim that they possessed occult powers and could get superhuman information. From this standpoint the king's demand that they reproduce his dream was not unreasonable. When the king saw that they could not reproduce his dream he lost all confidence in their claims, and naturally and justly charged them as being impostors, and with "sparring for time" until the "time be changed," that is, until the matter had passed from his memory and he was no longer solicitous about it.

That the claim of the Chaldeans that they could communicate with the "gods" was false is evident from their own confession.

> "The Chaldeans answered before the king, and said, There is not a man upon the earth that can shew the king's matter: therefore there is no king, lord, nor ruler, that asked such things at any Magician, or Astrologer, or Chaldean. And it is a rare thing that the king requireth, and there is none other that can shew it before the king, **EXCEPT THE GODS**, whose dwelling is not with flesh." Verses 10-11.

When the Chaldeans confessed that no one—**"except the gods,"** could reproduce the Dream, they acknowledged, because they could not reproduce it, that they had no power with the gods, thus justifying the king's charge that they were impostors.

> "For this cause the king was angry and very furious, and commanded to destroy all the wise men of Babylon. And the decree went forth that the wise men should be slain; and they sought Daniel and his fellows to be slain." Verses 12-13.

Whether the severity of the sentence pronounced upon them was justifiable we may question. The Magicians, Astrologers, Sorcerers, and Chaldeans were numerous, wealthy, and influential bodies. They were composed of the learned and cultivated classes of Babylon, and to cause their destruction was to weaken the Empire. What the execution of the sentence would have resulted in we can only imagine, but happily it was averted. When the magicians and wise men of Egypt could not interpret Pharaoh's dreams, God had a Hebrew captive, named Joseph, prepared for the task. So when the wise men of Babylon could not recall or interpret the King's dream, God had a Hebrew captive, Daniel, on the scene. Why Daniel was not among those first consulted we are not told. He does not seem to have known anything about the matter until Arioch, the king's captain, came to arrest him. But God's hand doubtless was in all this. He first wanted to show up the false claims of those heathen systems represented by the wise men of Babylon, and have them confess their incompetency. If Daniel had been called first the wise men would have escaped the test. When Daniel learned the mission of Arioch, he protested.

> "Then Daniel answered with counsel and wisdom to Arioch the captain of the king's guard, which was gone forth to slay the wise men of Babylon. He answered and said to Arioch the king's captain, Why is the decree so hasty from the king? Then Arioch made the thing known to Daniel. Then Daniel went in, and desired of the king that he would give him time, and that he would shew the king the interpretation." Verses 14-16.

Notice the faith of Daniel. He did not ask the king to describe his dream, he simply asked for time, and with sublime confidence promised the king that he would not only reproduce the dream, but give its meaning. His request was granted.

THE ALL-NIGHT PRAYER MEETING

> "Then Daniel went to his house, and made the thing known to Hananiah, Mishael, and Azariah, his companions: that they would desire mercies of the God of Heaven concerning this 'secret;' that Daniel and his fellows should not perish with the rest of the wise men of Babylon." Verses 17-18.

That was an epoch marking "Prayer Meeting." Doubtless Daniel would have been heard if he had gone off by himself and prayed, but he believed in united prayer, and then his three companions were as much interested in the matter as he, for their lives were suspended in the same balance as his. If Daniel could not keep his promise to the king all four would perish. But something more than their lives was at stake. If Daniel had failed God, the world would have missed that great **"REVELATION"** that was locked up in that Dream and its interpretation, the prophetic and historical outline of the

"TIMES OF THE GENTILES."

We are not told when the "Prayer Meeting" began, but we know that it lasted far into the night, and did not close until they had the assurance of a favorable answer. Then they retired. Whether Daniel fell asleep and the Dream of Nebuchadnezzar was repeated to him with the interpretation, or as he lay on his couch he saw in vision the Image, and the angel Gabriel appeared, as in later visions, and revealed its meaning, we are not told. We simply read—"Then was the **'secret' revealed unto Daniel in a 'NIGHT VISION.'"** Verse 19.

Daniel was not elated because the dream was revealed to him. He did not rush off in haste to the king to inquire if it corresponded with what the king had seen. But his soul unburdened itself in one of the most wonderful and beautiful outbursts of praise recorded in the Bible. Daniel believed in giving thanks for answered prayer. It contains a sevenfold paean of praise.

"Then Daniel blessed the God of Heaven. Daniel answered and said, Blessed be the name of God forever and ever: for—

1—**Wisdom and Might** are His:

2—And He **changeth the 'Times and the Seasons:'**

3—**He removeth kings, and setteth up kings:**

4—**He giveth Wisdom unto the Wise,**

5—And **Knowledge to them that know understanding:**

6—He **revealeth the deep and 'Secret Things:'**

7—He **knoweth what is in the darkness, and the light dwelleth with Him.**

"I thank Thee, and praise Thee, O Thou God of my fathers, who hast given me wisdom and might, and **hast made known unto ME now what WE desired of Thee: for Thou hast now made known unto US the KING'S MATTER."** Verses 19-23.

While to Daniel alone the revelation was made, he did not take all the credit to himself, but associated his companions with himself in his thanksgiving.

With no unseemly haste, yet doubtless as soon as it was day, Daniel hunted up Arioch.

"Therefore Daniel went in unto Arioch, whom the king had ordained to destroy the wise men of Babylon: he went and said thus unto him: Destroy not the wise men of Babylon: bring me in before the King, and I will shew unto the King the interpretation." Verse 24.

Daniel's first request of Arioch was that he—"Destroy not the wise men of Babylon." Thus they were saved because there was a "Man of God" among them, just as the prisoners and sailors on that "corn ship" were saved for Paul's sake. Acts 27:23-24.

The teaching of the Scriptures is that "The Wicked are blest for the Righteous' sake." The house of Potiphar was blessed for Joseph's sake. Gen. 39:5. The Lord would have spared Sodom if there had been ten righteous people in it. The world has thus far been spared from judgment because of the righteous people in it. When the Church is "caught out" the world will be ripe for judgment. And as the wise men of Babylon were spared for Daniel's sake, so we are saved for **JESUS' SAKE.**

"Then Arioch brought in Daniel before the king in haste, and said thus unto him, I have found a man of the captives of Judah, that will make known unto the King the interpretation." Verse 25.

It is characteristic of officials that they desire to ingratiate themselves with their sovereign. So here Arioch claims that he had discovered Daniel, saying, **"I have found a man,"** forgetting, if he knew, that Daniel had personally appeared before the King before and promised, if given time, that he would make known the interpretation.

"The King answered and said to Daniel, whose name was Belteshazzar, Art thou able to make known unto me the dream which I have seen, and the interpretation thereof? Daniel answered in the presence of the King, and said, The **'secret'** which the King hath demanded cannot the wise men, the Astrologers, the Magicians, the Soothsayers, shew unto the King; but there is a **GOD IN HEAVEN THAT REVEALETH SECRETS,** and maketh known to the King Nebuchadnezzar **what shall be in the**

LATTER DAYS.

Thy dream, and the visions of thy head upon thy bed, are these: as for thee, O King, thy thoughts came into thy mind upon thy bed, what should come to pass **HEREAFTER**: and he that revealeth secrets maketh known to thee what shall come to pass. But as for me, this secret is not revealed to me for any wisdom that I have more than any living, but for their sakes that shall make known the interpretation to the King, and that thou mightest know the thoughts of thy heart." Verses 26-30.

The King's question to Daniel, "Art thou able to make known unto me the 'Dream' which I have seen, and the interpretation thereof?"—for the King classed Daniel among the "wise men" and doubtless was somewhat suspicious that he was any abler than they to make known the "Dream" and interpret it—gave Daniel the opportunity to explain why the "wise men" could not make known the dream. It was beyond their province. It was something that only God, the **"REVEALER OF SECRETS,"** could do, because it had reference to things that were to come to pass in the **"LATTER DAYS."** And lest the King should give him the credit Daniel declared that the "Secret" was not revealed to him for any wisdom of his own, but that the King might not only know what the future of his Kingdom was to be, but that he might know what was to come to pass in the far distant future.

THE DREAM

"Thou, O King, sawest, and behold a great Image. This great Image, whose brightness was excellent, stood before thee: and the form thereof was terrible. This Image's head was of fine gold, his breast and his arms of silver, his belly and his thighs of brass, his legs of iron, his feet part of iron and part of clay. Thou sawest till that a stone was cut out without hands, which smote the Image upon his feet that were of iron and clay, and brake them to pieces. Then was the iron, the clay, the brass, the silver, and the gold, broken to pieces together, and became like the chaff of the summer threshing floors: and the wind carried them away, that no place was found for them: and the stone that smote the Image became a great Mountain, and filled the whole earth." Verses 31-35.

We can imagine the King's feelings when he had his "Dream" repeated to him. The "Image" stood out in every detail just as he had seen it in his sleep. And what must he have thought of Daniel. He must have been amazed at his spiritual insight and wisdom, which would give him confidence in the interpretation of the "Dream" when it was unfolded unto him.

THE INTERPRETATION

"This is the 'Dream:' and we will tell the interpretation thereof before the King. Thou, O King, art a king of kings: for the God of heaven hath given thee a kingdom, power, and strength, and glory. And wheresoever the children of men dwell, the beasts of the field and the fowls of the heaven hath He given into thine hand, and hath made thee ruler over them all.

I. THE HEAD. THE BABYLONIAN EMPIRE.

THOU ART THIS HEAD OF GOLD.

II. THE ARMS AND BREAST. THE MEDO-PERSIAN EMPIRE.

"And after thee shall arise another kingdom inferior to thee,

III. THE ABDOMEN. THE GRECIAN EMPIRE.

and another third kingdom of brass, which shall bear rule over all the earth.

IV. THE LEGS. THE ROMAN EMPIRE.

"And the fourth kingdom shall be strong as iron: forasmuch as iron breaketh in pieces and subdueth all things: and as iron that breaketh all these, shall it break in pieces and bruise.

THE FEET AND TOES.

"And whereas thou sawest the feet and toes, part of potter's clay, and part of iron, the kingdom shall be divided; but there shall be in it of the strength of the iron, forasmuch as thou sawest the iron mixed with miry clay. And as the toes of the feet were part of iron, and part of clay, so the kingdom shall be partly strong, and partly broken. And whereas thou sawest iron mixed with miry clay, they shall mingle themselves with the seed of men: but they shall not cleave one to another, even as iron is not mixed with clay.

V.
THE STONE.
THE MILLENNIAL KINGDOM OF CHRIST.

"And in the days of these kings (the kings represented by the Ten Toes) shall the God of Heaven set up a Kingdom, which shall **never be destroyed**: and the Kingdom shall not be left to other people, but it shall break in pieces and consume all these kingdoms, and it shall stand **FOREVER.**

THE PURPOSE OF THE DREAM.

"Forasmuch as thou sawest that the stone was cut out of the mountain without hands, and that it brake in pieces the iron, the brass, the clay, the silver, and the gold: the great God hath made known to the King **what shall come to pass HEREAFTER**: and the dream is certain, and the interpretation thereof sure." Verses 36-45.

If Nebuchadnezzar was astonished when he heard Daniel repeat his "Dream," he must have been thunder-struck when he heard the interpretation, and learned how his own Kingdom would fall and be succeeded by inferior ones, until all world kingdoms should be destroyed. The interpretation of the "Dream" is certainly one that human ingenuity could not have hit upon. The wise men and flatterers of the Chaldean court would never have dared to announce the downfall of Nebuchadnezzar's Kingdom, and the final termination of Gentile supremacy.

In the Golden Headed Image of Nebuchadnezzar's "Dream" we have a **"Visualized Portraiture"** of the "Times of the Gentiles." The phrase "The Times of the Gentiles" is not found in the Book of Daniel, but is a New Testament phrase used by the Lord. It was used by Him in His "Olivet Discourse" in reference to the destruction of Jerusalem in A. D. 70, where He said—"And Jerusalēm shall be trodden down of the Gentiles, until the **'TIMES OF THE GENTILES'** be fulfilled." Luke 21:24. In the phrase, "The Times of the Gentiles," Jesus had reference to a **"PERIOD OF TIME"** of certain **chronological limits,** that corresponds to the time that the Jewish Nation shall be without a king. It is foretold by Hosea.

> "The Children of Israel shall abide **MANY DAYS** without a king, and without a prince, and without a sacrifice, and without an image, and without an ephod, and without teraphim: **AFTERWARD** shall the Children of Israel return, and see the Lord their God, and David their King; and shall fear the Lord and His goodness **IN THE LATTER DAYS."** Hosea 3:4-5.

The "Times of the Gentiles" did not begin at the "Destruction of Jerusalem" in A. D. 70, but at the time when Daniel was carried captive to Babylon in B. C. 606, and will continue until Christ comes back and sets up His Millennial or "Stone Kingdom," represented by the "Stone" cut out of the mountain in

Nebuchadnezzar's Dream. We must not confound the phrase **"The Times of the Gentiles"** with the phrase the **"Fulness of the Gentiles,"** used by the Apostle Paul in Rom. 11:25. The "Fulness of the Gentiles" has no reference to the "Times of the Gentiles," but to the Gentiles who are being "called out" in this Dispensation by the Holy Spirit as members of Christ's Body—"The Church." When their number is complete, or **FULL,** then Christ will take out His Church, and the "Fulness of the Gentiles" will be complete. This "Divine Program" is outlined in Acts 15:13-17.

MAN'S DAY

While this present Dispensation is spoken of distinctively in the Scriptures as **"MAN'S DAY"** (see 1 Cor. 4:3, margin), the term applies to the whole period of the "Times of the Gentiles." This is the day of the **"DEIFICATION OF MAN."** From the day when Nebuchadnezzar set up in the Plain of Dura that "Golden Image," typical of himself, and commanded all the people of his realm to worship it (Dan. 3:1-7), until the False Prophet shall command that the people shall make an "Image to the Beast" (The Antichrist) and worship the same (Rev. 13:13-17), the only suitable symbol to describe the character of the "Times of the Gentiles" is the "Image of a Man." How suitable then was the "Golden Headed Image" of Nebuchadnezzar's "Dream" to describe the character of the "Times of the Gentiles." The deterioration of the "Times of the Gentiles" is seen in the **DIMINISHING VALUE OF THE METALS** from gold, to silver, to brass, to iron, to iron and clay. Whereas if the world is growing better the metals should have been in reverse order. The weight of the Image also declines. The specific gravity of gold is 19.5, of silver 10.47, of brass 8, of cast-iron 5, of clay 1.93. The "Image" is **TOP-HEAVY.** From this we see that Gentile dominion is represented by a huge **"METALLIC MAN"** that degenerates in character from head to foot.

THE HISTORICAL FULFILMENT

The "Image" symbolizes the four great World Empires in their **UNITY** and **HISTORICAL SUCCESSION.** There are to be four, and only four, great World Empires on the earth from the accession of Nebuchadnezzar to the throne of Babylon, to the Second Coming of Christ. They are represented by the four metals of the Image. Men like Napoleon have hoped, plotted and warred to establish a "Fifth" World Empire, and have failed. These Empires are not only made known as to **number,** but their **NAMES,** in the **ORDER OF THEIR SUCCESSION,** are given.

1. THE BABYLONIAN EMPIRE

The First Empire is pointed out by Daniel, in his interpretation of the Image, as **BABYLON,** in his words to Nebuchadnezzar—**"THOU art the HEAD OF GOLD."** It will be noticed in studying the "Interpretation" that Daniel uses the words "King" and "Kingdom" interchangeably. The writer uses the word "Empire" instead of "Kingdom" because there was a succession of kings in each Empire while it lasted, and in profane history those kings were called Emperors. The title of Emperor today is rare, because the Empires of the world have been broken up into small Kingdoms. This is a fulfilment of the teaching of the "Image," whose feet are divided into **"Ten Toes"** called Kingdoms. Nebuchadnezzar, after reigning forty-four years, died in B. C. 561. He was succeeded by his son Evil-Merodach, who after an ignoble reign of two years was assassinated by his brother-in-law, Neriglissar, who seized the throne, and after reigning for about four years was killed in battle in B. C. 556. He was succeeded by his son Laborosoarched, an imbecile child, who after nine months' reign was beaten to death, and Nabonidus, another son-in-law of Nebuchadnezzar, who had married the widow of Neriglissar, seized the throne and reigned for seventeen years, during the whole of which period Babylon was threatened with invasion by the Persians, and it was while Nabonidus was on a military expedition that Babylon was taken, he having made his son Belshazzar the **"second ruler"** and left him in charge of the city. That was why Belshazzar had to make Daniel the **"third ruler,"** because he himself was the second. Thus we see that Nebuchadnezzar was properly called the **"HEAD OF GOLD,"** because all his successors were inferior men. With the death of Belshazzar the Babylonian Empire ceased to exist.

2. THE MEDO-PERSIAN EMPIRE

The Second Empire, the **MEDO-PERSIAN,** is pointed out by Daniel in his account of the "Fall of Babylon" in the words—"In that night was Belshazzar the king of the Chaldeans slain, and Darius the **MEDIAN** took the Kingdom." Dan. 5:30-31.

It is also pointed out in the "Vision of the Ram and He-Goat" (Dan. 8:20), where the two horns of the Ram, that correspond to the two arms of the Image (see chart), are called the kings of Media and Persia. Thus we see that while the Babylonian Empire was single-headed, the Medo-Persian was a dual Empire, represented by the "two arms" of the Image and the "two horns" of the Ram. The left arm of the Image representing Media the weaker, and the right arm Persia the stronger Kingdom. The fact that the Medo-Persian Empire is represented by the "Silver" of the Image indicates that, as silver is inferior to gold, so the Medo-Persian Empire was inferior to the Babylonian. This we know was true, not in extent, for Cyrus conquered more territory, but in wealth, luxury, and magnificence.

Cyrus has the honor of being named in the Scriptures 175 years before he took Babylon. In Isa. 44:28 and 45:1-4, we read—

"That saith of **CYRUS,** He is my shepherd, and shall perform all my pleasure: even saying to

JERUSALEM—Thou shalt be built; and to the **TEMPLE—Thy foundation shall be laid.** Thus saith the Lord to His anointed, to **CYRUS,** whose right hand I have holden, to subdue nations before him; and I will **loose the loins of kings** (as those of Belshazzar) to **open before him** (Cyrus) **the TWO LEAVED GATES** (of Babylon); and the gates **shall not be shut** (which was true of the inner gates of Babylon, in the river walls, on the night of the siege); . . . For Jacob my servant's sake, and Israel mine elect, I have even called thee by thy name: **I have surnamed thee, though thou hast NOT KNOWN ME."**

From this Scripture we see that Cyrus was foreordained, over a hundred years before he was born, to do two things. First to besiege and take Babylon, and secondly to issue an Edict, at the close of the "Babylonian Captivity," in B. C. 536, for the return of the Jews and the rebuilding of the Temple.

At the taking of Babylon, B. C. 538, Cyrus, as an act of courtesy, because Media was the older of the two Kingdoms Media and Persia, and because he had some other military campaigns to finish, assigned the governorship of Babylon to his uncle Darius, the king of Media, who ruled for two years. The same year (B. C. 536) Cambyses, king of Persia, Cyrus' father, also died, thus making Cyrus the sole monarch of the Dual Kingdom. After a reign of seven years, Cyrus left the Empire to his son Cambyses, who reigned seven years and five months, to B. C. 522. Eight monarchs, whose reigns varied from seven months to forty-six years each, followed in succession until B. C. 335, when Darius Codomanus became the last of the long line of Persian kings. He was a noble person, and a long and splendid career would undoubtedly have been his, but it was his misfortune to have ascended the throne when the time had come for the "Silver" of the Image to give place to the "Brass," and nothing could prevent the change, and in B. C. 330 Alexander the Grecian conquered the Persian Empire.

3. THE GRECIAN EMPIRE

The Third Empire, the **GRECIAN**, is identified in Dan. 8:21, by the angel Gabriel as the **"He-Goat,"** that destroyed the **"Ram,"** which represented the Medo-Persian Empire.

> "The 'Ram' which thou sawest having two horns are the kings of **MEDIA** and **PERSIA.** And the 'Rough Goat' (the He-Goat) is the king of **GRECIA** (Greece): and the **'Great Horn'** that is between his eyes is the first king." (Alexander the Great). Dan. 8:20-21.

Again we see inferiority, for "Brass" is an inferior metal to "Silver." The Grecian Empire, as a World-Wide Empire, with Alexander as its head, was of short duration. After eight short years he died of intemperance and marsh fever in B. C. 323, in his thirty-third year, and his Empire was divided among four of his generals. See the exposition of chapter eight.

Right here we must not forget that the prophecy does not say that the Four World Empires are to succeed each other **without a break.** From the death of Alexander the Great, B. C. 323, to B. C. 30, when the Roman Empire succeeded the Grecian, the Grecian Empire was not a **single** Empire, but a **fourfold** Empire, composed of the Kingdoms of Thrace, Macedonia, Syria, and Egypt. These fell one by one until the Romans conquered Egypt in B. C. 30, which made them the conquerors of the world. This division of the Grecian Empire into four parts is not shown on the Image, as there is no break in the "Brass," between the "Silver" and the "Iron" of the Image, but the fact is revealed in the story of the "He-Goat" in chapter 8:21-25.

Another explanation is necessary at this point. The words—"his **belly** and **thighs** of brass," are a mistranslation. The word translated **"thighs"** is singular, and should be translated the "Thigh-part." A little explanation will make this clear. As we have already seen, the Grecian Empire was divided into four parts, that disappeared one by one, until the last, Egypt, was conquered in B. C. 30, and the fourth or Roman Empire came into existence. Now as the Roman Empire was not divided into its Eastern and Western Divisions, which represent the two legs of the Image, until A. D. 364, all that went before of the Roman Empire belongs to the **BODY** of the Image, and not the legs, as shown on the Chart. The Scripture would be clearer, and better express what we now know from history it was intended to express, if we read the passage as follows—"His belly (abdomen) of brass, and his Thigh-parts (buttocks) and legs of iron, his feet part of iron and part of clay." Verses 32-33.

4. THE ROMAN EMPIRE

The Fourth Empire, the **ROMAN,** is not named in the Book of Daniel, but it is pointed out. In Daniel's Vision of the "Seventy Weeks," chapter 9, verse 26, we read, that after the "cutting off" (Crucifixion) of the "Messiah the Prince" (Christ), Jerusalem and the Temple were to be destroyed by a **PEOPLE,** from whom later should come a **"Prince,"** whom we shall see will be the **ANTICHRIST.** Now we know that Jerusalem and the Temple were destroyed by the Romans in A. D. 70, and that Antichrist is to be the last Emperor of the Roman Empire, and as Antichrist is the **"LITTLE HORN"** of the "Fourth Wild Beast," that corresponds to the **"Iron"** of the Image, then the "Fourth Empire" is the "Roman." Thus we see that all four of the Empires symbolized by the metals of the Image were pointed out in their historical succession to Daniel, three of them before they ever came into existence. If this does not prove the Divine Inspiration of the Book of Daniel, what could?

There are three things that we are to note about the "Fourth Empire." First, as represented by the legs, it takes up in length at least half of the Image, and therefore in proportion the Roman Empire was to last longer than the other Empires. This we know from history to be true. Second, the Image is divided into **"two legs,"** this would imply that the Roman Empire would be divided into **TWO PARTS.** This we also know to be true, for the Roman Empire was divided into its "Eastern Division" with Constantinople as the Capital, and its "Western Division" with Rome as the Capital, in A. D. 364. Third, the two feet of the "Image" are divided into **"five toes"** each. These **"TEN TOES"** have not as yet manifested themselves, so the historical fulfilment of the Image is not yet complete. From what has been said we see that the First Empire was a **UNIT,** the Second **DUAL,** the Third became **QUADRUPLE,** and the Fourth, in its final form, will be **TEN-TOED.** While the Roman Empire, as a visible Empire, does not exist today, yet its laws, etc., are a controlling power among the nations, and the Empire in a visible form is to be revived, and in its revived and last form it will consist of "Ten Federated Kingdoms," represented by the "Ten Toes" of the Image, at the head of which shall be the last Roman Emperor and Gentile Ruler, the **ANTICHRIST.**

THE FEET AND TOES

While the legs of the Image are of iron, the feet and toes are of iron and potter's clay. There is a mingling, but not a commingling. That is, there is no union of the iron and the clay, and this condition is to continue until the feet of the Image are smitten by the "Stone" cut out of the Mountain.

The character of the Government of the different Empires reveals the fact that the Image will become increasingly unstable. The Babylonian Empire was an **ABSOLUTE AUTOCRACY.** It was said of Nebuchadnezzar, **"Whom he would he slew; and whom**

he would he kept alive: and whom he would he set up: and whom he would he put down." Dan. 5: 19. The Medo-Persian Empire was not an autocracy. The Emperor was bound by certain laws, called the "Laws of the Medes and Persians." Having once issued an Edict he could not recall it. As illustrations we have the case of Darius, who earnestly sought to deliver Daniel from the "lion's den," and of Ahasuerus, who could not rescind his order for the slaughter of the Jews, but could only issue a counter-decree permitting them to stand for their lives and slay those who would attempt to kill them. Esther 8: 1-17. The Grecian Empire was a Monarchy supported by a "Military Aristocracy," that was as weak as the ambitions of its leaders. The Roman Emperors were nominally elected by the people, but the people were neither allowed to legislate for them, nor to interfere with them, and so their despotic sway is well symbolized by "Iron," which in the form of **STEEL** will cut through every other metal. Rome was noted for her **IRON-RULE.**

But the form of Government grows weaker when we examine the "Feet" and the "Toes," composed of Iron and Clay. Here we see **"Imperialism"** mixed with **"Democracy."** The Iron representing "Imperialism," and the Clay "Democracy." In short the character of government passes from an **"ABSOLUTE AUTOCRACY"** to a **"DEMOCRATIC MONARCHY,"** to the rule of the "Head" by the "Feet," to a form of Government in which the masses, swayed by politicians and demagogues, who think only of their own selfish interests, control the Government. Such a form of government is the weakest that can be devised and opens the way for the growth and development of Socialism, Sovietism, Bolshevism, and Anarchy. The fact that such phases of government are becoming more prominent seems to indicate that, historically, we are now living in the time indicated by the "Feet" of the "Image," and that it will not be long before the "Toes" will appear in the form of "Ten Federated Nations," over which a Roman Emperor will rule.

5. THE STONE KINGDOM

"Thou sawest till that a **STONE** was cut out **without hands,** which smote the Image upon his **FEET** that were of iron and clay, and brake them to pieces. Then was the **iron,** the **clay,** the **brass,** the **silver,** and the **gold,** broken to pieces **TOGETHER,** and became like the chaff of the summer threshing floors; and the wind carried them away, that no place was found for them: and the **STONE** that smote the Image became a **GREAT MOUNTAIN, AND FILLED THE WHOLE EARTH."** Dan. 2:34-35.

The interpretation of this is given in verse 44.

"In the days of these kings shall the God of Heaven set up a **KINGDOM, which shall never be destroyed**: and the Kingdom shall not be left to other people (that is, it shall not be succeeded by other kingdoms), but it shall **break in pieces and consume all these Kingdoms** (the Kingdoms represented by the Metals of the Image), and it shall **STAND FOREVER."**

The climax of the Dream is the smiting of the Image by a **"STONE"** cut out of a mountain without hands, thus showing the "Stone's" supernatural origin. The "Stone" does not "fill the earth" by degrees and thus **"crowd out"** the Image, it at **one blow DEMOLISHES IT,** and its remains are blown away. The action of the "Stone" is **JUDGMENT,** not Grace. Not the spread of a "Spiritual Kingdom" by the preaching of the Gospel, but the immediate setting up of an outward and visible earthly Kingdom. The "Stone" therefore cannot mean Christianity, for it is a **PROCESS,** whereas the action of the "Stone" is **SUDDEN AND CALAMITOUS.** Again the **TIME** of the destruction is not until **AFTER THE FORMATION OF THE TOES OF THE IMAGE.** We know that the "Legs" of the Image did not appear until A. D. 364, when the

Roman Empire was divided into its Eastern and Western Divisions, and the "Ten Toes" have not yet developed. The time when the "Stone" falls on the feet of the Colossus is distinctly given in the interpretation as—**"IN THE DAYS OF THESE KINGS."** What kings? Not the kings of the Four World Empires, represented by the four metals of the Image, that would only bring us down to the "First Advent," and would make Christianity the smiting Stone, but by "these kings" we are to understand the kings of the "Ten Federated Kingdoms," represented by the "Toes" of the Image. So we see that the **TIME** of the smiting was not when Christ came the First time, but when He comes the Second time.

The "Stone" is not Christianity but **CHRIST.** He is everywhere in Scripture spoken of as **"THE STONE."** To the Jews He was "A Stone of stumbling, and rock of offence." He was the Stone that the builders rejected, that was to become the head of the corner. Christ must have had in mind the "Falling Stone" of Nebuchadnezzar's Dream when he prophetically uttered the words—"And whosoever shall fall on this Stone (Christ) shall be broken (melted into repentance), but on whomsoever it shall fall, it will **GRIND HIM TO POWDER."** Matt. 21:44. The "Stone" smites the Image, the Image does not smite the Stone. Did Christ when He came the First time smite and destroy the Roman Empire? No. The Roman Empire smote Him and was the cause of His death. So we see that the First Coming of Christ was not the "Falling of the Stone," for it is still future and cannot be until His Second Coming.

Some object that because it says—"Then was the **iron,** the **clay,** the **brass,** the **silver,** and the **gold,** broken to pieces **TOGETHER,"** that that cannot be, because the Empires represented by the "Gold," the "Silver," the "Brass," and the "Iron" have passed away. As outward visible Empires this is true. But we must not forget that those Empires were incorporated into their successors, and that all of them will be found in the last phase of the revived Roman Empire. As proof of this we have the description of the "Beast" that comes up out of the sea (and the sea is a symbol of the nations) in Rev. 13:1-2, where we read—

> "And the Beast which I saw was like a **LEOPARD,** and his feet were as the feet of a **BEAR,** and his mouth as the mouth of a **LION:** and the Dragon (Satan) gave him his power, and his seat, and great authority."

Now we shall see in our study of Daniel's Vision of the "Four Wild Beasts," chapter seven, that the "Wild Beasts" correspond to the metals of the Image. That is, the "Gold" corresponds to the "Lion," the "Silver" to the "Bear," the "Brass" to the "Leopard," and the "Iron" to the Fourth Beast. In John's description of the "Beast" out of the sea, given above, which is a description of the last phase of the revived Roman Empire, we see that the "Beast" is a "composite beast," composed of a body like that of a "Leopard," with the feet of a "Bear," and the mouth of a "Lion," the "Fourth Wild Beast" being represented by the whole of the Beast. Now we see from this that the revived Roman Empire will be a composite Empire, composed of the "Lion" (Babylon), the "Bear" (Medo-Persia), the "Leopard" (Greece), and the Beast itself (Rome). As the body, which is the largest part of a beast, in John's Beast is that of a Leopard, the inference is that the last phase of the Roman Empire will be mainly Grecian.

The Mountain out of which the "Stone" is cut by invisible hands represents Israel, for of Israel Christ came. This is confirmed by the words of Jacob in blessing his sons, where he speaks of—"The Shepherd, the **STONE OF ISRAEL**" (Gen. 49:24), which can refer to no other than Christ. The Mountain into which the "Stone" grows and fills the whole earth is the "Stone" or "Millennial Kingdom" of Christ. The four Empires or Kingdoms symbolized by the Image were **LITERAL** Kingdoms. It follows then that the "Stone Kingdom," which is to take their place, must also be a **LITERAL** Kingdom, for it is to conquer and control the whole earth. It is for this Kingdom, and not a spiritual Kingdom, that Christ taught His Disciples to pray in the words—**"Thy Kingdom Come."** If a Spiritual Kingdom was meant, and such a Kingdom is now present, then we should no longer pray—"Thy Kingdom **COME,"** for it is already here.

THE EFFECT UPON THE KING

"Then the King, Nebuchadnezzar, fell upon his face, and worshipped Daniel, and commanded that they should offer an oblation and sweet odors unto him. The King answered unto Daniel, and said, Of a truth it is, that **YOUR GOD** is a **'GOD OF GODS,'** and a **'LORD OF KINGS,'** and a **'REVEALER OF SECRETS,'** seeing thou couldst reveal this **SECRET** (of the Dream). Then the King made Daniel a great man, and gave him many great gifts, and made him Ruler over the whole province of Babylon, and 'Chief of the Governors' over all the Wise Men of Babylon. Then Daniel requested of the King, and he set Shadrach, Meshach, and Abed-nego, over the affairs of the province of Babylon: but Daniel sat in the gate of the King." Verses 46-49.

It took courage for Daniel to stand before a proud monarch like Nebuchadnezzar and announce to him that his Empire would not long survive his death. But Daniel was too loyal to his God to keep back the truth. The effect upon the King was the reverse of that which naturally was to be expected. Instead of professing to not believe a word of the interpretation, he falls upon his face and worships Daniel, thus testifying to Daniel's superhuman wisdom. Only God could have wrought such a change in the King. He also commanded that they should offer an oblation and sweet odors unto Daniel. That Daniel protested seems clear from the words—"The King **answered** unto Daniel." The King then gave testimony to the character of Daniel's God. The language is striking, in that it bears witness to the Trinity. Your God is a **"God of Gods"** (the Father), and a **"Lord of Kings"** (the Son), and a **"Revealer of Secrets"** (the Holy Spirit). What effect the reproduction of the Dream and its Interpretation had upon the Magicians, Astrologers, Sorcerers, and Chaldeans, we are not told, but they must have realized that they were not in Daniel's class, that what they professed he possessed.

DANIEL'S REWARD

Daniel's reward was twofold. He was made a "Great Man." There are two things in this world that are supposed to make a man "Great." The first is **"RICHES,"** the second is **"POWER."** Daniel received both. He was loaded with gifts, and made a Ruler over the Province of Babylon, and "Chief of the Governors" over the "Wise Men." But Daniel did not forget his companions, Shadrach, Meshach, and Abednego, in his exaltation. They had helped him by their prayers to secure the needed information as to the King's Dream, and he was determined that they should share in his honors, so he besought the King in their behalf, and they were given prominent offices, while Daniel sat in the "Gate of the King," the place where Councils were held, and matters of chief moment decided.

This chapter is one of the most remarkable in the Bible. It gives us a prophetical outline of the history of the Gentile nations, in their relation to the nation of Israel, from the time of Nebuchadnezzar on down to the Second Coming of Christ. If the statesmen and kings of the earth knew about it, and would heed its teaching, they would not be so ambitious to become world rulers, and would see in the rise of lawless organizations that we are nearing the end of the "Times of the Gentiles," and that the Second Coming of the Lord is not so far away.

CHAPTER THREE

The Golden Image

THE IMAGE

"Nebuchadnezzar the King made an 'Image of Gold,' whose height was three-score cubits, and the breadth thereof six cubits: he set it up in the plain of Dura, in the Province of Babylon." Dan. **3:1.**

The events recorded in this chapter happened about twenty-three years after Nebuchadnezzar had his Dream of the "Golden Headed Image." It is hardly likely therefore that that Dream suggested "The Golden Image." If it did, Nebuchadnezzar in his pride resolved to go one better, and, instead of erecting an image the head only of which was of gold and the remainder of the image of baser metals, resolved to make the whole of his image of **"Gold."** Nebuchadnezzar had reached a point in his career when he wished to emulate the kings of Egypt, who, while still alive, sought to perpetuate their memory, and the glory of their reign, by having carved out of the solid rock a statue or image of themselves. But as Babylon was located in a level country where there was no rocky formation, Nebuchadnezzar had to resort to a different kind of image or statue, and so he resolved, in harmony with the magnificent buildings of Babylon, as the "Tower of Bel," and the "Hanging Gardens," to make it of "Gold." The fact that it was erected on the "Plain of Dura," and not in the city of Babylon, reveals the fact that Nebuchadnezzar had a twofold purpose in its erection there. First, he did not want it to be overshadowed by the great buildings of Babylon, and in the second place, he had reached the conclusion that, if he was to keep his Great Empire intact, composed as it was of peoples from many nations, with various religious beliefs, he must cement them together by some form of "State Religion," and as he proposed to invite all the great men of the many provinces of his Empire, there would not be any place sufficiently large in the city of Babylon, so he chose the "Plain of Dura."

The critics of the Book of Daniel claim that everything in it bears the stamp of "Reckless Exaggeration," and that an image ninety feet high, and nine feet wide (counting a cubit as eighteen inches) is not only enormous in size, but is out of proportion, and that there was not enough gold in that country to make such an image of solid gold. But they forget that the riches and splendor of those days, and of Egypt and Babylon, put our time in the shade, and that Nebuchadnezzar had conquered Egypt, and taken back with him vast quantities of gold.

But it does not say that the Image was of solid gold. It doubtless was a wooden image plated with gold, which would have the same appearance as an image of solid gold, and answer the same purpose. Again, the height of the Image in proportion to its width seems to indicate that the Image stood on a pedestal, high in the air, so it could be seen above the heads of the multitude all over the "Plain of Dura," and that the height of the "Image" included the pedestal, and as there would be no need of making the pedestal of gold, this would reduce the golden part of the Image. Whatever Nebuchadnezzar did was **"Colossal."** The stupendous walls of Babylon have never been equalled, neither have its public buildings. See the chapter on "The Fall of Babylon."

The dimensions of the Image are not without significance. Its height was sixty cubits, and its breadth six cubits. Now six is the **"NUMBER OF MAN."** Six stops short of seven, which is the "Perfect Number," or the number of Completeness. Six then is the number of human incompleteness. Man was made on the sixth day. His appointed days of labor are six, the seventh day is God's day. The number six reminds us of the number of the "Beast" in Rev. 13·18, which is 666. Little did Nebuchadnezzar know that the erection of that "Golden Image" on the Plain of Dura was a "Prophetic Fore-Shadowing" of that Image that the "False Prophet" shall command the people to make to the "Beast," or "Antichrist." An Image that shall be given **life,** and the **power to speak.** And all who will not worship the Beast shall be **killed,** not by being thrown into a "Fiery Furnace," but by the "Guillotine." They will be beheaded. Rev. 20:4. In that day no one shall be able to buy or sell unless he has the "Mark of the Beast," which is his **"Number,"** which is **666,** the **"NUMBER OF MAN."** Rev. 13:13-18. The worship of the "Image of the Beast" will be the culmination of the **"Deification of Man,"** and the outcome of all such idolatry will be the bringing to an end of **"MAN'S DAY,"** or the "Times of the Gentiles," and the setting up of the "Stone Kingdom."

DEDICATION OF THE IMAGE

> "Then Nebuchadnezzar the King sent to gather together the princes, the governors, and the captains, the judges, the treasurers, the counsellors, the sheriffs, and all the rulers of the provinces, to come to the **'Dedication of the Image'** which Nebuchadnezzar the King had set up. Then the princes, the governors, and captains, the judges, the treasurers, the counsellors, the sheriffs, and all the rulers of the provinces, were gathered together unto the 'Dedication of the Image' that Nebuchadnezzar the King had set up." Verses 2-3.

The arrangements for the Dedication of the Image were very elaborate. All the nations of the earth that had become subject to Babylon were called upon to send representatives to the great ceremony. Babylon was crowded with the great men and rulers of the nations and their retainers. Everything was on a scale of great magnificence. It was probably the greatest day in all Babylon's history.

"Then a herald cried aloud, To you it is commanded, O people, nations, and languages, that at what time ye hear the sound of the cornet, flute, harp, sackbut, psaltery, dulcimer, and all kinds of music, ye fall down and **WORSHIP** the 'Golden Image' that Nebuchadnezzar the King hath set up: and whoso falleth not down and **WORSHIPPETH** shall the same hour be **cast into the midst of a burning 'Fiery Furnace.'** Therefore at that time, when all the people heard the sound of the cornet, flute, harp, sackbut, psaltery, and all kinds of music, all the people, the nations, and the languages, fell down and **WORSHIPPED** the 'Golden Image' that Nebuchadnezzar the King had set up." Verses 4-7.

It is not clear from the text that those who were invited to the "Dedication of the Image" understood that the "Dedication" would be of a religious character and take the form of **WORSHIP.** They probably expected the ceremonies to be of the usual character of such celebrations. The presence therefore of bands and orchestras did not make them suspicious. They probably had been informed that the Image was in honor of the King, and to memorialize the Golden character of his reign. But King Nebuchadnezzar had something else in mind. He was at the head of a vast Empire, composed of many kingdoms, speaking different languages, and of various religions. He knew for a nation to have but one religion would have a unifying effect. Such unification had probably become a political necessity. So he decided to set up a "State Religion," of a Babylonish type, to be known as the

"RELIGION OF BABYLON,"

and of an idolatrous character, as were the religions of the surrounding nations. But in doing this he was guilty of "Religious Intolerance," in that the penalty of refusal was death in a "Fiery Furnace," a type of the "Inquisition."

All men are religious by nature, and are easily carried away by anything that stirs their religious feelings. Knowing this, Nebuchadnezzar took advantage of it. Everything was done to excite and stir the religious emotions of that vast multitude on the "Plain of Dura." Large orchestras, with their various musical instruments, were stationed at convenient places, and all the paraphernalia and ritualistic ceremony of idolatrous worship, with the most gorgeous display of religious trappings, such as were used by the "Babylonian Cults," were doubtless used to impress the bystanders, and get them to worship the Image. The same method has its advocates today. And for argument they point to the Roman Catholic Church, and claim that its unity and success is largely due to the spectacular character of its religious services, which are of Babylonian origin. See the writer's work on the Book of Revelation, pages 149 to 153, for confirmation.

There are movements on foot today for a union of all religious denominations and sects in one vast organization. The purpose is to establish one "Universal Religion" that will appeal to the "Artistic" and "Esthetic" in man. A religion that is "Cainite" in character because there is no **BLOOD** in it, and that exalts man and his works, which the Scriptures declare will be the character of the closing days of the "Times of the Gentiles," when men shall have "the form of Godliness" without the **"POWER."** 2 Tim. 3:1-7. When the true Church is "caught out," those who are left behind will drift into the Papacy, that will then be the "Universal Church," the last phase of which is Babylonish, and is seen in the "Purple Clad Woman," that, in Rev. 17:1-5, rides the "Scarlet Colored Beast"—**"MYSTERY, BABYLON THE GREAT, THE MOTHER OF HARLOTS AND ABOMINATIONS OF THE EARTH."**

To insure the success of his plan Nebuchadnezzar took one precaution. He was determined that there should be no lack of unity. The worship must be universal or there would be discord. An ounce of prevention was worth a pound of cure. It was best to forestall any rebellion, and so he had constructed near the Image a large "Furnace," like a blast furnace, in which a fire was kindled, into which he threatened to throw any person who would not bow down and worship his "Golden Image." He counted on the love of life, and the fear of suffering, to prevent any opposition. Doubtless those who were not in his confidence wondered why the "Furnace" was there and already lighted. But they did not long remain in doubt, for a herald announced that whosoever would not fall down and worship the "Golden Image" would be cast alive into the "Fiery Furnace." The result was, that, at the sound of the musical instruments, the vast multitude fell upon their faces. But not all. There were three men, all prominent officials, who refused to bow the knee. They were **JEWS**, and their names were Shadrach, Meshach, and Abed-nego. Where Daniel was we do not know. He may have been ill, or away on State business. But this we do know, that if he had been there he would have refused to worship the Image.

The failure to worship of the "Three Hebrew Children" was noticed by certain Chaldeans, who had either been appointed as spies, or who were officials or politicians whose schemes had been blocked by these faithful public servants, and being jealous of the influence and power of the Jews in the affairs of the Empire, were glad of an excuse for bringing a charge against them, that they might get them out of the way.

"Wherefore at that time certain Chaldeans came near, and accused the Jews. They spake and said to the King Nebuchadnezzar, O King, live forever. Thou, O King, hast made a decree, that every man that shall hear the sound of the cornet, flute, harp, sackbut, psaltery, and dulcimer, and all kinds of music, shall fall down and worship the 'Golden Image:' and whoso falleth not down and worshippeth, that he should be cast into the midst of a burning 'Fiery Furnace.' There are certain Jews whom thou hast set over the affairs of the Province of Babylon, Shadrach, Meshach, and Abednego; these men, O King, **HAVE NOT REGARDED THEE,** they **SERVE NOT THY GODS,** nor **WORSHIP THE GOLDEN IMAGE WHICH THOU HAST SET UP."** Verses 8-12.

When the King heard these three clearly-put charges he was furious. Furious that anyone had the temerity to show disrespect for him, and his gods, and disobey his command to worship the Golden Image. Surely there was some mistake. These men must either not have heard the command, or misunderstood it. So he immediately summoned them into his presence, and addressing them said—

"Is it true, O Shadrach, Meshach, and Abednego, do ye not serve **MY GODS,** nor **WORSHIP THE GOLDEN IMAGE THAT I HAVE SET UP?** Now if ye be ready that at what time ye hear the sound of the cornet, flute, harp, sackbut, psaltery, and dulcimer, and all kinds of music, ye fall down and worship the Image which I have made: well: but if ye worship not, ye shall be cast the **same hour** into the midst of a burning 'Fiery Furnace;' and **WHO IS THAT GOD THAT SHALL DELIVER YOU OUT OF MY HANDS?"** Verses 14-15.

This defiant challenge of the King—**"WHO is that God that shall deliver you out of MY hands?"** is so contrary to his confession made to Daniel at the time of the Interpretation of the King's Dream—**"YOUR God is a GOD of gods, and a LORD of kings, and a REVEALER OF SECRETS,"** that we are led to inquire what has caused this radical change against the God of the Jews. Was Nebuchadnezzar not sincere when he made his confession to Daniel, or had subsequent events caused him to change his mind? We must not forget that the Dream of Nebuchadnezzar had occurred twenty years before, and that in the meantime, he had taken Jerusalem the second time (B. C. 598) and carried captive the majority of its inhabitants, including many of the sacred vessels of the Temple, and furthermore, he had besieged the city the third time (B. C. 587), took and destroyed it, and burned the Temple, and left the Holy Land in desolation. As Oriental Monarchs believed that their victories were a triumph of their "gods" over the "gods" of their vanquished foes, it would be conclusive evidence to Nebuchadnezzar that his victories over the earthly Capital of Jehovah, and the destruction of the Temple, meant that Jehovah was not the supreme Deity, but that his own God "Merodach" was. Hence his challenge—**"WHO is that God that shall deliver you out of MY hands?"**

THE CHALLENGE ACCEPTED

"Shadrach, Meshach, and Abed-nego answered and said to the king, O Nebuchadnezzar, we are not careful to answer thee in the matter. If it be so, **OUR GOD** whom we serve is **ABLE TO DELIVER US FROM THE BURNING FIERY FURNACE,** and He **WILL DELIVER US OUT OF THINE HAND,** O King. **BUT IF NOT,** be it known unto thee, O king, that we **WILL NOT SERVE THY GODS, NOR WORSHIP THE GOLDEN IMAGE WHICH THOU HAST SET UP.**" Verses 16-18.

What a noble answer. What men of faith they were. It was not a presumptuous reply, for they knew their God. They spoke with a decision that is magnificent. They said—**"We are not CAREFUL."** That is, we have no **concern** as to the matter. Phil. 4:6-7. Our God is **ABLE** to deliver us, and He **WILL** deliver.

BUT IF NOT, that is if He does not see fit to deliver us, it will make no difference as to our decision, we **WILL NOT serve thy Gods, nor worship the Golden Image which thou hast set up.** They had the spirit of the Martyrs. They "loved not their **lives**" and were resolved to be faithful **UNTO** death." Not **until** the end of their natural lives, but **unto** the death of the "Fiery Furnace." They would not yield or compromise. There was no mistaking the meaning of their answer, and it made the King more furious than ever.

THE HARMLESS FURNACE

"Then was Nebuchadnezzar full of fury, and the form of his visage was changed against Shadrach, Meshach, and Abed-nego: therefore he spake, and commanded that they should heat the Furnace one **SEVEN TIMES MORE** than it was wont to be heated. And he commanded the most mighty men that were in his army to bind Shadrach, Meshach, and Abed-nego, and to cast them into the burning 'Fiery Furnace.' Then these men were bound in their coats, their hosen, and their hats, and their other garments, and were cast into the midst of the burning 'Fiery Furnace.' Therefore because the king's commandment was urgent, and the furnace exceedingly hot, the flame of the fire slew those men that took up Shadrach, Meshach, and Abed-nego. And these three men Shadrach, Meshach, and Abed-nego, fell down bound into the midst of the burning 'Fiery Furnace.' Then Nebuchadnezzar the king was astonished, and rose up in haste, and spake, and said unto his counsellors, Did not we cast **three men bound** into the midst of the fire? They answered and said unto the king, True, O king. He answered and said, Lo, I see **four men loose,** walking in the midst of the fire, and they have no hurt; and the form of the **fourth** is like the **SON OF GOD."** Verses 19-25.

That the deliverance of the "Three Hebrew Children" from the burning "Fiery Furnace" was a **MIRACLE** no one can question. That men could survive and remain uninjured in fierce flames that would have melted iron, and walk to and fro and breathe as if only surrounded by the genial warmth of the sun, seems incredible. But that such a miracle was necessary to counteract the worship of the "Golden Image," and stop the persecution of the Jewish captives in Babylon, who were loyal to their religion, is clear.

The king, in his rage, over-reached himself when he commanded the "Furnace" to be heated "seven times hotter." That would only shorten the sufferings of his victims and hasten their destruction, and it was the cause of the death of the mighty men who threw them in. But the hand of God was in it. The fact that the heat of the "Furnace" was increased sevenfold made the "Miracle" that much greater, and revealed the hand of God in their deliverance. It is evident that some supernatural intelligence controlled the flames, for while they consumed the cords with which they were bound, they did not touch their clothing or singe their hair, and when they emerged from the "Furnace" there was no smell of fire upon them. When the flames burned off their bonds they made no attempt to escape from the "Furnace." The king put them in, and it was up to him to call them out. Then they had no desire to leave the "Furnace," for they had therein the companionship of the "Son of God," and they would rather be in the "Furnace" with the "Son of God" than in the Palace with the king. To them was fulfilled the promise—

> "When thou passest through the waters (like the Red Sea), I will be with thee; and through the rivers (like the Jordan), they shall not overflow thee: when thou **WALKEST THROUGH THE FIRE THOU SHALT NOT BE BURNED; NEITHER SHALL THE FLAME KINDLE UPON THEE."** Isa. 43:2.

It was to the three Hebrew Children that the writer of the Hebrews referred when he said, they **"Quenched the violence of FIRE."** Heb. 11 : 34.

What a scathing rebuke to the king's arrogant assertion, **"WHO is that God that shall deliver you out of my hands?"** was the deliverance of these men from the power of the flames. Their deliverance was a vindication of the course they had taken. None of the gods of the heathen had ever wrought such a deliverance as that, nor were they able to do so. The "Miracle" converted the king. He recognized that the God of the Jews was more powerful than his own gods.

A CONVINCED KING

"Then Nebuchadnezzar came near to the mouth of the burning 'Fiery Furnace,' and spake, and said, Shadrach, Meshach, and Abed-nego, **ye servants of the 'Most High God,' COME FORTH, AND COME HITHER.** Then Shadrach, Meshach, and Abed-nego, came forth of the midst of the fire. And the princes, governors, and captains, and the king's counsellors, being gathered together, saw these men, upon whose bodies the fire had no power, nor was an hair of their head singed, neither were their coats changed, nor the smell of fire had passed on them." Verses 26-27.

When bidden, Shadrach, Meshach, and Abed-nego walked out of the burning "Furnace," and the princes, governors, and captains, and the king's counsellors, were gathered together that they might look upon, and have optical and tangible proof that a miracle had been wrought. The preservation of the men put a stop to the worship of the "Golden Image."

THE ROYAL DECREE

"Then Nebuchadnezzar spake, and said, Blessed be the **GOD** of Shadrach, Meshach, and Abed-nego, **who hath sent His ANGEL,** and delivered His servants that **trusted in Him,** and have changed the king's word, and yielded their bodies, that they might not serve nor worship any god, except their own God. Therefore I make a decree, That every people, nation, and language, which speak anything amiss against the God of Shadrach, Meshach, and Abed-nego, shall be cut in pieces, and their houses shall be made a dunghill: **because there is no other God that can deliver after this sort.** Then the king promoted Shadrach, Meshach, and Abed-nego, in the Province of Babylon." Verses 28-30.

Had these three Jews been "time servers," the name of the true God would not have been exalted in Babylon, they would not have been promoted, and the "Decree of Toleration" by the king would not have been issued. The purpose then of the Miracle was not merely the deliverance of those three men, but the conviction of the king and the issuing of his "Royal Decree." That "Decree of Toleration," which God brought about by the Miracle, was not intended by God as a temporary attitude by the Gentile nations of Nebuchadnezzar's day, but is the attitude that God requires of all Gentile nations toward the Jews during the whole "Times of the Gentiles," and for which He will judge them at the **"Judgment of Nations,"** when the nations shall be judged for their treatment of Christ's **brethren—THE JEWS.** Matt. 25:31-46.

TYPICAL TEACHING OF THE MIRACLE

As we have seen that Nebuchadnezzar's **"Golden Image"** was a type of the **"IMAGE OF THE BEAST"** (Rev. 13:13-15), that is to be set up in Jerusalem in the closing days of this Dispensation, so the **"Three Hebrew Children,"** who would not worship the "Golden Image" of Nebuchadnezzar, are a type of the **"JEWISH REMNANT,"** the 144,000 **"Sealed**

Ones" of Rev. 7:3-8, who will pass unscathed through "The Great Tribulation." They are seen later in the Book of Revelation (Rev. 15:1-3) standing on a **"Sea of Glass," MINGLED WITH FIRE,** typical of the **"FIERY TRIALS"** (1 Pet. 1:7) through which they had passed. They had come out of "The Great Tribulation," for they had gotten the victory over the **"Beast,"** and over his **"Image,"** and over his **"Mark,"** and they are **"Israelites,"** for they sing the "New Song" of **"MOSES and of the LAMB,"** which only redeemed Israelites can sing. And as Shadrach, Meshach, and Abed-nego were not only delivered but **promoted,** so the "Jewish Remnant" of the "End Time" will be promoted and given positions of power and influence in the Millennial Kingdom of Christ.

CHAPTER FOUR

The Tree Dream

THE PROCLAMATION

"Nebuchadnezzar the king unto all people, nations, and languages, that dwell in all the earth;

PEACE BE MULTIPLIED UNTO YOU.

"I thought it good to shew the **signs** and **wonders** that the **HIGH GOD** hath **WROUGHT TOWARD ME.** How great are His signs! And how mighty are His wonders! His Kingdom is an Everlasting Kingdom, and His Dominion is from generation to generation." Verses 1-3.

This chapter is a "Babylonian State Document." It is a "Proclamation" of King Nebuchadnezzar to the **whole world.** It was issued in B. C. 562, the year he recovered from his insanity, and a year before his death. It was intended as a confession of his sin of Pride, and an explanation of the cause of his insanity, and of his conversion to the service of the Most High. The tone of it is in marked contrast with his previous utterances. And the salutation, **"Peace be multiplied unto you,"** are the words of a Christian, and sound strange coming from the lips of a heathen king whose life had been spent in warfare for the purpose of building up a world-wide Empire. But his Dreams and experience had taught him that his Kingdom was not to last forever, and that the "Stone Kingdom" of the "Most High God" was to be an **"EVERLASTING KINGDOM,"** whose dominion would last from **generation to generation.**

The main part of the Proclamation is taken up with an account of a "Dream" which the King had, and its interpretation and fulfilment in his own **experience.**

A TROUBLED KING

"I Nebuchadnezzar was at rest in mine house, and flourishing in my palace: I saw a **'Dream'** which made me afraid, and the thoughts upon my bed and the visions of my head **troubled me.** Therefore made I a decree to bring in all the 'Wise Men' of Babylon before me, that they might make known unto me the **interpretation of the 'Dream.'** Then came in the Magicians, the Astrologers, the Chaldeans, and the Soothsayers: and I told the **'Dream'** before them; but they did not make known unto me the Interpretation thereof." Verses 4-7.

The Proclamation begins with the significant words—"I Nebuchadnezzar was at rest in mine house, and flourishing in my palace." Like the rich man in the Parable, he was clothed in purple and fine linen and fared sumptuously every day, and cared little for the misery of others, for his thoughts were self-centered, and taken up with his own greatness. He was at **"rest"** because he had conquered all his enemies. He was familiar with all the perils of the battlefield, and had faced them without fear. And now in the quiet and rest of his Palace, with no enemy to fear, he is troubled by a "Dream." If the "Dream" had to do with his Empire, he probably would not have cared so much, but he realized that it in some way had to do with himself. He was anxious therefore to have it interpreted. So he sent for the "Wise Men" of Babylon, and while he this time had not forgotten his "Dream," and repeated it to them, they failed him as before. Then Daniel appeared upon the scene. Where he had been, or why he had not been called in the first place, we are not told.

"But at the last Daniel came in before me, whose name was Belteshazzar, according to the name of my god, and in whom is the Spirit of the Holy Gods: and before him I told the 'Dream,' saying, O Belteshazzar, 'Master of the Magicians,' because I know that the Spirit of the Holy Gods is in thee, and no **'secret'** troubleth thee, tell me the visions of my 'Dream' that I have seen, and the Interpretation thereof." Verses 8-9.

THE DREAM

"Thus were the 'Visions' of mine head in my bed: I saw, and behold a **TREE** in the **midst of the earth,** and the height thereof was great. The **TREE** grew, and was strong, and the height thereof **reached unto heaven,** and the sight thereof to the **end of all the earth**: the leaves thereof were fair, and the fruit thereof much, and in it was meat for all: the beasts of the field had shadow under it, and the fowls of the heaven dwelt in the boughs thereof, and all flesh was fed of it." Verses 10-12.

While Nebuchadnezzar was wondering what the "Vision of the Tree" meant, he saw descend from Heaven a **"WATCHER,"** or **"HOLY ONE."** From verse 17 we learn that there is in Heaven a "Court," known as the

"COURT OF THE WATCHERS"
or
"HOLY ONES,"

and that it was by a **"DECREE"** of that Court, to which the case of Nebuchadnezzar had been referred, that he was condemned to live as a "Beast" for a period of seven years. The purpose of the "Decree" was that the inhabitants of the earth might know that the **"Most High" ruleth in the kingdoms of men, and giveth them to whomsoever He will.** The Book of Daniel reveals the close connection between the earth and the "Spirit World." In chapter 9: 10 we read of the visit of the angel Gabriel to Daniel, and in chapter 10: 4-12 of other heavenly beings. In Eph. 6: 11-12 we are told to put on the whole "Armor of God," for, "we wrestle not against flesh and blood (earthly beings), but against **'Principalities,'** against **'Powers,'** against the **'Rulers of the Darkness of this World,'** against **'Spiritual Wickedness'** in high (heavenly) places." There are three heavens spoken of in the Scriptures. The first is the atmosphere of our earth, the third is the Heaven where God dwells, and the second is an intermediate heaven where the "Principalities and Powers of Evil," comprising the "Kingdom of Satan," dwell. Satan is the **"PRINCE"** of the "Powers of the Air," and he has many subordinate Princes who are delegated to do his obstructive work. Two of them are mentioned by Daniel, the **"PRINCE OF PERSIA"** and the **"PRINCE OF GRECIA."** Dan. 10:13, 20. From this it would look as if Satan had a delegated Prince for every nation to superintend his work there. So great and powerful are these Princes that it takes the power and strength of **"MICHAEL"** the Archangel, the Commander-in-Chief of the "Armies of Heaven," to overcome them. Dan. 10:13; Jude 9; Rev. 12:7-9. That the "Powers of Evil" in the Heavenlies, as well as the conduct of earthly powers, may be properly controlled, and officially passed upon, there is a "Judicial Court" in Heaven before which their cases are tried, that the Book of Daniel calls the **"COURT OF THE WATCHERS,"** and whose decrees, as in the case of Nebuchadnezzar, are executed on the earth.

What troubled Nebuchadnezzar was not the "Vision of the Tree," but the **PERSONIFICATION** of it by the "Watcher" or "Holy One," who changed the word **"it"** to the personal pronoun **"HIS."**

'I saw in the visions of my head upon my bed, and, behold, a **'WATCHER'** and a **'HOLY ONE'** came down from Heaven; he cried aloud, and said thus. **Hew down the TREE, and cut off HIS branches, shake off HIS leaves, and scatter HIS fruit: let the beasts get away from under it. and**

the fowls from HIS branches: nevertheless, leave the stump of HIS roots in the earth, even with a band of iron and brass, in the tender grass of the field; and let it be wet with the dew of heaven, and let HIS portion be with the BEASTS in the grass of the earth: let HIS HEART be changed from MAN'S, and let a BEAST'S HEART be given unto HIM: and let 'SEVEN TIMES' pass over HIM. This matter is by the **Decree of the 'WATCHERS,'** and the demand by the word of the **'HOLY ONES:'** to the intent that the living may know that the **'MOST HIGH'** ruleth in the 'Kingdom of Men,' and giveth it to whomsoever He will, and setteth up over it the basest of men. This 'Dream' I King Nebuchadnezzar have seen. Now thou, O Belteshazzar, declare the Interpretation thereof, forasmuch as all the 'Wise Men' of my Kingdom are not able to make known unto me the Interpretation: **but thou art able**: for the Spirit of the Holy Gods is in thee." Verses 13-18.

When Daniel heard the Dream he was greatly troubled, and for one hour was too astonished to speak. Not that he did not know the meaning of the Dream, but he dreaded to tell the King the unpleasant news. When however the King, who seemed to realize the personal character of the Dream, assured him that he need not fear to tell him, then Daniel, to prepare the King for the judgment that was to come upon him, said—"My lord, the Dream be to them that hate thee, and the Interpretation thereof to thine enemies." That is, I wish that the calamity that is to fall on you might fall on your enemies. It was a wise answer, and paved the way for

THE INTERPRETATION.

"The **TREE** that thou sawest, which grew, and was strong, whose height reached unto the heaven, and the sight thereof to all the earth;

whose leaves were fair, and the fruit thereof much, and in it was meat for all; under which the beasts of the field dwelt, and upon whose branches the fowls of the heaven had their habitation: it is **THOU,** O King, that art grown and become strong: for thy greatness is grown, and reacheth unto heaven, and thy dominion to the end of the earth. And whereas the King saw a **'WATCHER'** and a **'HOLY ONE'** coming down from Heaven, and saying, Hew the **TREE** down, and destroy it; yet leave the stump of the roots thereof in the earth, even with a band of iron and brass, in the tender grass of the field; and let it be wet with the dew of heaven, and let **HIS** portion be with the beasts of the field, till **'SEVEN TIMES'** pass over him; this is the Interpretation, O King, and this is the **DECREE** of the Most High, which is come upon my Lord the King: that **THEY SHALL DRIVE THEE FROM MEN, AND THY DWELLING SHALL BE WITH THE BEASTS OF THE FIELD, AND THEY SHALL MAKE THEE TO EAT GRASS AS OXEN, AND THEY SHALL WET THEE WITH THE DEW OF HEAVEN, AND 'SEVEN TIMES' SHALL PASS OVER THEE, TILL THOU KNOW THAT THE MOST HIGH RULETH IN THE KINGDOM OF MEN, AND GIVETH IT TO WHOMSOEVER HE WILL.** And whereas they commanded to leave the stump of the tree roots: thy Kingdom shall be sure unto thee, after that thou shalt know **THAT THE HEAVENS DO RULE."** Verses 20-26.

From the Interpretation the King could not mistake the meaning of his Dream. Then Daniel, like the faithful prophet that he was, took advantage of the opportunity and counselled the King to forsake his sinful ways.

"Wherefore, O King, let my counsel be acceptable unto thee, and break off thy sins by righteousness, and thine iniquities by shewing mercy to the poor; if it may be a lengthening of thy tranquility." Verse 27.

THE DREAM FULFILLED

But the King did not take Daniel's advice, and later had to make the humiliating confession that all that had been foretold about him had come to pass. But it did not come at once God gave him a year's grace. Because the sentence was not executed at once Nebuchadnezzar may have thought that Daniel was mistaken, or that God had forgotten. But at the end of twelve months, as the King was walking in his palace, and beheld the great city of Babylon as it spread out before him from his Palace window, he exclaimed in his pride—

"Is not this GREAT BABYLON, that I have built for the 'House of the Kingdom' by the might of MY POWER, and for the honor of MY MAJESTY?" Verse 30.

That was the fatal moment. The time of probation was up.

"While the word was in the King's mouth, there fell a voice from Heaven, saying, O King Nebuchadnezzar, to thee it is spoken: The Kingdom is departed from thee. And they shall drive thee from men, and thy dwelling shall be with the beasts of the field: they shall make thee to eat grass as oxen, and **'SEVEN TIMES'** shall pass over thee, until thou know that the Most High ruleth in the 'Kingdom of Men,' and giveth it (probably the Babylonian Kingdom) to whomsoever he will." Verses 31-32.

The sentence was immediately executed. Not another moment of grace was given the King.

"The **same hour** was the thing fulfilled upon Nebuchadnezzar: and he was driven from men, and did eat grass as oxen, and his body was wet with the dew of heaven, till his hairs were grown like eagle's feathers, and his nails like bird's claws." Verse 33.

The type of insanity that befell Nebuchadnezzar is a disease called **"lycanthropy,"** in which the patient imagines that he is some sort of a **beast.** Nebuchadnezzar imagined he was an **ox.** He was not confined but was allowed to roam in the fields, probably the grounds of the Palace, for we are told that he did eat grass as oxen, and his body was wet with the dew of heaven, and to complete the delusion he probably went about on all fours.

Nebuchadnezzar's insanity lasted for **seven years,** for that is what the **"Seven Times"** mean. The period is not without its prophetical significance. It does not signify the length of the "Times of the Gentiles," for a **"Time"** is not a period of 360 years, but only of one year. See chapter nine. The "Seven Times" foreshadow the **"SEVEN YEARS"** of the rule of Antichrist, or the "Seventieth Week" of Daniel's "Seventy Weeks," when the **"One" that hindereth — THE HOLY SPIRIT,** shall have left the earth, having gone back with the Church, and when men in their madness and bestiality will act like beasts, and give their service and worship to Antichrist, that John in the Apocalypse calls—**"THE BEAST."** At the end of the "Seven Times" (years), Nebuchadnezzar's reason was restored to him.

THE KING'S RECOVERY

"And at the end of the days I Nebuchadnezzar lifted up mine eyes unto heaven, and mine understanding returned unto me, and I blessed the Most High, and I praised and honored Him that liveth forever, whose dominion is an everlasting dominion, and His Kingdom is from generation to generation: and all the inhabitants of the earth are reputed as nothing: and He doeth according to His will in the Army of Heaven, and among the inhabitants of the earth: and none can stay His hand, or say unto Him, What doest Thou?" Verses 34-35.

At the end of the "Seven Years" Nebuchadnezzar lifted up his eyes to Heaven. A beast does not do that. It, particularly an ox, looks downward. What Nebuchadnezzar meant was that he looked upward in prayer to God, and acknowledged His supremacy. In the doing of that his reason was restored, and he was fit to resume his kingly duties.

"At the same time my reason returned to me; and for the glory of my Kingdom, mine honor and brightness (glory) returned unto me; and my counsellors and my lords sought unto me; and I was established in my Kingdom, and excellent majesty was added unto me. Now I Nebuchadnezzar praise and extol and honor the King of Heaven, all whose works are truth, and His ways judgment: and those that walk in pride He is able to abase." Verses 36-37.

Nebuchadnezzar's restoration to his kingly rights was in fulfilment of the promise that his insanity should only last seven years, and that his Kingdom should then be made **"sure,"** or restored to him. Verse 26. During his insanity, his son, Evil-Merodach, is said to have reigned as Regent in his stead. The fact that he was graciously received back by his counsellors and lords is an indication that they looked upon his insanity as only temporary, and yet, if that be true, it seems strange that they did not confine him to the palace, instead of **"driving"** (vs. 25) him out into the fields away from the haunts of men. This is the last we read in the Scriptures of Nebuchadnezzar. He lived only about a year after his restoration to his throne, but it was a year during which great honors were heaped upon him, and in which he glorified God. He died after a brief illness in B. C. 561, and was succeeded by his son Evil-Merodach.

CHAPTER FIVE

The Fall of Babylon

THE CITY OF BABYLON

The founder of Babylon was Nimrod, the great-grandson of Noah, over 2000 years before Christ.

> "And Cush begat Nimrod: he began to be a mighty one in the earth. He was a mighty hunter before the Lord: wherefore it is said, Even as Nimrod the mighty hunter before the Lord. And the beginning of his kingdom was **BABEL** (margin Babylon), and Erech and Accad, and Calneh, in the land of Shinar." Gen. 10:8-10.

Nimrod was a Hamite. Nineveh was founded by Asshur, a son of Shem. Gen. 10:11, 22. Nineveh became the capital of Assyria. About B. C. 1270, the Assyrian kings became masters of Chaldea, or Babylonia, of which Babylon was the capital. For several centuries the history of Babylon was overshadowed by that of Nineveh. In the time of Tiglath-pileser of Assyria, Nabonassar ascended the throne of Babylon in B. C. 747. About B. C. 720 Berodach-baladan became king of Babylon, and sent ambassadors to Hezekiah, king of Judah. 2 Kings 20:12-18. Isa. 39:1-7. A few years later Sargon, king of Assyria, defeated and dethroned Berodach-baladan. Sennacherib completed the subjection of Babylon, which he annexed to the Assyrian Empire about B. C. 690. The conquest of Nineveh and the overthrow of the Assyrian Empire, which was effected about B. C. 625, by Cyaxeres the Mede, and his ally Nabopolassar, the rebellious governor of Babylon, enabled the latter to found the Babylonian Empire. He reigned from B. C. 625 to B. C. 605. He was succeeded by his more famous son

Nebuchadnezzar, the greatest king of ancient times, who rebuilt and beautified the city of Babylon until it was the most magnificent city the world has ever seen.

The city of Babylon was built in an exact square of 15 miles on a side, or 60 miles around. It was surrounded by a brick wall 87 feet thick, which, according to Herodotus, was 350 feet high. On the walls were 250 towers, and the top of the wall was wide enough to permit six chariots to drive abreast. Outside this wall was a vast ditch or moat surrounding the city, kept filled with water from the river Euphrates, and crossed by draw-bridges in front of the gates. Inside the wall, and not far from it, was another wall, not much inferior, but narrower, extending around the city. Twenty-five magnificent avenues, 150 feet wide, ran across the city from north to south, and the same number crossed them at right angles from east to west, making 676 great squares, each nearly three-fifths of a mile on a side. A wide avenue also ran around the city inside the walls, and close to them, into which the cross avenues emptied. At the ends of these cross avenues magnificently burnished two-leafed gates of brass were built in the city walls, that shone, as they were opened or closed, in the rising or setting sun, like leaves of flame.

The city was divided into two equal parts by the river Euphrates, that flowed diagonally across it, and its banks were walled and pierced with brazen gates at the main avenues. Outside these river walls, and between them and the river, splendid wharves lined the river on each side within the city. Ferry boats crossed the river at each of the main avenues, and at the central avenue a magnificent bridge spanned the river, at each end of which was a beautiful Palace. These Palaces were connected by a subterranean passageway, or "**tube**," underneath the bed of the river, in which, at different points, were located sumptuous banqueting rooms constructed entirely of brass. Near one of these Palaces stood the

TOWER OF BEL,

consisting of eight towers, each 75 feet high, rising one upon the other, with an outside winding stairway to its summit, which towers, with the Chapel on the top, made a height of 660 feet. This Chapel contained the most expensive furniture of any place of worship in the world. One "Golden Image" alone, 45 feet high, was valued at $17,500,000, and the whole of the sacred utensils used in worship were reckoned to be worth $200,000,000. Babylon also contained one of the "Seven Wonders" of the world, the famous **"HANGING GARDENS."** These "Gardens" were 400 feet square, and were raised in terraces one above the other, to the height of 350 feet, and were reached by stairways ten feet wide. The top of each terrace was covered with large stone slabs on which were laid a bed of rushes, then a thick layer of asphalt, next two courses of brick, cemented together, and finally plates of lead to prevent leakage; the whole was then covered with earth and planted with shrubbery and large trees. The whole had the appearance from a distance of a forest-covered mountain, which would be a remarkable sight in the level plain of the Euphrates. These "Gardens" were built by Nebuchadnezzar simply to please his wife, who was Amyitis, daughter of Cyaxares, king of the mountainous country of Media, and who was thus made more contented with her surroundings. The rest of the city was, in its glory and magnificence, in keeping with these palaces, towers, and "Hanging Gardens." It contained many beautiful parks, and there was much unoccupied land that could be tilled, and help support the over 1,000,000 population. The character of its inhabitants, and of its official life at the zenith of its history, is seen in the description of "Belshazzar's Feast." Never before or since has this earth seen its equal. The Prophet Isaiah speaks of it as—**Babylon, the glory of kingdoms, the beauty of the Chaldees' Excellency."** Isa. 13: 19.

BELSHAZZAR'S FEAST

> "Belshazzar the king made a great Feast to a thousand of his lords, and drank wine before the thousand. Belshazzar, whiles he tasted the wine, commanded to bring the golden and silver vessels which his father Nebuchadnezzar had taken out of the Temple which was in Jerusalem; that the king, and his princes, his wives and his concubines, might drink therein. Then they brought the golden vessels that were taken out of the Temple of the House of God which was at Jerusalem; and the king, and his princes, his wives, and his concubines, drank in them. They drank wine, and praised the gods of gold, and of silver, of brass, of iron, of wood, and of stone." Verses 1-4.

Nebuchadnezzar was succeeded at his death, B. C. 561, by his son Evil-Merodach, who at once liberated Jehoiachin, king of Judah, from prison and fed him from his own table. 2 Kings 25:27-30. Jer. 52:31-34. After a reign of two years Evil-Merodach was put to death by conspirators, headed by Neriglissar, his brother-in-law, who ascended the throne and reigned for about four years, being killed in battle in the year B. C. 556. His son, and successor, Laborosoarchod, an imbecile child, was king for less than a year, when he was beaten to death, and the throne was seized by a usurper, Nabonidus (or Nabonnaid), another son-in-law of Nebuchadnezzar, who had married the widow of Neriglissar, and who reigned from B. C. 555 to the Fall of Babylon in B. C. 538. According to Daniel, Belshazzar, and not Nabonidus, was King of Babylon when it fell. But Berosus, a heathen historian, who lived about 250 years after Daniel, in his list of the kings of Babylon, omits the name of Belshazzar, and gives the name of Nabonnaid (Nabonidus) as the last king of Babylon. On account of this the critics attack the truthfulness of the Book of Daniel. But its truthfulness has been vindicated by the deciphering of a number of clay tablets taken from the ruins of Babylonia, on which the name of Belsharuzzar frequently appears as the son of Nabonnaid, and as sharing the government with him. Thus we see that the Belsharuzzar of the tablets is the Belshazzar of the Bible, and that Daniel is historically correct.

As the Prophet Jeremiah had foretold—"All nations shall serve **HIM** (Nebuchadnezzar), and his **SON,** and his **SON'S SON, until the very time of his land come"** (Jer. 27 : 7), it is clear that Belshazzar must have been a **GRANDSON,** and a son, not of a daughter, but of a **son** of Nebuchadnezzar. But as we have seen that his reputed father, Nabonidus, was not a son of Nebuchadnezzar, the only solution seems to be that Belshazzar was a **son of a son** of Nebuchadnezzar, and was adopted by Nabonidus to conciliate the royal family, and because of his adoption could be legally called the **son** of Nabonidus.

Belshazzar, at the time the incidents in this chapter took place, was reigning in conjunction with his father Nabonidus, who was away on some military expedition and had left Belshazzar in charge of the city of Babylon. Feasts were not uncommon in Babylon, but the "Feast of Belshazzar" was no common Feast. There is no feast like it recorded in all history. The only feast that approaches it is the Feast given by Ahasuerus, King of Persia, to the Princes of the 120 Provinces of his Kingdom, given in Shushan the Palace in B. C. 521, and recorded in the first chapter of Esther. Belshazzar's Feast was the turning point in the history of Babylon. It marked the transition from the "Head of Gold" to the "Arms and Breast of Silver" of the "Image," and from the "Lion" to the "Bear" phase of Gentile rule. Dan. 7: 1.5. It took place in B. C. 538, twenty-three years after the death of Nebuchadnezzar. As these years were taken up with events that had no relation to the Jews they are passed over in silence. Even Daniel drops out of sight. But he is not forgotten by God, who gives him "Visions" of coming events.

The Feast of Belshazzar was **given in a spirit of**

contempt and defiance. The city of Babylon was in a state of siege. The armies of the Medes and Persians were encamped outside its walls. But Belshazzar felt secure, for the drawbridges had been drawn up, the brazen gates barred, and Belshazzar knew that the walls of the city were impregnable; and he was confident that his soldiers from their position on the lofty walls would be able to destroy any who should attempt to batter down the gates. The city also was provisioned for several years' siege, and with the tillable ground within the city walls its capture could be postponed indefinitely. So Belshazzar to show his contempt of the besieging army gave his great Feast. The character of the Feast is seen in the conduct of the guests. **"They drank wine, and praised the gods of gold, and of silver, of brass, of iron** (reminding us of Nebuchadnezzar's Dream), **of wood, and of stone."** It was a Feast of licentiousness, drunkenness, and idolatrous worship.

In the midst of the Feast, the King, Belshazzar, his brain befuddled with wine, and desirous of doing something unique and sensational, surpassed all his previous blasphemous and sacrilegious acts by ordering to be brought into the Banqueting Hall the sacred vessels of gold and silver that his grandfather Nebuchadnezzar had taken from the Temple at Jerusalem, sixty-eight years before. When these vessels were brought in they were distributed among the drunken guests, and they drank wine from them to the gods of gold, silver, brass, iron, wood, and stone, and thus desecrated those sacred vessels of the Lord. That was the fatal moment, the turning point of the Feast. It filled Babylon's **"CUP OF INIQUITY" to the brim.** Her doom was sealed.

THE FINGER OF GOD

"In the **SAME HOUR** came forth the fingers of a man's hand, and wrote over against the Candlestick upon the plaster of the wall of the King's

Palace: and the King saw the part of the hand that wrote. Then the King's countenance was changed, and his thoughts troubled him, so that the joints of his loins were loosed, and his knees smote one against another." Verses 5-6.

No flash of supernatural light, nor deafening peal of thunder, startled the drunken revelers, thus announcing the interference of God in their impious carousal. But out of the "sleeve of the night" the Hand of God appeared, and with its finger silently wrote, in mystic characters, on the wall over against the lighted Candlestick, where it could readily be seen by all the assembled guests, the doom of Babylon. The fact that the writing remained indelibly fixed on the wall showed that it was no hallucination of an intoxicated man's fancy. It sobered the King, and filled him with fear, and he at once called for the "Wise Men" of Babylon to interpret its meaning.

AN INTERPRETER SOUGHT

"The King cried aloud to bring in the Astrologers, the Chaldeans, and the Soothsayers. And the King spake, and said to the 'Wise Men' of Babylon, Whosoever shall read this writing, and shew me the interpretation thereof, shall be clothed with scarlet, and have a chain of gold about his neck, and shall be the third ruler in the Kingdom. Then came in all the King's 'Wise Men:' but they could not read the writing, nor make known to the King the interpretation thereof. Then was King Belshazzar greatly troubled, and his countenance was changed in him, and his lords were astonished." Verses 7-9.

Again the "Wise Men" of Babylon fail in their office, as they failed in the days of Nebuchadnezzar. Dan. 2:1-13. They could not interpret the writing. Whether it was in a language with which they were not familiar we are not told. The true reason was that it was a message from **GOD**, and it takes a **"MAN OF GOD"** to interpret the **WORDS OF GOD**. The failure of the "Wise Men" to interpret the handwriting greatly troubled the King, and his countenance was changed. All the mirth and hilarity left it, and it presented the aspect of fear and terror. So marked was the change that the assembled lords were astonished, for they saw that the "handwriting on the wall" was not a part of the program, arranged by the King to entertain them, but was something supernatural and unexpected, and that the King was not needlessly alarmed. At once the boisterousness of the Feast was changed to cries of terror, and so great was the uproar and commotion the Queen came in to find out what it was all about. It is hardly likely that the Queen mentioned was the wife of Belshazzar. If he was married his wife's place was with him at the Feast. Neither is it likely that the Queen was the widow of Nebuchadnezzar. She probably was dead. Otherwise she would be very old, and indifferent to such an occasion. It would appear therefore that the Queen mentioned was the wife and Queen of King Nabonidus, who was still the "First Ruler" of the land, though away at the time, and who had a perfect right to be living in the Palace at that time, and who as a daughter of Nebuchadnezzar would still have a fresh and vivid memory of the wonderful part Daniel had taken in the affairs of the Empire during her father's reign. This view is confirmed by the use the Queen made of the word "father." The use of the word "father," instead of "grandfather," in the Queen calling Nebuchadnezzar the "father" of Belshazzar, is in accord with the usage of Old Testament times, and was made necessary because in the Semitic language there are no words for "grandfather," or "grandson."

"Now the Queen by reason of the words of the King and his lords came into the Banquet House:

and the Queen spake and said, O King, live forever: let not thy thoughts trouble thee, nor let thy countenance be changed: there is a man in thy Kingdom, in whom is the **Spirit of the Holy Gods;** and in the days of thy father light and understanding and wisdom, like the wisdom of the Gods, was found in him: whom the King Nebuchadnezzar thy father, the King, I say, thy father, made Master of the Magicians, Astrologers, Chaldeans, and Soothsayers; forasmuch as an excellent spirit, and knowledge, and understanding, interpreting of dreams, and shewing of hard sentences, and dissolving of doubts, were found in the same Daniel, whom the King named Belteshazzar: now let Daniel be called, and he will shew the interpretation." Verses 10-12.

While others had forgotten Daniel, not so the "Queen Mother." At once Daniel was sent for. He could not have been far away, or he could not have appeared so quickly. He was doubtless aroused from his slumbers, for it was far in the night. This would be no light matter, for he was now an old gray-haired man. Sixty-five years had passed by since he had interpreted Nebuchadnezzar's Dream, and if he was twenty years old when taken to Babylon, counting the three years in the "Palace School," he was now eighty-eight years of age.

"Then was Daniel brought in before the King. And the King spake and said unto Daniel, Art thou that Daniel, which art of the Children of the Captivity of Judah, whom the King my father brought out of Jewry? I have even heard of thee, that the **Spirit of the Gods** is in thee, and that light and understanding and excellent wisdom is found in thee. And now the 'Wise Men,' the Astrologers, have been brought in before me, that they should read this writing, and make known unto me the interpretation thereof: but they could not shew the interpretation of the thing: and I have heard of thee, that thou canst make interpretations, and dissolve doubts: now if thou canst read the writing, and make known to me the interpretation thereof, thou shalt be **clothed with scarlet,** and have **a chain of gold about thy neck,** and **shalt be the 'THIRD RULER' in the Kingdom."** Verses 13-16.

Daniel knew how empty were all these promises, for he saw by the "Handwriting on the Wall" that the Empire of Babylon was doomed, and that King Belshazzar was powerless to fulfil them. So he replied—

"Let thy gifts be to thyself, and give thy rewards to another; yet I will read the writing unto the King, and make known to him the Interpretation. O thou King, the **Most High God** gave Nebuchadnezzar thy father a Kingdom, and majesty, and glory, and honor: and for the majesty that He gave him, all people, nations, and languages trembled and feared before him: **whom he would he slew; and whom he would he kept alive; and whom he would he set up; and whom he would he put down.** But when his heart was lifted up, and his mind hardened in pride, he was deposed from his kingly throne, and they took his glory from him: and he was driven from the sons of men; and his heart was made like the beasts, and his dwelling was with the wild asses: they fed him with grass like oxen, and his body was wet with the dew of heaven; till he knew that the **MOST HIGH GOD ruled in the 'Kingdom of Men,' and that He appointeth over it whomsoever He will."** Verses 17-21.

Then Daniel, faithful prophet as he was, took advantage of the situation to reprove the King. Hear his fearless and sublime words—

A PROPHET'S REBUKE

"And thou his **son,** O Belshazzar, **hast not humbled thine heart, though thou KNEWEST ALL THIS;** but hast lifted up thyself against the Lord of Heaven; and they have brought the vessels of His House (the Temple at Jerusalem) before thee, and thou and thy lords, thy wives and thy concubines, have drunk wine in them; and thou hast praised the gods of silver, and gold, of brass, iron, wood, and stone, which see not, nor hear, nor know: and the God in whose hand thy breath is, and whose are all thy ways, hast thou not glorified: then was the part of the hand sent from Him; and this writing was written." Verses 22-24.

In this scathing rebuke Daniel charges Belshazzar with knowing all that had happened to his grandfather Nebuchadnezzar as a punishment for his pride. Belshazzar was probably fifteen years old when Nebuchadnezzar recovered from his insanity. Anyway he knew all about it from his mother's lips, and as heir apparent to the throne had been warned to avoid his grandfather's sin. But he failed to profit by the lesson, and added to his guilt what his grandfather never dared to do, the sin of the profanation of the "Sacred Vessels" of the Temple, thus mocking and defying God. It is a peculiar coincidence that when Daniel was called, Belshazzar took particular pains to find out if he was a Jew (verse 13), as if his presence had something to do with the King's desecration of the "Sacred Vessels" of the Temple. It seemed fitting therefore that Belshazzar's doom should be pronounced by Daniel the **Jew.** For it was because of the desecration of the "Sacred Vessels" that the "Handwriting" appeared on the wall, and the doom of Belshazzar pronounced, for if he continued on the throne there was little hope of the return of the Jews and the sacred vessels to Jerusalem two years later, as the prophets had foretold.

THE DOOM OF BABYLON

"And this is the writing that was written,

'MENE, MENE, TEKEL, UPHARSIN.'

"This is the interpretation of the thing: **MENE; God hath numbered thy Kingdom, and finished it. TEKEL; Thou art weighed in the balances, and art found wanting. PERES; Thy Kingdom is divided, and given to the Medes and Persians."** Verses 25-28.

In the interpretation Daniel changes the word **"UPHARSIN"** to **PERES,** which is the singular of "Upharsin." The change helps the interpretation, because the consonants written P–R–S on the wall were the same as those used for "Persians," showing where Daniel got the words, the "Medes" and "Persians," the Medes and Persians at that time being a dual Kingdom. The words **"MENE, MENE, TEKEL, UPHARSIN,"** translated into English, mean—**"Numbered," "Numbered," "Weighed," "Divisions."** Daniel interpreted them thus—

MENE—"God hath numbered thy Kingdom, and finished it."

TEKEL—"Thou (Belshazzar) **art weighed in the balances and art found wanting."**

PERES—"Thy Kingdom is divided, and given to the Medes and Persians."

The writing was in Aramaic, and the letters may have been arranged in Acrostic style, and so mystified the "Wise Men." The illustration below, taken from the Talmud, will show how this could have been done.

P	T	M	M
R	K	N	N
S	L	A	A

The Chaldeans (Wise Men), reading the letters from right to left, as in Hebrew and Aramaic, or from left to right, as in other languages, could make no sense of the words: but Daniel read from top to bottom, beginning at the right. That Belshazzar did not believe the Prophet, or that while he believed him, he did not expect the prophecy to come true in his day, is probable from the fact that—

> "Then commanded Belshazzar, and they clothed Daniel with scarlet, and put a chain of gold about his neck, and made a proclamation concerning him, that he should be the **'THIRD RULER'** in the Kingdom." Verse 29.

Belshazzar had to make Daniel the "Third Ruler," because he himself was the "Second," for his father Nabonidus was the "First." But the honor for Daniel was an empty one, for if God's word was true Belshazzar had no Kingdom to share with when he clothed him in scarlet, and put a chain of gold about his neck, for that Kingdom had already been given to the Medes and Persians, for we read—

> "In that night was Belshazzar the king of the Chaldeans slain. And Darius the Median took (received) the Kingdom, being about threescore and two years old." Verses 30-31.

Darius the Mede did not take Babylon. It was captured by Cyrus. But as an act of courtesy, and because Media was the older of the two Kingdoms Media and Persia, and because he had some other military campaigns to finish, Cyrus committed the governorship of Babylon to his uncle Darius, the king of Media, who ruled for two years.

THE TAKING OF BABYLON

Two years after the death of Nebuchadnezzar a war broke out between the Babylonians and the Medes that continued off and on for over twenty years. At last Cyaxares, king of the Medes, who is called "Darius" in verse 31, summoned to his aid his nephew,

Cyrus, of the Persian line. And in the seventeenth year of Nabonidus, and the third year of Belshazzar, Cyrus laid siege to the city of Babylon. The Babylonians entrenched behind the impregnable walls of the city, with provisions to last them for years, and sufficient tillable soil to supplement the supply, scoffed at Cyrus, and made light of the siege. Hence they breathed as freely and slept as soundly as though no foe was waiting and watching for their destruction. But it was a false security, for God had decreed over 175 years before that the city should be taken by a man not then born, Cyrus (Isa. 44:28—45:1-4), who was then knocking at its gates, and when God **sets the time** for the fulfilment of His word, the most impregnable fortress must fall.

Realizing the futility of taking the city by siege, Cyrus decided to use strategy. He decided to drain the river Euphrates, that flowed through the city, and march his soldiers in on its bed. To this end some say he constructed a large artificial lake, miles above the city, into which he drained the river. Others say, and it seems the most likely, that he constructed a new channel for the river, far away and invisible from the tops of the Towers on top of the walls, and into this new channel he diverted the water of the river above the city, so that the water that flowed through the city flowed away and left the river bed through the city dry. Having made all arrangements to carry out his plan, Cyrus waited a suitable occasion. Hearing of the Feast that Belshazzar was going to give to a thousand of his lords, and knowing the character of such Feasts, and that Belshazzar's soldiers would be off their guard, Cyrus divided his army into three Divisions. One Division was to divert the water of the river Euphrates, at the proper time, into the new channel. The second Division was stationed where the river entered the city on the north. And the third Division was stationed where the river left the city on the south. The second and third Divisions were instructed to enter the channel of the river as soon as the water was low enough, and march toward each other until they met in the centre of the city where the Palace was located. The plan worked to perfection. But it would have been a failure if the city had not been given over to debauchery. Through the carelessness of the guards, the brazen gates in the walls that lined the banks of the river inside the city were left unbolted, thus giving easy entrance to the soldiers of Cyrus, who quickly took the city. If it had been otherwise Cyrus' soldiers would have been trapped, or had to march out again. But the Hand of God was in it. God had said that Cyrus should take the city, and as its time was come, the plan of Cyrus was doubtless inspired of God, and He saw to it that the gates on the river's banks were not closed. If the guards of the river gates had been on duty, and had noticed the subsidence of the water of the river, they could have given the alarm, and probably saved the city. But God had ordered otherwise. The soldiers of Cyrus immediately took possession of the city, stormed the Palace, and slew the King. That night's revelry cost Belshazzar his life, and the Fall of Babylon.

As proof of the inspiration of the Scriptures it is worthy of note that the "Fall of Babylon" was foretold, and the manner of its capture described, and the name of its captor given, 175 years before the event took place. The Prophecy is found in Isa. 44:28—45:1-4.

> "That saith of **CYRUS**, He is my shepherd, and shall perform all my pleasure: even saying to **JERUSALEM—Thou shalt be built;** and to the **TEMPLE—Thy foundation shall be laid.** Thus saith the Lord to His anointed, to **CYRUS,** whose right hand I have holden, to subdue nations before him; and I will **loose the loins of kings** (as those of Belshazzar) to **open before him** (Cyrus) **the TWO LEAVED GATES** (of Babylon); and the gates **shall not be shut** (which was true of the inner gates of Babylon, in the river walls on the

night of the siege); **I will go before thee** (Cyrus), **and make the crooked places straight: I will break in pieces the GATES OF BRASS** (of Babylon), **and cut in sunder the bars of iron.** And I will give thee the treasures of darkness, and hidden riches of secret places, that thou (Cyrus) mayest know that I, the **LORD, which call thee by thy NAME** (over a hundred years before he was born), am the **GOD OF ISRAEL.** For Jacob my servant's sake, and Israel mine elect, I have even called thee (Cyrus) **by thy name: I have SURNAMED THEE** (given him his name), **THOUGH THOU HAST NOT KNOWN ME.**"

The last sentence may mean that Cyrus was not a believer in God when he besieged the city of Babylon, and was not aware that he was chosen of God as His agent in the downfall of the city. From this Scripture we see that Cyrus was foreordained, over one hundred years before he was born, to do two things. First, to besiege and take Babylon, and secondly, to issue an Edict, two years later, when the term (70 years) of the Babylonian Captivity had expired (B. C. 536), for the return of the Jews to Jerusalem.

THE REBUILDING OF BABYLON

That the ancient city of Babylon restored is to play an important part in the startling events of the last days of this Dispensation is very clear. This is seen from what is said of it in the seventeenth and eighteenth chapters of the Book of Revelation. At first sight the two chapters, which contain some things in common, are difficult to reconcile, but when we get the "**Key**" the reconciliation is easy. The seventeenth chapter speak of a "**WOMAN,**" called "**MYSTERY, Babylon the Great, the Mother of Harlots and Abominations of the Earth.**" The eighteenth chapter speaks of a **CITY, a literal city,** called "**Babylon the Great.**" That the "**WOMAN**" and the "**CITY**" do not symbolize the same thing is clear, for what is said of the "**Woman**" does not apply to a city, and what is said of the "**City**" does not apply to a woman. The **"WOMAN"** is destroyed by the **TEN KINGS,** while the **"Kings of the Earth"** in the next chapter, **"bewail and lament"** the destruction of the **"CITY,"** which is not destroyed by them, but by a **MIGHTY EARTHQUAKE AND FIRE.** Again, the **"WOMAN"** is destroyed **THREE AND A HALF YEARS BEFORE THE CITY;** and the fact that the first verse of chapter eighteen says—"**After these things,**" that is **after the destruction of the "WOMAN"** what happens to the **"CITY"** occurs, shows that the **"WOMAN"** and the **"CITY"** are not one and the same.* That the two chapters refer to different things is further verified by the fact that they are announced by **different angels.** The events of chapter seventeen are announced by one of the "**Vial**" Angels, while those of the eighteenth are announced by **"another"** angel; probably the "Second Angel Messenger," who by way of Anticipation, announced in Rev. 14:8, the "Fall of Babylon," that is there called—**"That Great City."**

If "Mystical Babylon" was destroyed in chapter seventeen, she cannot appear in chapter eighteen, therefore the **"CITY"** described in chapter eighteen must be a **literal city** called **BABYLON.** As there is no city of that name on the earth today, nor has been since the ancient city of Babylon was destroyed, the reference must be to some **future city of Babylon.** The city of Babylon is so intimately connected with the history of the God's People, the Jews, that the Scriptures have much to say about it. A large part of the book of Daniel has to do with it; and it is mentioned in twelve other books of the Old Testament, and in four of the New Testament. And that the Book of Revelation is a continuation of the Book of Daniel is proven by the fact that the city of Babylon is again spoken of in it, and its prominence in the affairs of the world at the

---

*For a description of "Ecclesiastical Babylon" of chapter seventeen, see the author's book on Revelation, pages 149-153.

"End Time" disclosed, and its final and complete destruction foretold.

That the ancient city of Babylon was destroyed there can be no question, but when we affirm that it is to be **rebuilt** and **again destroyed** we are met with two objections.

1. That all the Old Testament prophecies in reference to its destruction have been **literally** fulfilled, and that it cannot be rebuilt.

2. As there is no city of Babylon now in existence, the references in the Book of Revelation to the destruction of such a city must be symbolical and not refer to a literal city.

Let us take up the first objection that all the prophecies in reference to its destruction have been literally fulfilled. For a description of Babylon and her destruction we must turn to Isaiah, chapters 13 and 14, and Jeremiah 50 and 51. In these two prophecies we find much that has not **AS YET** been fulfilled in regard to the city of Babylon. This will appear as we proceed. But first we will review the history of Babylon from its capture by Cyrus, B. C. 538, until the present time. So quietly and quickly was the city captured by Cyrus that some of the inhabitants did not know until the **third day** that the King had been slain and the city taken. There was no destruction of the city at that time. Some years after it revolted against Darius Hystaspis, and after a fruitless siege of nearly twenty months was taken by strategy. This was in B. C. 516. About B. C. 478 Xerxes, on his return from Greece, plundered and injured, if he did not destroy, the great "Temple of Bel."

In B. C. 331 Alexander the Great approached the city, which was then so powerful and flourishing that he made preparation for bringing all his forces into action in case it should offer resistance, but the citizens threw open the gates and received him with acclamations. After sacrificing to "Bel," he gave out that he would rebuild the vast Temple of that god, and for weeks he kept 10,000 men employed in clearing away the ruins from the foundations, doubtless intending to revive the glory of Babylon and make it his Capital, when his purpose was defeated by his sudden death of marsh fever and intemperance in his thirty-third year. During the subsequent wars of his generals Babylon suffered much, and finally came under the power of Seleucus, who, prompted by ambition to build a Capital for himself, founded Seleucia in its neighborhood about B. C. 293. This rival city gradually drew off the inhabitants of Babylon, so that Strabo, who died in A. D. 25, speaks of the latter as being to a great extent deserted. Nevertheless the Jews left from the Captivity still resided there in large numbers, and in A. D. 60 we find the Apostle Peter working among them, for it was from Babylon that Peter wrote his First Epistle (1 Pet. 5: 13), addressed to "The strangers scattered throughout Pontus, Galatia, Cappadocia, Asia and Bethynia."

About the middle of the fifth century Theodoret speaks of Babylon as being inhabited only by Jews, who had still **three Jewish Universities,** and in the last year of the same century the **"Babylonian Talmud"** was issued, and recognized as authoritative by the Jews of the whole world.

In A. D. 917 Ibu Hankel mentions Babylon as an insignificant village, but **still in existence.** About A. D. 1100 it seems to have again grown into a town of some importance, for it was then known as the **"Two Mosques."** Shortly afterwards it was enlarged and fortified and received the name of Hillah. In A. D. 1898 Hillah contained about 10,000 inhabitants, and was surrounded by fertile lands, and abundant date groves stretched along the banks of the Euphrates. Certainly it has never **AS YET** been true that—"neither shall the **Arabian pitch tent there,** neither shall the **shepherds make their fold there."** Isa. 13: 20. Nor can it be said of Babylon—"Her cities are a desolation, a dry land, and a wilderness, a land **wherein no man dwelleth, neither doth any son of man pass**

thereby." Jer. 51:43. Nor can it be said—"And they shall not take of thee a **stone for a corner,** nor a **stone for foundations,** but thou shalt be desolate forever, saith the Lord" (Jer. 51:26), for many towns and cities have been built from the ruins of Babylon, among them **four Capital Cities:** Seleucia, built by the Greeks; Ctesiphon, by the Parthians; Al Maiden, by the Persians; and Kufa, by the Caliphs. Hillah was entirely constructed from the debris, and even in the houses of Bagdad, Babylonian stamped bricks may be frequently noticed.

But Isaiah is still more specific, for he locates the **TIME** when his prophecy will be fulfilled. He calls it the **"DAY OF THE LORD."** Isa. 13:9. The "Day of the Lord" takes in the "Tribulation Period" and the "Millennium." See the chart of the Prophetic Days of Scriptures. Isaiah says when Babylon shall be destroyed—

> "The **stars of heaven** and the **constellations thereof shall not give their light;** the **sun shall be darkened** in his going forth, and the **moon shall not cause her light to shine."** Isa. 13:10.

None of these things happened when Babylon was taken by Cyrus in B. C. 538. Nor have they happened since. This darkening of the "Heavenly Bodies" locates the **TIME** of the destruction of Babylon as at the **close of "The Great Tribulation,"** as foretold by Christ in His "Olivet Discourse" (Matt. 24:29-30), and at the **pouring out of the "Seventh Vial"** of the Book of Revelation. Rev. 16:17-19.

In the description of the destruction of the city of Babylon given in Rev. 18, we read that her judgment will come in **ONE HOUR** (verse 10), and that in **ONE HOUR** she shall be made **desolate** (verse 19), and as an illustration of the **suddenness** and **completeness** of her destruction, a mighty angel took up a **stone** like a **"Great Millstone,"** and cast it into the sea, saying—"Thus with **VIOLENCE** shall that great city Babylon be thrown down and shall be **found no more at all."**

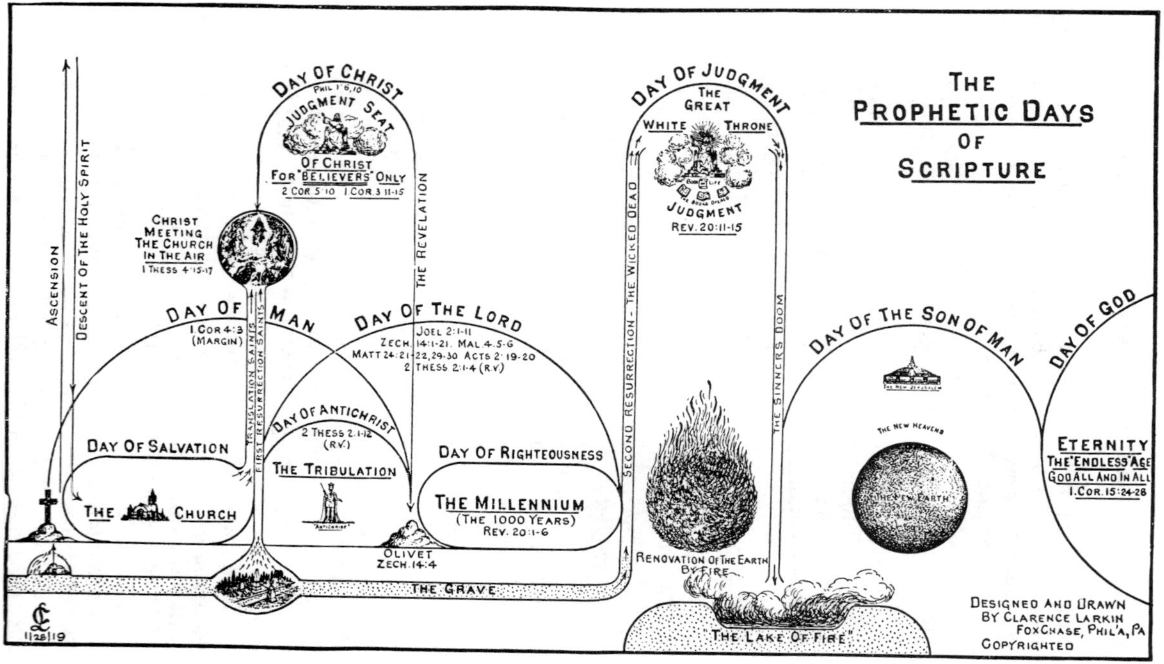

THE PROPHETIC DAYS OF SCRIPTURE
ASCENSION
DESCENT OF THE HOLY SPIRIT
DAY OF CHRIST
PHIL 1:6,10
JUDGMENT SEAT OF CHRIST
FOR "BELIEVERS" ONLY
2 COR 5:10 1 COR.3 11-15
CHRIST MEETING THE CHURCH IN THE AIR
1 THESS 4:15-17
THE REVELATION
DAY OF MAN
1 COR 4:3 (MARGIN)
TRANSLATION SAINTS
FIRST RESURRECTION SAINTS
DAY OF THE LORD
JOEL 2:1-11
ZECH. 14:1-21. MAL.4.5-6
MATT 24:21-22,29-30 ACTS 2:19-20
2 THESS 2:1-4 (R.V.)
DAY OF SALVATION
THE CHURCH
DAY OF ANTICHRIST
2 THESS 2:1-12 (R.V.)
THE TRIBULATION
"ANTICHRIST"
DAY OF RIGHTEOUSNESS
THE MILLENNIUM
(THE 1000 YEARS)
REV. 20:1-6
OLIVET
ZECH. 14:4
THE GRAVE
DAY OF JUDGMENT
THE GREAT WHITE THRONE JUDGMENT
REV. 20:11-15
SECOND RESURRECTION - THE WICKED DEAD
THE SINNERS DOOM
RENOVATION OF THE EARTH BY FIRE
"THE LAKE OF FIRE"
DAY OF THE SON OF MAN
THE NEW JERUSALEM
THE NEW HEAVENS
THE NEW EARTH
DAY OF GOD
ETERNITY
THE "ENDLESS" AGE
GOD ALL AND IN ALL
1 COR. 15:24-28
DESIGNED AND DRAWN BY CLARENCE LARKIN FOX CHASE, PHIL'A, PA
COPYRIGHTED
CL 1/28/19

Rev. 18:21. We are also told in the same chapter that she is to be destroyed by **FIRE.** Rev. 18:8, 9, 18. This is in exact harmony with the words of Isa. 13:19-22.

> "And Babylon, the glory of Kingdoms, the beauty of the Chaldees excellency, shall be as when God overthrew **SODOM AND GOMORRAH.**"

The Prophet Jeremiah makes the same statement. Jer. 50:40. The destruction of Sodom and Gomorrah did not extend through many centuries, their glory disappeared in a few hours (Gen. 19:24-28); and as ancient Babylon was not thus destroyed, the prophecies of Isaiah and Jeremiah cannot be fulfilled unless there is to be a future Babylon that shall be thus destroyed.

In Rev. 16:17-19, we are told that Babylon shall be destroyed by an **EARTHQUAKE,** attended with most vivid and incessant lightning and awful thunder. It would appear then, that as Sodom and Gomorrah were first set on fire and then swallowed up by an earthquake, that the rebuilt city of Babylon will be set on fire, and as the site of ancient Babylon is underlaid with **Bitumen** (Asphalt), that an earthquake will break up the crust of the earth, and precipitate the burning city into a **"Lake of Fire,"** and the city, like a **MILLSTONE** (Rev. 18:21) sink below the surface of the earth as into the sea, and be swallowed up so that it will be impossible to ever take of her stones for building purposes, and the land shall become a **Wilderness** where no man shall ever dwell.

The Vision of the **"Ephah,"** seen by the Prophet Zechariah (Zech. 5:5-11) is further confirmatory evidence that the ancient city of Babylon is to be rebuilt and become the **COMMERCIAL CENTRE OF THE WORLD.** The **"Ephah"** is the largest of Hebrew dry measures, and is often used as a symbol of **Commerce.** In the vision the **"Ephah"** is seen being carried by two women who had the wings of a stork, and flew with the swiftness of the wind, and the Prophet was told that they were transporting it to the **"LAND OF SHINAR,"** where a **"House"** would be built for it. Now the **"Land of Shinar"** is the place where the **"Tower of Babel"** was built (Gen. 11:1-9), and the site of Babylon. The inference is that the **"HOUSE"** that is to be built for the **"Ephah"** in the **"Land of Shinar"** will be the rebuilt city of Babylon, and that Babylon is to become the great **"Commercial Centre"** of the world. The fact that the occupant of the "Ephah" was a **"Woman"** called **WICKEDNESS** implies that the **"Commercialism"** of those days will be characterized by all manner of dishonest schemes and methods, which surely will be the business methods of those who only can buy or sell who have the **"MARK OF THE BEAST."** Rev. 13:16-17.

As to the probability of the ancient city of Babylon being rebuilt, we have only to consider the events that in recent years have been happening in that part of the world looking to just such a thing. China, Japan, and India have risen from their sleep and isolation and become world commercial nations. There must therefore be some transcontinental means of transportation between the East and the West of the Eastern Hemisphere, and the logical route is through Mesopotamia, with rebuilt Babylon as the "Commercial Centre." In the "Department of War" of France, at Paris, there are to be seen the records of valuable surveys and maps made, by order of Napoleon I, in Babylonia, and among them is a plan for a **New City of Babylon,** thus showing that the vast schemes of Napoleon contemplated the **Rebuilding of the Ancient City of Babylon,** and the making it his Capital, as his ambition was to conquer the whole of Europe and Asia, and he recognized to that end the **strategical position** of ancient Babylon as a governmental and commercial centre. The same was the dream of the late Emperor William of Germany. It was that desire that made him and Abdul Hamid, of Turkey, the closest of political friends, and he secured from Abdul Hamid a concession to build a railroad from the

Asiatic side of the Bosphorus, by way of Aleppo, to the Tigris River, and from there to Bagdad, and from Bagdad **via Babylon** (via Babylon, mark that) to Koweit on the Persian Gulf, and **most of the road has been built to Bagdad.** And if the truth was known the Kaiser's precipitation of the "World's Great War" was largely due to his desire to carry out his plans for a **"Trans-European-Asiatic-Indian Air Line"** that would connect Europe with India, China, and Japan, and would have necessitated the building of a city on the site of ancient Babylon. But his and Napoleon's plans were **premature,** and were brought to naught by God, until His time arrives for the rebuilding of Babylon.

The whole country of Mesopotamia, including Assyria and Babylonia, only needs a system of irrigation, such as it once had, as revealed by the unearthing of numerous irrigation canals, to make it again the most fertile country in the world. As early as 1850 the British Government sent out a military officer, with his command, to survey and explore the river Euphrates at a cost of $150,000, and when the European war broke out the great English Engineer who built the "Assouan Dam" in Egypt was engaged in making surveys in the Euphratean valley for the purpose of constructing a series of irrigation canals that would restore the country and make it again the great grain-producing country it once was. With these facts in mind, it can readily be seen that it is the desire of European capitalists to revive the country of Babylonia and rebuild its cities, and when the time comes in the purpose of God the city of Babylon will be rebuilt almost in a night, and on a scale of magnificence such as the world has never seen.

But I hear a protest. How, you say, can we be expecting Jesus to come at **"any moment,"** if the city of Babylon must be rebuilt before He can come? We reply that Jesus' "Second Coming" will be in "Two Stages." At the "First Stage" He will not come all the way to the earth but will stop in the **"Air,"** and all believers who have been **"Born Again"** will be caught up to Him. 1 Thess. 4:13-18. They will then be judged for their **"Works,"** that they may receive a proper reward, at the "Judgment Seat of Christ." 2 Cor. 5:10. 1 Cor. 3:11-15. This will take some time. Then the Church will be married to Christ, after which He will come **WITH** the saints (the Church) to **"Judge the Nations"** (Matt. 25:31-46) and set up His Millennial Kingdom. This will be the "Second Stage" of His Coming, and will be visible. Between these "Two Stages" there will be a **"Time Space"** of at least **SEVEN YEARS,** the last **"Week"** of Daniel's **"Seventy Weeks."** (See chapter 9.) But there is not a word in Scripture that says He cannot come **before the beginning** of those "Seven Years." He may come five, ten, or even twenty-five years before, which would give ample time for the rebuilding of Babylon before the rise of the last Gentile Ruler, the **ANTICHRIST.** Some claim that Babylon will be rebuilt during the first three and a half years of the "Seven," and Antichrist will make it his Capital during the last three and a half years. And when we consider how rapidly cities spring up in these days, or are rebuilt, as were Chicago and San Francisco, from the catastrophes that overtook them, it would take but a very few years to rebuild the city of Babylon when once the capitalists of the world decide to do it.

BABYLON THE GREAT

Let us take the description of **"Babylon the GREAT"** as given to us in Rev. 18:1-24, and try to visualize it. It will be an immense city, the greatest in every respect the world has ever seen. It will be a typical city, the London, the Paris, the Berlin, the Petrograd, the New York, the Chicago of its day. It will be the greatest "Commercial City" of the world. Its merchandise will be of gold and silver, and precious stones and pearls, of purple, and silk, and scarlet and costly wools. Its fashionable society will be clothed in the most costly raiment and decked with the most costly jewels. Their homes will be filled with the most costly furniture of precious woods, brass, iron and marble, with the richest of draperies, mats and rugs. They will use the most costly of perfumes, cinnamon, fragrant odors, ointments and frankincense. Their banquets will be supplied with the sweetest of wines, the richest of pastries, and the most delicious of meats. They will have horses, and chariots, and the swiftest of fast-moving vehicles on earth and in the air. They will have their slaves, and they will traffic in the **"souls of men."** That is women will sell their bodies, and men their souls, to gratify their lusts.

The markets will be crowded with cattle, sheep, and horses. The wharves will be piled with goods from all climes. The manufactories will turn out the richest of fabrics, and all that genius can invent for the comfort and convenience of men will be found on the market. It will be a city given over to pleasure and business. Business men and promoters will give their days and nights to scheming how to make money fast, and the pleasure-loving will be constantly planning new pleasures. There will be riotous joy and ceaseless feasting. As it was in the days of Noah and of Lot, they will be marrying and giving in marriage, buying and selling, building and planting. The blood will run hot in their veins. Money will be their god, pleasure their high-priest, and unbridled passion the ritual of their worship.

It will be a city of music. Amid the noise and bustle of its commercial life will be heard the music of its pleasure resorts and theatres. There will be the sound of "harpers and musicians, of pipers and trumpeters" (verse 22). The world's best singers and players will be there. Its theatres and places of music will be going day and night. In fact there will be no night, for the electric illumination of the city by night will make the night as bright and shadowless as the day, and its stores and places of business will never close, night or day, or Sunday, for the mad whirl of pleasure, and the absorbing desire for riches will keep the wheels of business constantly moving. And all this will be easy because the **"God of this World"** (Age)—**SATAN,** will possess the minds and bodies of men, for we read in verse 2, that Babylon at that time will be the **"Habitation of Devils,"** and the **"Hold of Every Foul Spirit,"** and the **"Cage of Every Unclean and Hateful Bird."** The city will be the seat of the most imposing **"OCCULTISM,"** and mediums, and those desiring to communicate with the other world, will then go to Babylon, as men and women now go to Paris for fashions and sensuous pleasures. In that day **"demons,"** and **"unclean spirits"** will find at Babylon the opportunity of their lives to **materialize themselves in human bodies,** and from the atmospheric heavens above, and from the Abyss below, they will come in countless legions until Babylon shall be full of **demon-possessed men and women.** And at the height of its glory, and just before its fall, Babylon will be ruled by **SATAN HIMSELF,** incarnate in the **"Beast"—ANTICHRIST.**

But before its destruction God will mercifully deliver His own people, for a voice from Heaven will cry—

> **"Come out of her, MY PEOPLE, that ye be not partakers of her sins, and that ye receive not of her plagues."** Rev. 18:4.

As Sodom and Gomorrah could not be destroyed until righteous Lot had escaped, so Babylon cannot be destroyed until all the righteous people in it have fled.

The destruction of the city will be sudden and without warning. A fearful storm will sweep over the city. The lightning and thunder will be incessant. The city will be set on fire and a **great earthquake** will shake it from centre to circumference. The tall office buildings and apartment houses, the "Hanging Gardens" and the great towers will totter and fall, the crust of the earth will crack and open, and the whole city with its inhabitants will sink like a **MILLSTONE** (verse 21) into a lake of burning bitumen, and the smoke will ascend as of a **"burning fiery furnace,"** and the horror of the scene will be intensified by vast clouds of steam, generated by the waters of the river Euphrates pouring into that lake of fiery asphalt, and when night comes on those clouds of steam will reflect the light of the burning city so it can be seen for miles in all directions in that level country. And the kings of the earth, and the merchants, and the shipmasters, and sailors, and all who have profited by her merchandise, will stand afar off and cry, and wail because of her destruction, but the heavens will rejoice, for God will have rewarded her **"Double"** according to her works, and Babylon will be **NO MORE.**

CHAPTER SIX

The Lions' Den

THE PRIMACY OF DANIEL

"It pleased Darius to set over the Kingdom a hundred and twenty princes, which should be over the whole Kingdom: and over these three presidents of whom **Daniel was first**: that the princes might give accounts unto them, and the King should have no damage. Then this Daniel was preferred above the Presidents and Princes, because an excellent spirit was in him; and the King thought to set him **over the whole realm."** Verses 1-3.

This chapter introduces us to the "Second World Empire" of the "Times of the Gentiles," the "Medo-Persian Empire." The "Head of Gold" had lasted for sixty-seven years, and now the "Arms and Breast of Silver" of the "Image" appear. As the Fall of Babylon occurred in B. C. 538, and Darius immediately took the throne, and died in B. C. 536, the event narrated in this chapter must have taken place inside those two years. Daniel was at this time **nearly ninety years old.** It is remarkable that for his age he was equal to such a task as Darius placed upon him. He made him not only one of the three Presidents, but their chief. What prompted Darius to do this we are not told. But he must in some way have become acquainted with Daniel's integrity and superior statesmanship. The Medo-Persian Empire was not an "Absolute Monarchy" such as had been the Babylonian. The Presidents and Princes composed a sort of congress or parliament that had a voice in the making of laws, which had to be ratified by the King, and once ratified the law was **unalterable.**

It was not long before Darius found out the worth of Daniel, and preferred him above the Presidents and

Princes, because of his **"excellent spirit,"** and the King thought to set him **over the WHOLE REALM.** When this became known, the other Presidents and Princes were filled with envy and fear. For they well knew that Daniel would not stand for any graft or dishonesty in the administration of the affairs of the Empire, and they did not want to lose either their positions or their opportunity for gain, so they sought for some charge of malfeasance in office that they might make against the old Jew, but they found no occasion or fault. Then they hatched a hellish and

A DIABOLICAL PLOT.

> "Then the Presidents and Princes sought to find occasion against Daniel concerning the Kingdom; but they could find **none occasion nor fault; forasmuch as he was faithful, neither was there any error or fault found in him.** Then said these men, We shall not find any occasion against this Daniel, except we find it against him concerning the **LAW OF HIS GOD.** Then these Presidents and Princes assembled together to the King, and said thus unto him, King Darius, live forever. All the Presidents of the Kingdom, the Governors, and the Princes, the Counsellors, and the Captains, have consulted together to establish a 'Royal Statute,' and to make a firm Decree, that **whosoever shall ask a petition of any God or man for thirty days, SAVE OF THEE, O KING, he shall be cast into the 'DEN OF LIONS.'** Now, O King, establish the Decree, and sign the Writing, that it be **not changed, according to the Law of the Medes and Persians, which ALTERETH NOT.** Wherefore King Darius signed the Writing and the Decree." Verses 4-9.

The plot reveals the cunning of the "Serpent." They knew that Daniel was a deeply religious man, and that nothing would cause him to be disloyal to his God. They also knew that it would never do to let

Darius know that they were after Daniel, because of his fondness for the "Old Jew," whom they considered as "superannuated" and in his "dotage." If they had made the "Decree" read that no petition should be asked of the "God of the Hebrews," the King would have divined that it was aimed at Daniel, and would have refused to sign it. So they made it general, and thus heaped insult on their own gods, for the sake of getting rid of the object of their hatred. They also knew that the King was not an absolute Monarch as was Nebuchadnezzar, that he was subject to the will of his Counsellors, and any unanimous suggestions or recommendations they should make he dare not ignore. They also knew that if their plan succeeded, and the King once signed and sealed such a "Decree" it could not be repealed by him, for under the Law of the Medes and Persians, the "Decree" would be irrevocable.

Having decided on their course of action, with lying tongues they went into the presence of the King and told him that **ALL** the Presidents, the Governors, the Princes, the Counsellors, and the Captains had **CONSULTED TOGETHER** to establish such a "Royal Decree." But as Daniel, the **"Chief"** of the Presidents, had not been consulted, they lied. King Darius was doubtless flattered by their proposal, for in those days it was not uncommon to look upon their kings as gods, and for no one to pray to any other one than the King for thirty days was to exalt him to that position. So the King, not knowing that Daniel, whom he loved, had not been consulted, fell into the trap, and the "Decree" was prepared, signed by the King, stamped with the "Royal Seal," and publicly proclaimed according to the Law of the Medes and Persians, and therefore unalterable.

A FEARLESS OFFICIAL

Soon what had been done came to Daniel's ears. What was he to do? He knew that the "Royal Decree" was aimed at him. To pray to his God was to break it.

He must choose between loyalty to his God or loyalty to his King. Should he be faithless to his God, and thus save his life? That would be to deny all his past faithfulness. But was there no way to pray to his God **in secret?** Could he not enter into some secret chamber in his own home and lock the door, and stuff the keyhole, and close the shutters, and pray inaudibly, so his enemies would have no evidence against him? Most of us would be tempted to do that. But Daniel was not made of that kind of stuff. He was no coward. He did not value his life when it came to a question of loyalty to his God. What did he do?

> "Now when Daniel knew that the Writing was signed, he went to his own house; and, his **windows being open** in his chamber toward Jerusalem, he kneeled upon his knees **three times a day,** and prayed, and gave thanks before his God, as he did **AFORETIME.**" Verse 10.

This was just what those conspirators expected Daniel to do. They knew that no "Decree," even one that would endanger his life, would prevent him from praying daily to his God. All they had to do then was to assemble on the Jerusalem side of his home at the hour of prayer, not only to see him in the attitude of prayer, but to hear his supplication.

> "Then these men assembled, and found Daniel praying and making supplication before his God." Verse 11.

Daniel's enemies had not misjudged him, and they were delighted at the success of their scheme, and at once they brought the matter to the notice of the King.

A HELPLESS KING

> "Then they came near, and spake before the King concerning the King's 'Decree;' Hast thou not signed a 'Decree,' that every man that shall ask a petition of any God or man within thirty

days, save of thee, O King, shall be cast into the 'Den of Lions?' The King answered and said, The thing is true, according to the Law of the Medes and Persians, which altereth not. Then answered they and said before the King, **That DANIEL, which is of the 'Children of the Captivity of Judah,' REGARDETH NOT THEE,** O King, **nor the 'Decree' that thou hast signed,** but maketh his petition three times a day. Then the King, when he heard these words, **was sore displeased with HIMSELF,** and set his heart on Daniel to deliver him: and he labored **till the going down of the sun to deliver him.** Then these men assembled unto the King, and said unto the King, Know, O King, that the Law of the Medes and Persians is, That no 'Decree' nor 'Statute' which the King establisheth may be changed." Verses 12-15.

Notice the contempt with which the conspirators speak of Daniel—**"THAT DANIEL, which is of the 'Children of the Captivity of Judah.'"** As much as to say, "That old Jew who is but a captive, and is dependent on you for his position, is so far from being grateful and appreciative of your favors, that he has disregarded your 'Decree' and thus shown his disrespect of thee." Instead of making the King angry with Daniel their charge had the opposite effect. When the King learned how he had been **tricked,** he was sore displeased with **HIMSELF.** He felt mortified that he had been trapped. He saw how his pride had overcome his insight and judgment, and he now knew that he ought to have been **suspicious** when they told him that **ALL** the Presidents had agreed in the matter, for a moment's thought would have made it clear to him that Daniel would never have given his consent to such an idolatrous "Decree," and the King well knew that anything that Daniel did not favor was questionable. The King soon discovered that he was in a helpless position. He loved Daniel, and desired to save him, and though he **"labored until the going down of the sun"** he could devise no way of getting around the Law. At sundown the enemies of Daniel again assembled and demanded that Daniel pay the penalty of the Law. The King was powerless.

THE LIONS' DEN

"Then the King commanded, and they brought Daniel, and cast him into the 'Den of Lions.' Now the King spake and said unto Daniel, **Thy God whom thou servest continually, HE WILL DELIVER THEE.** And a stone was brought, and laid upon the mouth of the 'Den;' and the King **sealed it with his own signet, and with the signet of his Lords**; that the purpose might not be changed concerning Daniel." Verses 16-17.

Thus Daniel, the aged and faithful servant, was cast, as if he had been one of the vilest malefactors, into the "Den of Lions" to be devoured of them. The God who had permitted the three faithful "Hebrew Children" to be cast into the "Burning Fiery Furnace" that He might work a Miracle for their deliverance, permitted His aged servant Daniel to be cast into the "Den of Lions" for the same reason. The King had done his best to deliver Daniel and failed. Will Daniel's God, who now appears on the scene, fail?

A GREAT DELIVERANCE

"Then the King went to his Palace, and passed the night fasting: neither were instruments of music brought before him: and his sleep went from him. Then the King arose very early in the morning, and went in haste unto the 'Den of Lions.' And when he came to the 'Den,' he cried with a lamentable voice unto Daniel: and the King spake and said to Daniel, O Daniel, **servant of the 'Living God,' is THY GOD, whom thou servest continually, ABLE to deliver thee from**

the lions? Then said Daniel unto the King, O King, live forever. **MY GOD hath sent His Angel, and hath SHUT THE LIONS' MOUTHS, that they have not hurt me**: forasmuch as before Him innocency was found in me; and also before thee, O King, have I done no hurt. Then was the King exceeding glad for him, and commanded that they should take Daniel up out of the 'Den.' So Daniel was taken up out of the 'Den,' and **no manner of hurt was found upon him, because he BELIEVED IN HIS GOD."** Verses 18-23.

We see from the above that the King's interest in Daniel, and his condemnation of himself, were genuine, otherwise he would not have spent a "sleepless night." He was so impressed by Daniel's faithfulness to his God in refusing to obey the "Decree" that he felt that somehow Daniel's God would deliver him. With such a hope he hastened to the "Lions' Den" early in the morning to find his hope justified. Then was the King "exceeding glad," and commanded that Daniel be taken up from the "Den," and when he was examined no manner of hurt was found upon him. It was a repetition of the Miracle of the "Burning Fiery Furnace," from which the three "Hebrew Children" were delivered without a hair singed. The writer to the Hebrews refers to it in the words — **"stopped the mouths of lions."** Heb. 11 : 33. Thus was Daniel's faith vindicated.

There is a beautiful spiritual lesson in Daniel's deliverance. The "Den of Lions" prefigures the "Tomb of Joseph of Arimathea" in which our Lord was laid, and before which a stone was rolled, and sealed, and marked with the King's signet. But as the lions could not harm Daniel, so Jesus, who went into the **"jaws of Death,"** could not be **"holden of Death,"** and was delivered, like Daniel, by resurrection from his prison house. When Daniel was liberated from the "Lions' Den," he could not be thrown in again, he was free from that "Law," for he had paid its penalty. So when we accept Jesus as our personal Saviour we are free from the Law of "Sin and Death," because Jesus our Saviour paid its penalty on the Cross, and His deliverance from the "Tomb" by resurrection shows that He had fulfilled His sentence of three days, and the "Tomb" could no longer hold Him, any more than the criminal who has served his term can any longer be kept behind prison bars.

A JUST PUNISHMENT

But Daniel's deliverance did not satisfy the King. He felt that the conspirators who had thus selfishly and inhumanly imperiled Daniel's life should have a dose of their own medicine, and see if their gods would deliver them from the Lions' mouths. So—

"The King commanded, and they brought those men which had accused Daniel, and they cast them into the 'Den of Lions,' **them, their children, and their wives**; and the lions had the mastery of them, and **brake all their bones in pieces or ever they came at the bottom of the Den.**" Verse 24.

Here we see how the wicked involve their families in their wickedness and bring upon them sorrow and death. The argument that the "Lions" were **not hungry,** and therefore there was no miracle in the preservation of Daniel's life, is disproved by the ravenous manner in which they seized and devoured those wicked men and their families. The King was converted by the interposition of Daniel's God in his behalf, and issued a "Decree."

THE KING'S DECREE

"Then King Darius wrote unto all people, nations, and languages, that dwell in all the earth: Peace be multiplied unto you. I make a 'Decree,' That in every dominion of my Kingdom men tremble and fear before the 'God of Daniel:' for He is the 'Living God,' and steadfast forever, and His Kingdom that which shall not be destroyed, and his dominion shall be even unto the end. He delivereth and rescueth, and He worketh signs and wonders in Heaven and in earth, **WHO hath delivered Daniel from the POWER OF THE LIONS."** Verses 25-27.

This "Decree" amounted almost, if not quite, to incorporating the worship of Jehovah into the religion of the Empire. It at least did one thing, it proclaimed "Religious Toleration," and permitted the Jewish captives to henceforth worship their God without molestation. Again, Daniel's faithfulness to his God is rewarded by his promotion, and his life was spared not only through the reign of Darius, but into the reign of Cyrus the Persian.

"So this Daniel prospered in the reign of Darius, and in the reign of Cyrus the Persian." Verse 28.

Thus Daniel was delivered from the Lions' Den that he might be the "chief adviser" of the first two monarchs, one representing the Median (Darius), and the other the Persian (Cyrus), of the "Dual Kingdom," Medo-Persian, represented by the "Arms and Breast of Silver" of the "Image."

DEIFICATION OF MAN

In the erection of the "Golden Image" on the "Plain of Dura" we saw that the characteristic feature of the First, or "Babylonian" Empire, was the **"Deification of Man."** And here in this chapter, in the "Decree" that no one for thirty days should offer a petition to any God or man except King Darius, we see that the same characteristic feature, the "Deification of Man," was present in the Second, or "Medo-Persian" Empire. So it was in the "Grecian" and "Roman" Empires, and so it will be until the end of the "Times of the Gentiles," the last great example of it being the last great Gentile Ruler, the **"Beast,"** or **ANTICHRIST.** Rev. 13:4, 14-15. Daniel, like the three Hebrew Children, is a type of the Jewish Remnant, that, during the "Great Tribulation," will be miraculously delivered.

Second Division

Prophetical

Chapters 7 to 12

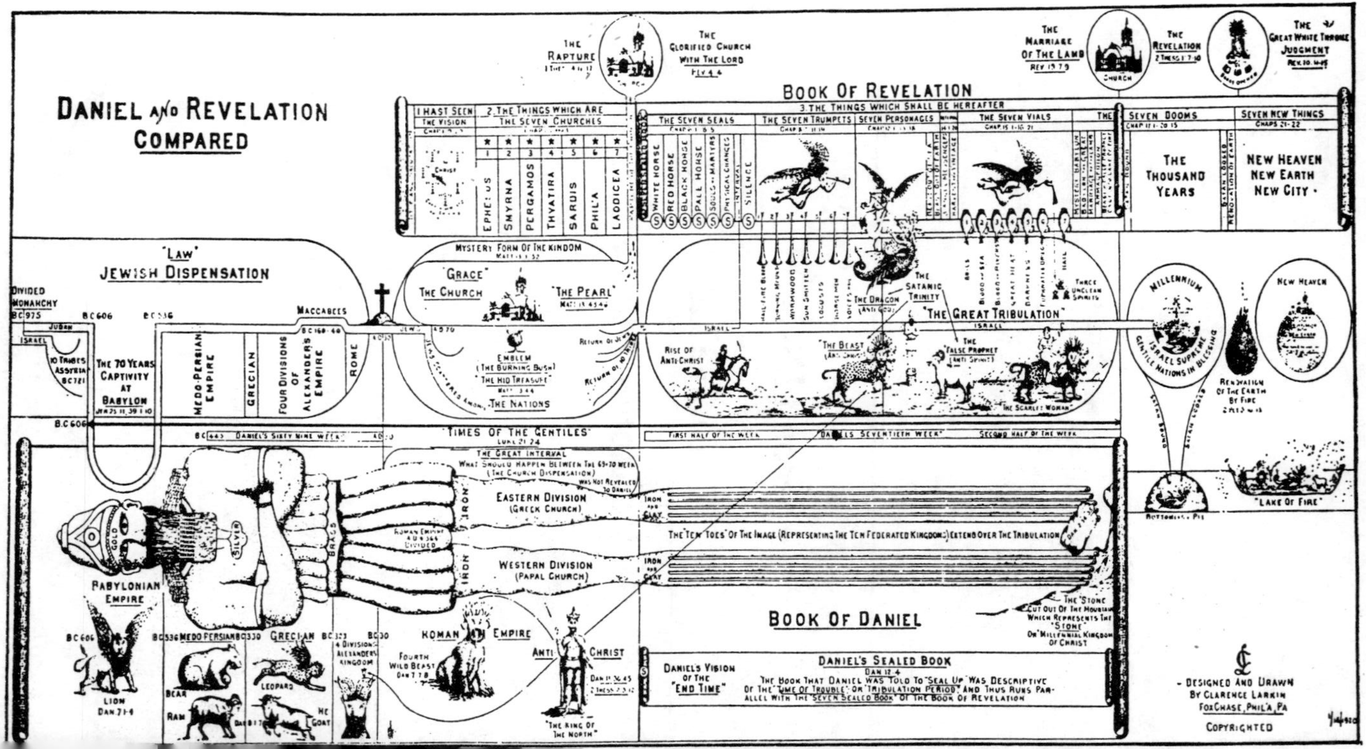
DANIEL AND REVELATION COMPARED
BOOK OF REVELATION
The Rapture
The Glorified Church With The Lord
The Marriage Of The Lamb
Rev 19:7-9
The Revelation
The Great White Throne Judgment
1 Hast Seen
The Vision
2. The Things Which Are
The Seven Churches
Ephesus
Smyrna
Pergamos
Thyatira
Sardis
Phila
Laodicea
3. The Things Which Shall Be Hereafter
The Seven Seals
White Horse
Red Horse
Black Horse
Pale Horse
Souls of Martyrs
Physical Changes
Interval
Silence
The Seven Trumpets
Seven Personages
The Seven Vials
Seven Dooms
Seven New Things
Chaps 21-22
The Thousand Years
Satan Loosed
Renovation of Earth
New Heaven
New Earth
New City
"Law"
Jewish Dispensation
Divided Monarchy
BC 975
Judah
Israel
10 Tribes Assyria BC 721
BC 606
BC 536
The 70 Years Captivity at Babylon
Medo-Persian Empire
Grecian
Four Divisions of Alexanders Empire
Rome
Maccabees
Mystery Form Of The Kingdom
"Grace"
The Church
"The Pearl"
Emblem
(The Burning Bush)
The Hid Treasure
The Nations
Jews Scattered Among The Nations
Return of Jews
Rise of Antichrist
The Beast
The Dragon
The Satanic Trinity
The False Prophet
"The Great Tribulation"
Israel
Three Unclean Spirits
The Scarlet Woman
Millennium
Israel Supreme
Gentile Nations In Blessing
Satan Bound
Satan Loosed
Renovation Of The Earth By Fire
New Heaven
Bottomless Pit
"Lake Of Fire"
B.C. 606
"Times Of The Gentiles"
Luke 21:24
Daniel's Sixty Nine Weeks
First Half Of The Week
Daniel's Seventieth Week
Second Half Of The Week
The Great Interval
What Should Happen Between The 69-70 Week (The Church Dispensation) Was Not Revealed To Daniel
Gold
Silver
Brass
Iron
Eastern Division
(Greek Church)
Roman Empire A.D. 364 Divided
Western Division
(Papal Church)
Iron and Clay
The "Ten Toes" Of The Image (Representing The Ten Federated Kingdoms) Extend Over The Tribulation
Babylonian Empire
BC 606
Lion
Dan 7:1-4
BC 536 Medo-Persian BC 330
Bear
Ram
Grecian
Leopard
He Goat
BC 323
4 Divisions Alexanders Kingdom
BC 30
Roman Empire
Fourth Wild Beast
Dan 7:7-8
Anti Christ
"The King Of The North"
Book Of Daniel
The "Stone" Cut Out Of The Mountain Which Represents The "Stone" Or Millennial Kingdom Of Christ
Daniel's Vision Of The "End Time"
Daniel's Sealed Book
Dan 12:4
The Book That Daniel Was Told To "Seal Up" Was Descriptive Of The "Time Of Trouble" Or "Tribulation Period" And Thus Runs Parallel With The "Seven Sealed Book" Of The Book Of Revelation
- Designed And Drawn By Clarence Larkin
FoxChase, Phil'a, Pa
Copyrighted

CHAPTER SEVEN

The Four Wild Beasts

THE TIME OF THE VISIONS

"In the **first year of Belshazzar** King of Babylon, Daniel had a **'Dream'** and **'Visions'** of his head upon his bed: then he wrote the **'Dream,'** and told the sum of the matters." Verse 1.

This chapter, chronologically, should precede chapters five and six, but chronological order has been disregarded so as to keep the "Historical" part of the Book separate from the "Prophetical." We now enter upon the second, or "Prophetical," part of the Book. The opening words of this chapter take us back to the **first** year of Belshazzar's reign, the date of which is uncertain. In all probability he was not associated with his father as King of Babylon over three years, and as he was slain in B. C. 538, the first year of his reign would have been the year B. C. 541, at which time Daniel would have been about eighty-five years old. The date then of the Visions of this chapter must have been sixty-two years after Nebuchadnezzar had his "Dream" of the "Golden Headed Image." During the **"Years of Silence,"** from the death of Nebuchadnezzar (B. C. 561), to the "Fall of Babylon" (B. C. 538), a period of twenty-three years, Daniel appears to have lived a retired life. How blessed must have been those years of rest and communion with God. They were largely spent in the study of the writings of Moses, and such of the Psalms and Prophets as were then in existence. This is clear from his reference to the **"books"** in Dan. 9:2. It was during those quiet years, while Daniel was seeking more light from the Scriptures as to the "Times of the Gentiles," and their relation to his own people, the Jews, that he had this "Vision" of the "Four Wild Beasts." It is a noteworthy fact that the Apocalyptic writers of the Old and New Testaments, Daniel and John, were **old men** when they received their **"Revelations"** from God. They were also both **"greatly beloved"** of the Lord, and it was because of their faithfulness that they received these "Revelations."

This chapter records "Three Visions" that Daniel had.

1. The Vision of the **"Four Wild Beasts."**
2. The Vision of a **"Judgment Scene."**
3. The Vision of the **"Son of Man Receiving the Kingdom."**

The fact that these "Visions" are interwoven implies that they were all three seen on the same occasion.

THE FIRST VISION

THE FOUR WILD BEASTS

"Daniel spake and said, I saw in my 'Vision' by night, and, behold, the **'Four Winds'** of the heaven strove upon the **'Great Sea.'** And **FOUR GREAT BEASTS** came up from the sea, **diverse** one from another." Verses 2-3.

The scene of this "Vision" was on the shore of the **"Great Sea."** This is an important statement. For in the Old Testament the term "Great Sea" stands for the Mediterranean Sea, and this locates the geographical position of the Nations symbolized by the "Four Wild Beasts." For while the "Babylonian" and "Medo-Persian" Empires were not located on the Mediterranean Sea, as were the "Grecian" and "Roman" Empires, they were greatly indebted for their wealth and power to their Mediterranean coast land which they had conquered. And as more and more of this coast land was absorbed as the "Grecian" and "Roman" Empires came into existence, the "Prophetic Earth," including "Palestine" as a centre, became the boundary of the Mediterranean Sea, and the "Great Sea" became little more than a "Roman Lake" within the Roman Empire.

In the **"raging waves"** we have a symbol of the unrest and tumult of the nations, for the **"sea"** in the Scriptures is a type of the nations. "The **waters** which thou sawest . . . are **peoples,** and **multitudes,** and **nations,** and **tongues."** Rev. 17:15. "Woe to the multitude of **many people,** which make a noise like the **NOISE OF THE SEAS,** and to the rushing of **nations,** that make a rushing like the rushing of mighty **WATERS."** Isa. 17:12-13. But the sea is never thrown into a commotion of itself. Its disturbance is caused by some outside force, as a hurricane or an earthquake. So the nations are never thrown into discord only from without. These outside influences are spoken of in the "Vision" as the **"Four Winds of Heaven."** The number four points out the direction of the winds as coming from the four points of the Compass, and denotes their universality. These **"Winds"** represent the **"POWERS OF THE AIR,"** the forces of the **"Evil One,"** of whom the Apostle says—

> "We wrestle not against **flesh** and **blood** (that is, human beings), but against **'PRINCIPALITIES,'** against **'POWERS,'** against the **'RULERS OF THE DARKNESS OF THIS WORLD,'** against **'SPIRITUAL WICKEDNESS'** in **HIGH** (the heavenly) **PLACES."** Eph. 6:12.

We are to understand then by the "Four Winds of Heaven," the "Evil Powers" of the air that Satan uses to cause unrest among the nations of the earth. And as the closing days of this Dispensation draw near, and Palestine is rèpeopled by the Jews, the nations that centre around it will be more and more thrown into commotion, as Satan in his last great effort to checkmate the plans of God will bring into play all the "Evil Forces" of the air.

We are now ready to study the meaning of the **"Four Beasts"** that Daniel saw in his "Vision." As we proceed we shall find that they correspond with the **"Four Metals"** of the "Image" that Nebuchadnezzar saw in his "Dream." Why, you ask, should there be a repetition of the same revelation? The answer is, that men and God see the nations from a different standpoint. Man sees in them the concentration of wealth, majesty, and power, as seen in the "Golden Headed Image." God sees them as a set of **RAPACIOUS WILD BEASTS DEVOURING ONE ANOTHER.** He sees them as **bestial** in character, and as maintaining their supremacy by **brute** force. The Lion **devours,** the Bear **crushes,** the Leopard springs upon its victim and **sucks its blood,** and the character of the "Fourth Wild Beast" is such that there is no beast in nature to which it can be compared. Unconsciously the nations affirm their beastly character by their national emblems, as the British Lion, the Russian Bear, the American Eagle, the Chinese Dragon, the Persian Ram, the Macedonian Goat, etc.

Then this Vision of the "Wild Beasts" was given to Daniel that he might have additional light on the "Times of the Gentiles." Light that God vas not willing to give to a heathen king like Nebuchadnezzar, nor even ready at that time to give to his servant Daniel.

THE FIRST BEAST

"The **first** was like a **LION,** and had **eagle's wings:** I beheld till the wings thereof were plucked, and it was lifted up from the earth, and made stand upon the feet **as a man,** and a **man's heart** was given to it." Verse 4.

The **"First Beast"** that Daniel saw emerge from the seething foam of the "Great Sea" was like a **LION,** with this difference, it had wings like those of an Eagle. Its appearance would recall to Daniel the colossal figures of lions, with the wings of an eagle, and the face of a man, that adorned the palaces of Nineveh and Babylon, and would suggest to him that the "First Beast" was a symbol of the Babylonian Empire, and its first king, Nebuchadnezzar, and that it corresponded to the "Head of Gold" of the "Image." In this "Eagle Winged Lion" we see a combination of the "King of Beasts" and the "King of Birds," typical of the "Absolute Monarchy" of Nebuchadnezzar, and his conquering flight over the nations. But as Daniel gazed upon the "Beast" its wings were **plucked.** That is, Nebuchadnezzar satisfied with his conquests gave himself up to building palaces, and to the pursuits of peace, and from that time the glory of the Empire began to wane. Then Daniel saw it lifted up and caused to walk on two feet, instead of four, **like a man,** and a **man's heart** was given it, but otherwise it was still a **beast.** That is, it no longer resorted to the use of its teeth and claws to overcome its enemies, but to its intellect. The plucking of the wings may also refer to the insanity of Nebuchadnezzar, and the standing on two feet like a man, and the receiving of a man's heart, to his recovery from his **beastly** state, and his humane conduct thereafter.

THE SECOND BEAST

> "And behold another beast, a second, like a **BEAR,** and it **raised up itself on one side,** and it had **three ribs in the mouth of it between the teeth of it;** and they (the heavenly Watchers, verse 16) said thus unto it—**ARISE, DEVOUR MUCH FLESH.**" Verse 5.

The **"Second Beast"** was like a **BEAR.** The Bear is the strongest beast after the Lion, and is distinguished for its voracity, but it has none of the agility and majesty of the Lion, is awkward in its movements, and effects its purpose with comparative slowness, and by brute force and sheer strength. These were characteristics of the Medo-Persian Empire. It was ponderous in its movements, and gained its victories by hurling vast masses of troops upon its enemies. Xerxes' expedition against Greece was undertaken with 2,500,000 fighting men. It is easy to be seen that the movements of such enormous bodies of men would **"devour much flesh."** Not merely in the shape of food, but by death by exposure and disease, and in battle. The side of the "Bear" which raised up, preparatory to attack, represented Persia, which of the Dual Empire was the stronger and the most aggressive. It corresponded to the **"right shoulder and arm"** of the "Image." The **"Three Ribs"** stood for the three Kingdoms of **Lydia, Babylon, and Egypt,** that formed a **"Triple Alliance"** to check the Medo-Persian power, but were destroyed by it. As the "Bear" is an inferior animal to the "Lion," we see that the Medo-Persian Empire was inferior to the Babylonian. Not however in power, but in wealth and magnificence, and in its form of government. Thus the "Four Wild Beasts" correspond with the "Metals" of the "Image," in that each succeeding "Beast" is **inferior** to the one that preceded it.

THE THIRD BEAST

"After this I beheld, and lo another (Beast), like a **LEOPARD,** which had upon the back of it **four wings of a FOWL;** the breast had also **four heads;** and dominion was given to it." Verse 6.

The **"Third Beast"** was like a **LEOPARD,** with this difference, that it had **"Four Heads"** and **"Four Wings."** The Leopard is the most agile and graceful of wild beasts. Slight in its frame, but strong, swift, and fierce, its characteristics render it a fitting symbol of the rapid conquests of the Greeks under Alexander the Great, who, followed by small but well-equipped and splendidly brave armies, moved with great celerity and in about ten years overthrew the unwieldy forces of Persia, and subdued the whole civilized world. While the **"Four Wings of a Fowl"** would add to the rapidity of its progress, they were only the wings of a **"fowl,"** and not those of an **"Eagle,"** indicating that its progress, though swift, would not be as royally victorious as the armies of Nebuchadnezzar. Why only **four** wings, when "Four Heads" call for **eight** wings, we do not know, unless the "Four Wings" were intended to devote the "four quarters" of the earth into which Alexander sought to extend his Empire. The **"Four Heads"** represent the **"Four Kingdoms"** into which the Empire of Alexander was divided, namely, **Thrace, Macedonia, Syria,** and **Egypt.** While Daniel, following out the correspondence between the "Beasts" and the "Image," would see that the **"Leopard"** corresponded to the **Abdomen and Thigh Parts"** (Hips) of the "Image," he must have been confused by the **"Four Heads"** of the Leopard, for there was no **"Fourfold Division"** of the lower part of the **"Brass"** of the Image, indicating that the "Grecian Empire" was to be divided into four parts. Thus we read that the "Visions of his Head" **troubled him** (verse 15), and his countenance was changed by his **"cogitations."** Verse 28. Daniel had to wait two years longer, until his Vision of the "Ram and the He-Goat," for a solution of his difficulty. See the exposition of chapter eight.

THE FOURTH BEAST

> "After this I saw in the 'Night Visions,' and behold a **FOURTH BEAST, dreadful and terrible, and strong exceedingly**; and it had great **IRON TEETH**; it devoured and brake in pieces, and stamped the residue (the three previous Beasts) with the feet of it: and it was **DIVERSE** from all the Beasts that were before it; and it had **TEN HORNS.** I considered the **'Horns,'** and, behold, there came up among them another **'LITTLE HORN,'** before whom there were **three** of the 'First Horns' **plucked up by the roots**: and, behold, in **this 'HORN'** (the Little Horn, Antichrist) were **eyes like the eyes of a man,** and a **mouth speaking great things."** Verses 7-8.

The words, **"After this,"** do not imply that the Vision of the "Fourth Wild Beast" was separate as to time from the Vision of the three preceding Beasts, for **the**

Vision of the "Third Beast" begins with the same words. The fact is, as stated in verse 4, that Daniel saw the "Four Beasts" emerge from the "Sea," not all at once, but one after the other, and that their separate appearances constituted but **one** Vision. This view seems correct. Otherwise the correspondence between the "Four Wild Beasts," and the "Four Metals" of the "Image" would not harmonize, for Nebuchadnezzar did not have two separate Visions of the "Image," seeing only half of it, the "Gold," "Silver," and "Brass" in one Vision, and the other half, the "Iron," in another, and later Vision.

The **"Fourth Beast"** was like no other beast that had ever been seen on the earth. It was hideous to behold, and had, what no natural beast has, teeth of **iron,** and nails of **brass.** Verse 19. The fact that the "Fourth Beast" had **IRON TEETH** and **TEN HORNS** would cause Daniel to see that the **"Iron Teeth"** corresponded to the **"Iron Legs"** of the "Image," and the **"Ten Horns"** to the **"Ten Toes,"** and therefore the **"Fourth Beast"** represented the **ROMAN EMPIRE.** But what mystified Daniel was the **"LITTLE HORN"** that sprang up amid the **"Ten Horns,"** for he had not seen a **"LITTLE TOE"** spring up among the **"Ten Toes"** of the "Image." Daniel at once saw that the **"LITTLE HORN,"** with its **"eyes of a man"** and its **"mouth speaking great things,"** meant some new and additional revelation that God did not see fit to reveal on the "Image" to Nebuchadnezzar, and that was reserved for Daniel and his people, for we must not forget that Daniel's own "Visions" in the last six chapters of the Book have to do with God's dealings with the **"Jewish People"** in the **"LATTER DAYS."** It is well then to remember that Daniel's "Fourth Wild Beast" is descriptive of the Roman Empire in both its "First" and "Last" Stages. Before Daniel could ask for an explanation of the **"Little Horn" he had another Vision.**

THE SECOND VISION

A JUDGMENT SCENE

"I beheld till the **'Thrones'** were cast down, and the **'ANCIENT OF DAYS'** did sit, whose garment was white as snow, and the hair of His head like the pure wool: His Throne was like the fiery flame, and His wheels as burning fire. A fiery stream issued and came forth from before Him: thousand thousands ministered unto Him, and ten thousand times ten thousand stood before Him: the Judgment was set, and the books were opened. I beheld then, because of the voice of the great words which the **'HORN'** (Little Horn) spake: I beheld even till the **'BEAST'** (the Fourth Wild Beast) **was slain,** and his **body destroyed, and given to the burning flame.** As concerning the **rest of the 'Beasts,'** they had their **dominion taken away**: yet their **lives were prolonged for a season and time."** Verses 9-12.

The introduction here of a **"Judgment Scene,"** and a Vision of Christ **"Receiving the Kingdom,"** was for the purpose of revealing to Daniel the Judgment that shall fall on the "Gentile Nations," and the manner in which Christ shall receive the Kingdom. This was information not imparted in Nebuchadnezzar's "Dream Vision" of the "Golden Headed Image," and helped Daniel to fill out God's Program as to the Gentile Nations. Thus step by step Daniel was receiving light as to the things that should come to pass in the **"Latter Times,"** or the **"TIME OF THE END."** Not the "end of time," but the end of this present Dispensation.

This "Judgment Scene" is not the "Great White Throne Judgment" of Rev. 20:11-15, that takes place at the close of the Millennium. Neither is it the "Judgment Seat of Christ" that is pictured. 2 Cor. 5:10. 1 Cor. 3:11-15. That Judgment takes place **before** the Millennium, and soon after the Church has been "caught out." This "Judgment Scene" is that of the "Gentile Nations" as represented by the "Four Wild Beasts," for as the outcome of the "Judgment" Daniel saw the **"BEAST," the "Fourth Wild Beast,"** the Roman Empire (not the "Little Horn," it is not called a **"Beast"** in Daniel), slain and its body destroyed and given to the burning flame. This is figurative language describing the destruction of the Roman Empire. The **"Little Horn,"** called by John **"THE BEAST"** (Rev. 13:1-8), is not **slain,** as is the **"Beast"** of Daniel, but is cast **ALIVE** into the **"Lake of Fire."** Rev. 19:20. While the "Fourth Wild Beast," the Roman Empire, will be destroyed as the result of this Judgment, the other **"Beasts,"** the "Lion," the "Bear," and the "Leopard," representing respectively the Babylonian, the Medo-Persian, and the Grecian Empires, simply have their **dominion** taken away, but their lives **are prolonged for a season and a time.** It is worthy of note right here, that the Persian and Grecian Kingdoms have been revived. Why not the Babylonian when Babylon is rebuilt?

It is well to recall that there is a **"Dispensation of Judgment"** between the Present Dispensation, and the Millennium, during which there shall be three Judgments. (1) The **"Judgment of Believers for their Works"** at the "Judgment Seat of Christ." 2 Cor. 5:10. (2) The **"Judgment of the Jews"** during "The Great Tribulation." The Jews are an earthly people, and as all promises to them are earthly, it follows that their Judgment must be of an earthly character, and it is called by Jeremiah and Daniel as the time of **"JACOB'S TROUBLE."** Jer. 30:4-7. Dan. 12:1. Christ calls it **"THE GREAT TRIBULATION."** Matt. 24:21-31. The result of this Judgment will be the conversion of the Jews. (3) The **"Judgment of Nations."** Matt. 25:31-46. This is a Judgment of the Nations after Christ's return to the earth. It will take place in the "Valley of Jehoshaphat" (Joel 3:1-2), and its purpose will be to separate the **"Sheep"** and **"Goat"** Nations, so that the **"Sheep"** Nations may enter into the **"Kingdom prepared for them from the Foundation of the World,"** which is the Millennium, or "Stone Kingdom" of Christ. The "Goat" Nations, **as nations,** will be destroyed.* From this we see that the "Judgment Scene" that Daniel saw in his "Second Vision" is a general description covering the whole "Dispensation of Judgment" period.

The statement — **"I beheld till the THRONES WERE CAST DOWN"** (verse 9) may refer to the **"Thrones"** of the "Ten Kings" that shall be reigning with the "Little Horn" at the time of this Judgment. Or they may refer, as the writer thinks more probable, to the **"Thrones"** of the **"EVIL POWERS OF THE AIR."** For we know that at the time of this Judgment, the **"DRAGON"** (Satan), with all the **"Principalities"** of the Air, will be cast out of the Heavenlies, and thus their **"Thrones"** will be cast down. Eph. 6:12. Rev. 12:7-9. The writer is aware that the words **"cast down"** are changed in the Revised Version to the word **"placed,"** but the marginal, or alternate reading, is **"cast down."**

Who is it that sits upon this "Throne of Judgment?" He is called the **"ANCIENT OF DAYS."** Who is the **"ANCIENT OF DAYS?"** He can be no other than the **"SON OF MAN," "For the FATHER judgeth no man, but hath committed all judgment unto the SON."** John 5:22. Then the description of Him corresponds to that of the **"Son of Man"** in Rev. 1:12-15, "whose **Head** and **Hairs** were **white like wool,** as **white** as **snow**: and His **Eyes** were as a **flame of fire**; and His **Feet** like unto **fine brass,** as if they **burned in a furnace**; and His **Voice** as the **sound of many waters."** The picture of the **"Son of Man"** in Revelation, chapter one, is that of Christ as **JUDGE,** not as **High Priest.** At that time Christ will have completed His High Priestly Office, and assumed the Office of **"JUDGE,"** preparatory to His entering upon His "Kingly" duties when the Millennial Kingdom is

*See the Chart of the Judgments in the Author's book on "Rightly Dividing the Word."

set up. This is seen in that He is not girdled around the waist like a Priest, but wears a sash over His shoulder and breast like a Judge, and His hair of **"White Wool"** corresponds to the **"Snow White Wig"** worn by English Judges.

THIRD VISION

THE SON OF MAN RECEIVING THE KINGDOM

"I saw in the night visions, behold, one like the **'SON OF MAN'** came with the clouds of heaven, and came to the **'ANCIENT OF DAYS,'** and they brought him near before Him. And there was given him **dominion,** and **glory,** and a **KINGDOM,** that all peoples, nations, and languages should serve him: his **Dominion** is an **EVERLASTING DOMINION, which shall not pass away,** and his **KINGDOM** that **which shall not be destroyed."** Verses 13-14.

We are met here with an apparent contradiction in titles. We learned in the preceding "Vision" that the **"Son of Man"** was the **"ANCIENT OF DAYS,"** here we are told that the **FATHER** is. How can we reconcile these statements? There is but one way, and that is that the "Title" is used interchangeably. Jesus said—"I and my Father are **ONE."** John 10:30. And Paul says—"And without controversy great is the **'Mystery of Godliness:'** God was **MANIFEST IN THE FLESH."** 1 Tim. 3:16. And John tells us—**"In the beginning was the WORD** (Christ), **and the WORD** was **with God,** and the **WORD WAS GOD."** John 1:1. Thus we see, that, without trying to explain the Mystery of the Trinity, God and the Son of Man are one and the same, and therefore their "Titles" can be used interchangeably. Now we know from other Scripture that Christ is to receive the Kingdom from **the FATHER.** Hence in this "Vision," the **"Ancient of Days"** must represent **GOD THE**

FATHER. When Pilate asked Jesus—**"Art Thou the KING of the Jews?"** He evaded the question by saying—"My Kingdom is **not of this world."** That is, it would be given to Him by God the Father, and therefore would be from Heaven. John 18:33-37. In Luke 19:11-12 we read—

> "Because He was nigh to Jerusalem, and because they thought that the **'Kingdom of God'** should **IMMEDIATELY** appear; He spake this Parable. A **certain nobleman** went into a **far country** to receive for himself a **KINGDOM,** and to **return."**

From this we see that Jesus is the **"Certain Nobleman"** who has gone into a **"Far Country"** (Heaven) to receive **THE KINGDOM,** and that, when He has received it, He will return. That He has not **as yet** received it is evidenced by the fact that He has not **as yet** returned. The time for receiving the Kingdom, as shown by this Vision, is still **future,** and is given by John in Rev. 11:15.

> "And the Seventh Angel sounded; and there were great voices in Heaven, saying. **The Kingdoms of THIS WORLD are become the KINGDOMS OF OUR LORD, AND OF HIS CHRIST; and He shall reign FOREVER AND EVER."**

This passage locates the **time** when Christ shall receive the Kingdom as being when the "Seventh Trumpet" shall sound, which locates it as near the Middle of Daniel's "Seventieth Week." Thus Daniel and Revelation are in agreement.

THE PERPLEXITY OF DANIEL

The effect of these "Three Visions" on Daniel was a **troubled spirit.**

> "I Daniel was grieved in my spirit in the midst of my body, and the 'Visions' of my head **troubled me."** Verse 15.

Daniel knew from the "Dream Vision" of Nebuchadnezzar of the "Golden Headed Image" that there were to be "Four Great World-wide Empires" to succeed each other before the "Times of the Gentiles" would end. He also knew that the first one, the Babylonian, was still in existence, with no signs at that time of a speedy ending, and if the three Empires to follow should each last as long, the end of the "Times of the Gentiles" was a long way off; which meant that the setting up of the "Stone" or "Messianic Kingdom" was that far away. But what troubled him the most was the character of the "Four Wild Beasts," and the meaning of the **"Little Horn."** So he says—

> "I came near unto one of them that stood by, and asked him the truth of all this. So he told me, and made me know the interpretation of the things." Verse 16.

The "Bystander" that Daniel approached was no human being, for Daniel was still in the "Vision State," and no human being could have revealed to him the meaning of the Visions. It was some celestial messenger, like those sent to him later, who was waiting to interpret the Visions.

THE INTERPRETATION OF THE VISIONS

> "These great **Beasts,** which are four, **are four Kings** (or Kingdoms), which shall arise out of the earth. But the **'Saints of the Most High'** shall take the Kingdom, and possess the Kingdom forever, even forever and ever." Verses 17-18.

The "Heavenly Bystander" informed Daniel that the "Four Wild Beasts" represented "Four Kings," or Kingdoms, which should rise in the earth, thus identifying them with the Four Kingdoms represented by the Metals of the "Image," and that their power would be wrested from them by the **"Saints of the Most High,"** whose Kingdom should last forever. Who are these "Saints of the Most High?" **They are not the**

"Saints of the Church," for the "Saints of the Church" are "caught out" **before** the "Little Horn" makes "War with the Saints." Verse 21. And as the location of that "War" is on the earth, and the time is during the reign of the "Little Horn," and is distinctly given as three and one-half years (verse 25), the "Saints of the Most High" must be Daniel's people the Jews. For the "Most High" is the "Son of Man," the Messiah of the Jews, and they therefore are His Saints of the "End Time," who shall with Him take the Kingdom. Verse 22. This is further confirmed in verse 27, where it says—

> "And the Kingdom, and Dominion, and the greatness of the Kingdom under the whole heaven, shall be given to the **People** of the **'Saints of the Most High,'** Whose (the Most High) Kingdom is an **'Everlasting Kingdom,'** and all 'Dominions' shall serve and obey Him."

Now the **"People"** of the "Saints of the Most High" are the Jews, for they are to be the **"Head"** of the Nations during the Millennium (Deu. 28:13), and the "Saints of the Most High" are the "God-fearing Jews" that shall escape destruction by the "Little Horn" during the "Great Tribulation."

The reply of the "Heavenly Bystander" was not full enough for Daniel. It did not explain the meaning of the "Fourth Wild Beast," and of the "Little Horn" who was to make war on the "Saints of the Most High," Daniel's people. It was the conduct of the "Little Horn" that perplexed and troubled him.

> "Then I would know the truth of the **'Fourth Beast,'** which was diverse from all the others, exceeding dreadful, whose **teeth were of IRON,** and his **nails of BRASS;** which devoured, brake in pieces, and stamped the residue with his feet; and of the **TEN HORNS** that were in his head, and of the **other** (Horn) which came up, and before whom three fell; even of that **'HORN'** that had **EYES,** and a **MOUTH** that spake **very great**

things, and whose **LOOK** was more stout than his fellows." Verses 19-20.

Here Daniel records what he did not mention in his first description of the "Fourth Wild Beast:"

"I beheld, and the same **HORN** (the Little Horn) made **war with the Saints,** and prevailed against them; until the **'Ancient of Days'** came, and judgment was given to the **'Saints of the Most High;'** and the time came that the Saints possessed the Kingdom." Verses 21-22.

This additional description of his Vision of the "Fourth Wild Beast" helps the explanation of the "Heavenly Bystander."

"The **'Fourth Beast'** shall be the **'Fourth Kingdom'** upon earth, which shall be diverse from all Kingdoms, and shall **devour the whole earth, and shall tread it down, and break it in pieces.** And the **'Ten Horns'** out of this Kingdom are **'Ten Kings'** that shall arise: and **another** (King) shall rise after them: and **HE** shall be diverse from the **first** (Kings), and **HE** shall subdue **Three Kings.** And **HE** shall speak great words against the **'MOST HIGH,'** and shall wear out the **'Saints of the Most High,'** and think to change **'Times'** and **'Laws:'** and they shall be given into his hand until a **'Time and Times and the Dividing of Time'** (three and one-half years). But the Judgment (verses 9-12) shall sit, and they shall take away his dominion, to consume and to destroy it unto the end. And the Kingdom and Dominion, and the greatness of the Kingdom **under the whole heaven,** shall be given to the **PEOPLE** of the **'Saints of the Most High,'** whose (the Most High) Kingdom is an **'Everlasting Kingdom,'** and all Dominions shall serve and obey **HIM.**" Verses 23-27.

There are two "Figures" in this Interpretation that demand our attention. The first is the **"Beast,"** and the second is the **"Little Horn."** We must distinguish between them.

TIMES AND LAWS

The "Little Horn" of Dan. 7 shall "think to change **Times** and **Laws**: and they shall be given into his hand until a **'Time'** and **'Times'** and the **'Dividing of Time'** " (or three and one-half years). Dan. 7:25. The Rabbis understood by "Times" and "Laws," the Hebrew Sabbaths and Festivals, and the Law (Levitical) which regulated them. Now as these "Times" and "Laws" will be re-established when the Jews return to their own land and rebuild the Temple, they will be in force when the Antichrist (the Little Horn) shall make a Covenant with them for **"One Week,"** or "Seven Years." But in the **"Middle of the Week"** the Antichrist will break the Covenant (Dan. 9:27), and substitute the worship of himself for the worship of Jehovah, thus causing the Jewish "sacrifices and oblations to cease," and in his desire to annihilate all Jewish institutions he will think to change all Jewish "Times" and "Laws," and this he will do for the remainder of the "Week," or for three and one-half years.

THE BEAST

The **"iron teeth"** of this "Fourth Beast" identifies it with the **"Iron Legs"** of the "Image," or as we have seen, with the Roman Empire in its **past stage.** The **"Ten Horns"** correspond to the **"Ten Toes"** of the "Image," or the **last stage** of the Roman Empire. So we see that this **"NONDESCRIPT BEAST"** represents the Roman Empire in its **first** and **last** stages, but does not reveal what happens between the two stages. Now as the Book of Revelation gives us, in chapters 6 to 19 inclusive, the details of what is to happen during Daniel's "Seventieth Week," the period covered by the **"Toes"** of the "Image," and that is represented on Daniel's "Fourth Wild Beast" by the

"Ten Horns," we must turn to the Book of Revelation to get further light as to the **"Beast,"** and the **"Little Horn."** Let us compare "Daniel's Beast," and "John's Beast."

DANIEL'S BEAST

"After this I saw in the night visions, and behold a **FOURTH BEAST, dreadful** and **terrible,** and **strong exceedingly;** and it had **great iron teeth;** it devoured and brake in pieces, and stamped the residue (the 3 preceding Beasts) with the feet of it; and it was **diverse from** all the Beasts that were before it; and it had **TEN HORNS.** I considered the **HORNS,** and, behold, there came up among them another **LITTLE HORN,** before whom there were **THREE** of the **FIRST HORNS plucked up by the roots;** and, behold, in **THIS HORN** were **eyes** like the **eyes of a MAN,** and **a mouth speaking** great things." Dan. 7:7-8.

"Thus he said, the **FOURTH BEAST** shall be the **FOURTH KINGDOM** upon earth, which shall be **diverse from all kingdoms,** and shall **devour the whole earth,** and shall **tread it down** and **break it in pieces.** And the **TEN HORNS** out of this Kingdom are **TEN KINGS** that shall arise; and another (King) shall rise after them; and he shall be **diverse** from the first, and he shall **subdue THREE KINGS.** And he shall speak great words against the Most High, and shall wear out the saints of the Most High, and think to **change times and laws**; and they shall be given into his hand until a **TIME** and **TIMES** and the **DIVIDING OF TIME."** Dan. *7*: 23-25.

JOHN'S BEAST

"I saw a **BEAST** rise up out of the **SEA,** having **SEVEN HEADS** and **TEN HORNS,** and upon his horns **TEN CROWNS,** and upon his heads the **NAMES OF BLASPHEMY.** And the **BEAST** which I saw was like unto a **LEOPARD,** and his **feet** were as the feet of a **BEAR,** and his **mouth** as the mouth of a **LION**; and the Dragon gave him his **power,** and his **seat,** and great **authority.** And I saw **one of his**

HEADS as it were **wounded to death**; and his **deadly wound was healed**; and all the world wondered after the **BEAST**. . . . And there was given unto him a mouth **speaking great things** and **blasphemies**; and power was given unto him to continue **FORTY AND TWO MONTHS**. And he opened his mouth in blasphemy against God, to blaspheme His Name, and His Tabernacle, and them that dwell in Heaven. And it was given unto him to make war with the saints, and to overcome them; and power was given him over all kindreds, and tongues, and nations." Rev. 13:1-7.

In comparing these two **"BEASTS"** we find that they both come up out of the **"Sea."** As **"Daniel's** Beast" came up out of the "Great Sea" (the Mediterranean) (Dan. 7:2), and John was a prisoner on the Isle of Patmos when he had his Vision, an island of the same sea, both "Beasts" came from the same locality. Both of these "Beasts" were utterly unlike any beasts we have ever heard of. **"Daniel's** Beast" was **dreadful** and **terrible**, and **strong exceedingly**; and it had **great IRON teeth**, and **nails of BRASS**; while **"John's** Beast" was like a **LEOPARD**, with the **feet of a BEAR**, and the **mouth of a LION**. As **"Daniel's** Beast" represented the "Fourth Kingdom," the Roman Empire, it is evident that its characteristics, as given above, describe the Old Roman Empire, while the characteristics of **"John's** Beast" describe the Future Roman Empire. We know that the Old Roman Empire was **"strong exceedingly"** and its grip and power were like a beast with **"great iron teeth"** and **"claws of brass;"** and from the description of **"John's** Beast" we learn that the Future Roman Empire shall embody all the characteristics of the "Four World Empires," as seen in its **LEOPARD**-like body, its feet of a **BEAR**, and its mouth of a **LION**. And as the body of an animal is the largest part of it, the "Leopard," or Grecian character of the "Beast," will probably preponderate. That both "Beasts" have **"TEN HORNS"** reveals the fact that they will both be in existence at the time indicated by the **"TEN TOES"** of the "Image," which will be just before the setting up of the "Stone," or "Millennial Kingdom of Christ." We are told that the **"Ten Horns"** of **"Daniel's** Beast" stand for **"TEN KINGS,"** and the **"Ten Horns"** of **"John's** Beast" stand for the same. Rev. 17: 12. From this we see that both Daniel and John foresaw that the Roman Empire was to be eventually divided into "Ten Federated Kingdoms."

While both "Beasts" have **"Ten Horns,"** they differ in that John's has **"SEVEN HEADS,"** while Daniel's had but **"ONE,"** and among the **"Ten Horns"** on **"Daniel's** Beast" there came up a **"LITTLE HORN,"** which is not seen amid the **"Ten Horns"** of **"John's** Beast." These, as we shall see, are features that refer to the **"Last Stage"** of the "Beast," and show that we cannot understand the "Last Stage" of the Beast without carefully comparing Daniel's and John's "Beasts," for the **"LITTLE HORN"** of **"Daniel's** Beast" plucks up **three** of the **"Ten Horns"** and destroys them, or takes their Kingdom away, a thing that John omits to tell us. Again the **"Antichristian"** character of **"Daniel's** Beast" is seen in its **"LITTLE HORN,"** whose conduct corresponds with not a part, but the whole of **"John's** Beast," and that for the **same length of time,** for Daniel's **"TIME** and **TIMES** and the **DIVIDING OF TIME"** (Dan. 7: 25) is equal to John's **"FORTY AND TWO MONTHS"** (Rev. 13: 5), or three and one-half years. And both Beasts make **"War"** on the "Saints of the Most High," and **blaspheme His Name.** From this comparison we see the similarity of the two Beasts, and that they must be studied together to fill out the picture.

THE LITTLE HORN

In our study of Prophecy we lay much stress on the **"Second Coming of Christ,"** forgetting that there are two other comings of **"Persons"** that are just as momentous as Christ's Coming. The first is that of

"ANTICHRIST," and the other is that of **"SATAN."** In both the Old and New Testaments we are told of a—**"MYSTERIOUS AND TERRIBLE PERSONAGE"** who shall be revealed in the **"LAST TIMES,"** or the closing days of this Dispensation. He is called by various names.

In the Old Testament

"The Assyrian." Isa. 10: 5-6; 14: 24-25; 30: 27-33.
"The Wicked." Isa. 11: 4.
"King of Babylon." Isa. 14: 4.
"Lucifer." Isa. 14: 12.
"King of Tyrus." Ezek. 28: 11-19.
"The Little Horn." Dan. 7: 8; 8: 9-12.
"A King of Fierce Countenance." Dan. 8: 23.
"The Prince That Shall Come." Dan. 9: 26.
"The Wilful King." Dan. 11: 36.

In the New Testament

"The Man of Sin." 2 Thess. 2: 3-8.
"Son of Perdition." 2 Thess. 2: 3-8.
"That Wicked." 2 Thess. 2: 3-8.
"Antichrist." 1 John 2: 18.
"The Beast." Rev. 13: 1-8.

The Prophet Isaiah sees the **"Antichrist"** as the **"ASSYRIAN."** Isa. 10: 5-6; 30: 27-33. In Isa. 11: 4, a chapter which is evidently Messianic, we read that, among other things which the Messiah will do, "He small smite the earth with the **'rod of His mouth,'** and with the **'breath of His lips'** shall He slay **'THE WICKED.'"** The word translated **"THE WICKED"** is in the singular number, and cannot refer to wicked persons in general, but to some **one person who is conspicuously wicked.** The expression is strikingly like that of Paul in 2 Thess. 2: 8. "Then shall that **'WICKED'** be revealed, whom the Lord shall consume with the **'Spirit of His Mouth,'** and shall destroy with the **'Brightness of His Coming.'"** It is evident that Isaiah and Paul refer to the same individual, who can be no other than the **"ANTICHRIST."** In Isa. 14:4-17 there is a description of a **"King of Babylon"** who shall smite the people in his wrath, and rule the nations in anger. He is called **"LUCIFER, Son of the Morning,"** and his fall is described. There has never as yet been such a King of Babylon. It must therefore refer to some future King of Babylon, when Babylon shall be rebuilt, as we have seen it is to be. Verses 12 to 14 evidently refer to **"Satan,"** here called **"LUCIFER,"** and are descriptive of him before his fall, but as he is to incarnate himself in the **"Antichrist"** (Rev. 13:1-2), who will be a future King of Babylon, they explain the source of the pride and presumption of Antichrist which will lead to his downfall, as it did to Satan's. The Prophet Ezekiel has a similar view of the "Antichrist," under the name of the **"King of Tyrus."** Ezek. 28:11-19. And as the Future Roman Empire will include both Tyrus (Tyre) and Babylon, the "Antichrist" will be both King of Babylon and King of Tyrus.

We now come to the **"LITTLE HORN"** of Daniel, and as Daniel had three Visions of him, we will have to anticipate in part the description given of him in chapters eight and eleven. We have already considered him in this chapter. In Dan. 8:3-12, 20-25, in the Vision of the **"Ram and He-Goat,"** Daniel saw a **"Great Horn"** between the eyes of the "He-Goat" broken off, and four **"Notable Horns"** came up in its place, and upon one of these there appeared a **"LITTLE HORN."**

"And out of one of them came forth a **'LITTLE HORN,'** which waxed exceeding great, toward the South (Egypt), and toward the East (Babylonia), and toward the 'Pleasant Land' (Palestine). And it waxed great, even to the **'Host of Heaven;'** and it cast down some of the **'Host'** and of **'Stars'** (angels) to the ground, and stamped upon them. Yea, **HE** magnified himself even to the 'Prince of the Host,' and by **HIM** (the Little Horn) **the** daily sacrifice was taken away, and the place of His (the Prince of the Host) Sanctuary was cast down." Dan. 8:9-11.

In his interpretation of the **"LITTLE HORN,"** the Angel Gabriel said—

"In the **'LATTER TIME'** of their Kingdom, when the transgressors are come to the full, a King of **'Fierce Countenance,'** and **understanding 'Dark Sentences,'** shall stand up. And his power shall be mighty, but not by his own power (it shall be Satanic): and he shall **destroy wonderfully,** and shall **prosper,** and **practice,** and shall **destroy the mighty,** and the **'Holy People'** (the Jews). And through his policy also he shall cause **craft to prosper in his hand;** and he shall **magnify himself in his heart,** and **by peace shall destroy many:** he shall also **stand up against the 'Prince of princes;'** but he **shall be BROKEN WITHOUT HAND."** Dan. 8:23-25.

Quite a few Bible scholars claim that this **"LITTLE HORN"** is not the same as the **"LITTLE HORN"** that arose amid the **"Ten Horns"** of the "Fourth Wild Beast," but that it represents Antiochus Epiphanes, who, in B. C. 166, desecrated the Temple Altar at Jerusalem by erecting an **"idol altar"** upon it, and offering **"swine flesh"** thereon. But the description of this **"LITTLE HORN"** and his conduct does not accord with that of Antiochus Epiphanes, but does with the **"LITTLE HORN"** of the "Fourth Wild Beast." Antiochus Epiphanes never cast down any of the **"Host of Heaven,"** or magnified himself against the **"Prince of the Host."** Neither did he stand up against the **"Prince of Princes"** (Christ), nor was he **"broken without hand,"** for he died a natural death at Tabae in B. C. 165. The Angel Gabriel distinctly states that the Vision belongs not to the time of Antiochus

Epiphanes, but to the **"TIME OF THE END."** Dan. 8:17. That is, to the end of the "Times of the Gentiles" which is still future. And Gabriel also added that his mission was to make known to Daniel what shall come to pass in the **"Last End of the Indignation"** (Dan. 8:19), or the **"GREAT TRIBULATION."** So we see that as the "Little Horn" of Dan. 8:9-12, 23-25, synchronizes as to **TIME** (the "Time of the End") with the "Little Horn" of the "Fourth Wild Beast" of Dan. 7:7-8, that they both refer to the **same person—THE ANTICHRIST.**

Daniel also had another "Foreview" of the "Little Horn" in his Vision of the "Wilful King," but we will not stop here to consider it, as it will be explained in the Exposition of chapter eleven. We now turn to—

PAUL'S FOREVIEW OF THE "LITTLE HORN."

> "Let no man deceive you by any means; for **'THAT DAY'** (the 'Day of the Lord') shall not come except there come a **falling away** first, and that **'MAN OF SIN'** be revealed, the **'SON OF PERDITION,'** who opposeth and exalteth himself above all that is called God, or that is worshipped; so that he **AS GOD** sitteth in the Temple of God (the rebuilt Temple of Jerusalem), showing himself that he **IS GOD.** . . . For the **'MYSTERY OF INIQUITY'** doth already work (in Paul's day); only He (the Holy Spirit) who now letteth (restraineth, R. V.) will let (restrain), until He be taken out of the way. And then shall **'THAT WICKED' be revealed,** whom the Lord shall consume with the **spirit** (breath) **of His Mouth,** and shall destroy with the **brightness** (manifestation, R. V.) **of His Coming.** Even him, whose coming is after the **working of Satan** with all **power** and **signs** and **lying wonders,** and with all **deceivableness of unrighteousness in them that perish;** because they received not the **love of the Truth** (Christ) that they might be saved. And

for this cause God shall send them **strong delusion** that they should believe **a lie** (THE LIE. American Standard 1911 Bible), that they all might be **damned** who believed not the truth, but had pleasure in unrighteousness." 2 Thess. 2: 3-12.

Here Paul calls the **"Little Horn"** of Daniel by three different names,

"THE MAN OF SIN."

"THE SON OF PERDITION."

"THAT WICKED."

The name **"SON OF PERDITION"** is not without significance. It may help us to locate the origin of the "Little Horn" or "Antichrist." The name is used but twice in Scripture. It is first used by Christ of **"Judas"** (John 17: 12), and here of **"Antichrist."** In Gen. 3: 15, God said to the **"Serpent"** (Satan), "I will put enmity between thee and the woman, and between **'THY SEED'** and **'HER SEED.'"** Now the Woman's **SEED** was **CHRIST**, then the Serpent's **SEED** must be **ANTICHRIST.** And as Christ was born of a **"virgin"** by the Holy Spirit, so Antichrist will be born of a **"woman"** (not necessarily a virgin) by Satan. This is no new view, for it has been held by many of God's spiritually minded children since the days of the Apostle John, who have been looking for a man to be born among men who should be a **"Demon Man,"** upon whose mother Satan would descend, and fill her totally, and surround her totally, and possess her totally within and without, so that the creature born of her would be totally depraved. If the "Sons of God" (Angels) could take on them the form of men, and cohabit with the "Daughters of Men" in the days just before the Flood, and the offspring of that union were **"mighty men,"** men of Satanic character, whose wickedness brought on the Flood (Gen. 6: 1-8), then why cannot Satan assume the form of a man and be the father, by some woman, of the Antichrist? And could not such a person be properly called the **"SON OF PERDITION,"** or of Satan? For while **"Perdition"** is a **PLACE** (Rev. 17:8, 11), Judas and Antichrist are the **"SONS OF PERDITION"** in a special sense, for they are the **SONS** of the author of **"Perdition"—SATAN.**

In John 6:70-71, we read that Jesus said—"Have not I chosen you Twelve, and one of you is a **DEVIL?** He spake of **'Judas Iscariot'** the son of Simon: for he it was that should betray Him, being one of the Twelve." In no other passage than this is the word **"Devil"** applied to anyone but to Satan himself. Here the word is **"diabolus."** The definite article is employed, and it should read—"and one of you is **THE DEVIL."** This would make Judas the Devil **incarnate,** and explains why Jesus called him the **"SON OF PERDITION."** It will not do to say that in the text he is called "the **son** of Simon," for the words "the son" are in italics, showing that they are not in the original, and the name "Simon" is given because he was the reputed father of Judas, while Judas might have been the son of someone else.

The **next** question that arises is, "If Judas and the Antichrist are both called the **'SON OF PERDITION,'** are they one and the same, or are there **two 'Sons of Perdition?'** " Here we must anticipate. Turning to Rev. 11:7, we read that the **"Beast"** that slays the "Two Witnesses" **ascends out of the** "Bottomless **Pit" (ABYSS),** and that **"Beast"** is the **ANTICHRIST.** Now how did he get into the **"ABYSS?"** Well, if there is only **one "SON OF PERDITION,"** and Judas and Antichrist are one and the same, then he got in the **ABYSS** when Judas went to his **"Own Place"** (the **ABYSS).** Acts 1:25. Of no other person is it said anywhere in the Scriptures that he went **"to his own place."** Again in Rev. 17:8 it is said—"The **'Beast'** that thou sawest **was,** and **is not:** and shall **ascend out of the 'Bottomless Pit'** (Abyss), and go into **PERDITION."** As this **"Beast"** is the same that slays the **"Two Witnesses"** he is the **ANTICHRIST.** Now there are four things said of him. First, he **"WAS."** Second, he **"IS NOT."** Third, he shall **"ASCEND OUT OF THE BOTTOMLESS PIT."** Fourth, he shall **"GO INTO PERDITION."** From this we learn that in John's day the **"Beast" "Was Not,"** but that he had been **before on the earth,** and was to **come again,** that he was to **ASCEND FROM THE BOTTOMLESS PIT.** This is positive proof that the **ANTICHRIST** has been on the earth **before,** and that when he comes in the **future** he will come from the **"ABYSS."**

The question then arises, when was **"Antichrist"** on the **earth before?** If Judas and Antichrist are one and the same the enigma is solved. When Judas was on the earth, he **WAS;** when Judas went to his **"Own Place"** he **"WAS NOT;"** when Judas comes back from the **"Abyss" he will be—THE ANTICHRIST.** The Author does not insist on this view of Judas and Antichrist being correct, but with open mind he accepts it, because it seems to be the only logical solution of both Judas and Antichrist being called the **"SON OF PERDITION."**

The Apostle Paul also calls the Antichrist the **"MAN OF SIN."** That is, all **"SIN"** will head up in him. The "Apostasy" will be not merely a corruption of Christianity, but a renunciation of it. It will be a denial of the Father and the Son. It will be the embodiment of all **"Lawlessness."** The "Mystery of Iniquity" (Lawlessness) was secretly working in Paul's day. The Antichrist will not be the **"cause"** of "Lawlessness," he will be the **"fruit"** of it. He will arise out of the seething cauldron of "Lawlessness" that is now becoming so pronounced and manifest in the world, and in him will be the consummation of all "Lawlessness."

It now remains in tracing the **"LITTLE HORN,"** or Antichrist, to compare the "Two Visions" that John had of the **"BEAST."**

JOHN'S TWO VISIONS OF THE BEAST

BEAST OUT OF THE SEA

Rev. 13:1-7

"I saw a BEAST rise up out of the SEA, having SEVEN HEADS and TEN HORNS, and upon his horns TEN CROWNS, and upon his heads the NAMES OF BLASPHEMY. And the BEAST which I saw was like unto a LEOPARD, and his **feet** were as the feet of a BEAR, and his **mouth** as the mouth of a LION; and the Dragon gave him his **power**, and his **seat**, and great **authority**. And I saw **one of his** HEADS as it were **wounded to death**; and his **deadly wound was healed**; and all the world wondered after the BEAST. . . And there was given unto him a mouth **speaking great things** and **blasphemies**; and power was given unto him to continue FORTY AND TWO MONTHS. And he opened his mouth in blasphemy against God, to blaspheme His Name, and His Tabernacle, and them that dwell in Heaven. And it was given unto him to make war with the saints, and to overcome them; and power was given him over all kindreds, and tongues, and nations."

SCARLET COLORED BEAST

Rev. 17:3, 7-17

"I saw a Woman sit upon a **scarlet colored** BEAST, full of **names of blasphemy**, having SEVEN HEADS and TEN HORNS. . . . I will tell thee the mystery of the Woman, and of the BEAST that carried her, which hath the SEVEN HEADS and TEN HORNS. The BEAST that thou sawest WAS, and IS NOT; and shall **ascend out of the** BOTTOMLESS PIT, and go into **perdition**. . . The SEVEN HEADS are SEVEN MOUNTAINS, on which the Woman sitteth. And they (the **Seven Heads**, R. V.) are SEVEN KINGS; **FIVE are fallen**, and **ONE is**, and the **OTHER is not yet come**; and when he cometh, he must continue a **short space**. And the BEAST that **WAS**, and **IS NOT**, even he is the EIGHTH, and is **of the SEVEN**, and goeth into **perdition**. And the TEN HORNS which thou sawest are TEN KINGS, which have received no kingdom as yet; but receive power as kings one hour with the BEAST. These have **one mind**, and shall give their **power** and **strength** unto the BEAST. . . . And the TEN HORNS which thou sawest upon the BEAST, these shall **hate** the WHORE, and shall make her **desolate** and **naked**, and shall **eat her flesh**, and **burn her with fire**. For God hath put in their hearts to fulfil His will, and to agree, and give their kingdom unto the BEAST, until the words of God shall be fulfilled."

In the two descriptions given above it is very important to see that the "Beast" has a "**Dual**" meaning. It represents both the Revived Roman Empire, and its "Imperial Head," the Antichrist. As the Revived Roman Empire it is seen coming up out of the **"sea of the nations"** (Rev. 13:1), as the Antichrist it comes up out of the **"ABYSS."** Rev. 11:7; 17:8. For instance, it cannot be said of the Roman Empire of John's day, that it **"WAS,"** and **"IS NOT,"** for it was at the height of its power in John's day. Neither can it be said of it that it shall **"ascend out of the pit (ABYSS) and go into PERDITION,"** that could only be said of a **person.** Again we must distinguish between the **"Body"** of the Beast and its **"Heads"** and **"Horns."** The **"Body"** being that of a **LEOPARD,** with the **feet** of a **BEAR,** and the **mouth** of a **LION** is to show that the Revived Roman Empire in its "Last Stage" will include the characteristics of the first "Three Wild Beasts" of Daniel. That is, of the **LION** (Babylon), the **BEAR** (Medo-Persia), and the **LEOPARD** (Greece), and as the largest part of the Beast, the **body,** is represented by the **LEOPARD,** the prevailing characteristic of the Revived Roman Empire will be **GRECIAN.**

The Beast that comes up out of the Sea (Rev. 13) has **SEVEN HEADS** and **TEN HORNS,** and the **"Horns"** are **CROWNED.** This represents the Beast, or Empire, at the height of its power, when it will have **all its "Heads,"** and when the **TEN KINGS,** the heads of the **TEN KINGDOMS** into which the Empire shall be divided, will have been crowned. The Beast that comes up out of the **"ABYSS"** also has **SEVEN HEADS** and **TEN HORNS,** but they are **not crowned,** for the Ten Kings represented by the "Ten Horns" have not **as yet** received their kingdom (Rev. 17:12). This implies that the Beast of Rev. 17 represents the Empire at the beginning of the "Week." As confirmation of this view the **"WOMAN"** is seen at this stage **RIDING THE BEAST.** For while the **"Scarlet Clothed Woman"** is not seen until chapter 17, it is clear that she rides the Beast from the **beginning** of the "Week," for she represents the **"PAPAL CHURCH"** that comes into power after the "Church" has been caught out. During the wars preceding the rise of Antichrist the nations that will then be found in the geographical limits of the Old Roman Empire will form an "Alliance" for mutual protection. Those nations will be ten in number, represented by the "Ten Horns" of the Beast. No doubt the "Papal Church" will play a prominent part in those proceedings. She will be rewarded by restoration to Political Power, and this union of Church and State, in which the Church will have control, is shown by the **WOMAN RIDING THE BEAST**, thus dominating it. But when the **"Ten Kings"** shall receive their Kingdoms and be **Crowned**, which shall be in the "Middle of the Week," they "shall **HATE THE WHORE**, and shall make her **desolate** and **naked**, and shall **eat her flesh** (confiscate her wealth), and **burn her with fire.**" That is, burn her churches and cathedrals. Rev. 17:16.

While we are told in Rev. 17:9 that the **"Seven Heads"** of the Beast represent **"SEVEN MOUNTAINS"** (this is to identify it with the Roman Empire), we are told in the next verse (R. V) that they (the "Seven Heads") also represent **"SEVEN KINGS"** of whom **"FIVE are fallen**, and **ONE is**, and the **OTHER is not yet come**; and when he cometh he must continue a **short space.**" That is, in John's day **"Five"** of these Kings had fallen, **"One"** was the then ruling Emperor, and the **"Seventh"** was **yet to come.** Who are meant by the first "Five Kings" that had fallen we do not know. They were doubtless Kings of the Nero type. The King that was on the throne in John's day was Domitian, who had banished John to the Isle of Patmos. The last, or **"SEVENTH KING,"** who is yet to come is undoubtedly the **ANTICHRIST.** We are told in Rev. 13:3, that one of the **"Seven Heads,"** or **"Kings,"** received a **deadly wound.** Which one is not stated. The inference is that it is the last, for the Beast has **ALL** of his **"Heads"** before one of them is wounded. In Rev. 17:11 he is called "the

Beast that **WAS,** and **IS NOT,** even he is the **'EIGHTH'** (Head), and is of the **'SEVENTH'** (Head), and **goeth into PERDITION."** The only clear explanation is that the **"Seventh Head"—THE ANTICHRIST,** is the one who receives the **"deadly wound,"** probably at the hand of an assassin, and who actually dies or simulates death, and as his body is lying in state, he rises from the dead, and thus becomes the **"EIGHTH"** (Head), though he is of the **"SEVENTH"** (Head) revived. By this apparent resurrection from the dead, the Antichrist imitates the Resurrection of Christ and makes the world **"WONDER AFTER THE BEAST"** (Rev. 13:3), and this will add to his prestige and power. If this happens at the "Middle of the Week," at the time the Dragon is cast out of Heaven (Rev. 12:7-9), it will account for the great change that takes place in the Antichrist, for before receiving his "deadly wound" he was sweet and lovable, but after his resurrection, or recovery, he becomes **"Satanic,"** the result of the "Dragon" (Satan) incarnating himself in him. It is at this time that he breaks the **"Covenant"** with the Jews (Dan. 9:27), and desecrates the rebuilt Temple at Jerusalem by setting up the **"Abomination of Desolation"** (Matt. 24:15), which is an **"Idol Image"** of himself—**THE DESOLATOR.** Rev. 13:13-15. As the **"Little Horn"** of Daniel's "Fourth Wild Beast" he will destroy three of the "Ten Kings" and firmly establish himself in the place of power, and as he as the **"LITTLE HORN"** does not appear until **after** the **"TEN HORNS,"** or **"Ten Federated Kingdoms,"** come into existence, it is clear that the Antichrist does not form the "Federation," but is the outgrowth of it.

When we compare these **"Foreviews,"** and note the similarity of conduct of Daniel's **"LITTLE HORN,"** Paul's **"MAN OF SIN,"** and John's **"BEAST,"** and that Daniel's **"LITTLE HORN"** and John's **"BEAST"** are to continue for the **same length of time—"Forty and Two Months,"** or three and one-half years, and that Daniel's **"LITTLE HORN,"** Paul's **"MAN OF**

SIN," and John's **"BEAST,"** are all to be destroyed in the **same manner at Christ's "Second Coming,"** we see that they all prefigure the same **"Evil Power"** which is after the **"Working of Satan,"** and which John in 1 John 2:18 calls **THE ANTICHRIST.** In other words, when we find in prophecy **"Three Symbolic Personages"** that come upon the stage of action at the **same time,** occupy the **same territory,** exhibit the **same character,** do the **same work,** exist the same **length of time,** and meet the **same fate,** they must symbolize the **SAME THING.**

THE ANTICHRIST

The Antichrist, or last "Gentile Ruler," will be a **"COMPOSITE MAN,"** as seen from the description of the **"Leopard Like Beast"** with its feet like a **"Bear,"** and its **"Lion"** mouth. Rev. 13:2. He will have the combined abilities and powers, augmented by the power that the Dragon will confer upon him (Rev. 13:2), of Nebuchadnezzar, Xerxes, Alexander the Great, and Caesar Augustus. He will have the marvellous gift of attracting unregenerate men, and the irresistible fascination of his personality, his versatile attainments, superhuman wisdom, great administrative and executive ability, along with his powers as a consummate flatterer, a brilliant diplomatist, a superb strategist, will make him the most conspicuous and prominent of men. All these gifts will be conferred on him by Satan, whose **"Masterpiece"** and **TOOL** he will be, thus making him

THE SUPERMAN.

He will intoxicate men with a strong delusion and his never-varying success. And when he shall be slain and rise again he will have lost none of these powers, but will be in addition the **embodiment of all kinds of wickedness and blasphemy.** There has never as yet appeared on this earth a person who answers the description of the "Little Horn." Such a character is almost inconceivable. No writer would have invented such a character. Yet the Scriptures clearly foretell the coming of such a **"Person."** The world that today is rejecting Christ for **"Eternal Salvation"** will readily accept the Antichrist unto **"ETERNAL DAMNATION."** Refusing the **"Lamb,"** they will receive the **"BEAST."**

THE FALSE PROPHET

While Daniel did not see the "Little Horn's" companion—**THE FALSE PROPHET,** that being an additional revelation given to John, and therefore does not belong to the Book of Daniel, yet because many confuse the "Two Beasts" of Rev. 13, calling the "First Beast" that comes up **out of the sea** the "Political Head" of the Revived Roman Empire, and the "Second Beast" that comes up **out of the earth** the "Ecclesiastical Head" or **THE ANTICHRIST,** it seems necessary that we should at this point distinguish between the two. John thus describes the "Second Beast:"

> "And I beheld **another** Beast coming up **out of the EARTH;** and he had **'Two Horns' like a LAMB,** and he **spake as a DRAGON.** And he exerciseth all the power of the First Beast before him, and causeth the earth and them which dwell therein to **worship the First Beast,** whose deadly wound was healed. And he doeth great wonders, so that he maketh **fire come down from heaven on the earth in the sight of men,** and deceiveth them that dwell on the earth by the means of those miracles which he had power to do in the sight of the Beast; saying to them that dwell on the earth, that they should make an **IMAGE TO THE BEAST,** which had the wound by a sword, and did live. And he had power to give **LIFE** unto the **'Image of the Beast,'** that the **'Image of the Beast'** should both **SPEAK,** and cause that as

many as **would not worship the 'Image of the Beast'** should be **KILLED.** And he causeth all, both small and great, rich and poor, free and bond, to receive a **'MARK'** in their **right hand,** or in their **foreheads;** and that no man might **BUY** or **SELL,** save he that had the **'MARK,'** or the **'NAME OF THE BEAST,'** or the **'NUMBER OF HIS NAME.'** Here is wisdom. Let him that hath understanding count the **'NUMBER OF THE BEAST:'** for it is the **'NUMBER OF MAN:'** and his number is **SIX HUNDRED THREESCORE AND SIX."** Rev. 13:11-18.

This "Second Beast," while John does not say **it was a Lamb,** had "Two Horns" **like a lamb,** that is, it was **LAMB-LIKE,** but it **spake as a DRAGON.** It had a name. It is called the **"FALSE PROPHET"** three times. Rev. 16:13; 19:20; 20:10. Twice it is associated with the "First Beast" (Antichrist), and once with the "Dragon" (Satan) and the "First Beast," and as they are **PERSONS** so must it be. The fact that the "Second Beast" is called the "False Prophet" is proof that he is not the Antichrist. Jesus had a foreview of him when He said—"There shall arise **'FALSE CHRISTS'** and **'FALSE PROPHETS,'** and shall show **GREAT SIGNS AND WONDERS:** insomuch that, if it were possible they shall deceive the very elect." Matt. 24:24. Here Jesus differentiates between "False Christs" and "False Prophets," therefore **ANTICHRIST** and the **FALSE PROPHET** cannot be the same.

That the "Second Beast" comes up **out of the EARTH** may signify that he will be a **resurrected person.** If, as we have hinted, Antichrist was Judas resurrected, why should not the "False Prophet" also be a resurrected person? There will be two persons who shall come back from Heaven in those days, the "Two Witnesses," Moses and Elijah. Rev. 11:3-7. Why not two persons come up from **"The Underworld,"** brought up by Satan to counteract the work of the "Two Witnesses?" The fact that both Beasts are cast **ALIVE** into the "Lake of Fire" (Rev. 19:20) is further proof that they are **more than ordinary mortals,** and that the "First Beast" is **more** than the last Emperor of the Revived Roman Empire, he is the **ANTICHRIST.** Again, the Antichrist is to be a **KING,** and rule over a **KINGDOM.** He will accept the **"Kingdoms of this World"** that Satan offered Christ, and that Christ refused. Luke 4:5-8. He will also **EXALT** himself, and claim to be God. 2 Thess. 2:4. But the "False Prophet" is not a King. He does not exalt himself, he exalts the "First Beast" (Antichrist). His relation to the "First Beast" is the same as the Holy Spirit's relation to Christ, which is to glorify Christ and not himself. John 16:13-15. He causeth the earth and them which dwell therein to worship the "First Beast." Rev. 13:12. And as the followers of Christ are **"sealed"** by the Holy Spirit until the **"Day of Redemption"** (Eph. 4:30), so the followers of the "First Beast" shall be sealed by the "Second Beast" (the "False Prophet") until the **"Day of Perdition."** Rev. 13:16-17. 2 Pet. 3:7.

The "False Prophet" will be a "Miracle Worker." While Jesus was a "Miracle Worker," He did all His "Mighty Works" in the power of the Holy Spirit. Acts 10:38. One of the miracles that the "False Prophet" will perform will be to bring down **FIRE FROM HEAVEN.** Rev. 13:13. As Moses and Elijah will be back on the earth at that time (Rev. 11:3-12), there will probably be a **"FIRE-TEST"** between Elijah and the "False Prophet," and the test of Mt. Carmel as to who is God, Jehovah or Baal, will be repeated. But the test this time will be as to whether Jehovah or Antichrist is God, and as both Elijah and the "False Prophet" shall bring down fire, the test will not be conclusive. The "False Prophet" will be able to do this because he will be energized by Satan. For Satan can bring down fire from heaven, as we know from the Book of Job. Job 1:16. As further proof that the "First Beast" is the Antichrist, the "False Prophet" commands the people to make an **"IMAGE OF THE BEAST,"** and worship it, which he would not do if the "First Beast" were not the Antichrist. The "False Prophet" will also cause all who buy or sell to receive a **"Mark,"** the **"BRAND OF HELL."** This **"BRAND"** will be either upon the **"Right Hand,"** or the **"Forehead,"** and will be of three kinds, the **"Mark"** (some peculiar mark), or the **"NAME OF THE BEAST,"** or the **"NUMBER OF HIS NAME,"** which is **666,** the **"NUMBER OF MAN."** Rev. 13:16-18. Now these several distinctions between the "First" and "Second Beast," and that they both come up from **"The Underworld"** (Rev. 17:8; 13:11), hence cannot be slain as mortals, but must be cast **ALIVE** into the "Lake of Fire" (Rev. 19:20), differentiates them, and clearly shows that the "False Prophet" is not the Antichrist, but that the "First Beast" is. In other words the "False Prophet" is introduced, without any preliminary explanation, as an ecclesiastical companion and subordinate of the "First Beast," having no power of his own, but only that which is delegated to him (Rev. 13:12), and he claims no worship for himself, but causeth all to **worship the "First Beast,"** and those who will not he punishes as heretics, emphasizing his authority by miracles and "lying wonders" so as to get the people to accept **"THE LIE."** 2 Thess. 2:8-12.

THE SATANIC TRINITY

In the **"Dragon,"** the **"Beast,"** and the **"False Prophet,"** we have the **"SATANIC TRINITY,"** Satan's imitation of the "Divine Trinity." In the unseen and invisible "Dragon" we have the **FATHER** (the **ANTI-GOD).** In the "Beast" we have the **"SON OF PERDITION"** (the **ANTI-CHRIST), begotten of the Dragon,** who appears on the earth, dies, and is resurrected, and to whom is given a "Throne" by his Father the Dragon. Rev. 13:2. In the "False

Prophet" we have the **"ANTI-SPIRIT,"** who **proceeds from the "Dragon Father" and the "Dragon Son,"** and whose speech is like the **DRAGON'S.** The "Dragon" then will be the **"ANTI-GOD,"** the "Beast" the **"ANTI-CHRIST,"** and the "False Prophet" the **"ANTI-SPIRIT,"** and the fact that all three are cast **ALIVE** into the "Lake of Fire" (Rev. 20:10) is proof that they together form a **"Triumvirate"** which we may well call—**"THE SATANIC TRINITY."**

CHAPTER EIGHT

The Ram and the He-Goat

THE TIME AND PLACE OF THE VISION

"In the third year of the reign of King Belshazzar a '**Vision**' appeared unto me, even unto me Daniel, after that which appeared unto me at the first. And I saw in a '**Vision**;' and it came to pass, when I saw, that I was at Shushan in the Palace, which is in the province of Elam; and I saw in a '**Vision,**' and I was by the river of Ulai." Verses 1-2.

It is worthy of note that, beginning with this eighth chapter, the remainder of the Book of Daniel is written in **Hebrew.** The first chapter, and the first four verses of the second, are also in **Hebrew,** because this section gives the account of the Fall of Jerusalem and the Captivity of Israel. But from chapter 2:4 to the end of chapter seven, the language is **Aramaic,** because that part of the Book relates to the Gentile World Powers. From chapter 8:1 to the end of the Book is in **Hebrew** because it has direct reference to the **Jews, Jerusalem,** and the **Sanctuary** (Temple), and the terrible Roman Emperor (Antichrist) who will desecrate the Sanctuary and persecute the Jews. The purpose was to show Daniel what shall befall his People (the Jews) in the **"Latter Days."**

This Vision of the **"RAM"** and **"HE-GOAT"** occurred in the **"Third Year"** of the reign of Belshazzar, B. C. 538, or two years after the previous Vision of the Four Wild Beasts. It occurred in the same year as the "Fall of Babylon," and probably **before** its "Fall," and its purpose was to inform Daniel what Empires were to succeed the Babylonian, and to further trace the Little Horn, for it is worthy of note that while the prophecies of Isaiah relate mainly to the **"Christ,"** the Visions of Daniel are for the purpose of unveiling the **ANTICHRIST.** The Prophet was in Babylon when he received the Vision, but was transported in spirit to Shushan, the Capital of Persia, in the Province of Elam, where as he stood by the side of the river Ulai, he saw a wonderful sight.

THE VISION

THE RAM

"Then I lifted up mine eyes, and saw, and, behold, there stood before the river a **RAM** which had **'TWO HORNS:'** and the 'Two Horns' were **high,** but one was **higher** than the other, and the higher came up **last.** I saw the **RAM** pushing **Westward,** and **Northward,** and **Southward;** so that no beasts might stand before him, neither was there any that could deliver out of his hand; but he did according to his will, and became great."

THE HE-GOAT

"And as I was considering, behold, a **HE-GOAT** came from the **West** on the face of the whole earth, and **touched not the ground**: and the **GOAT** had a **'Notable Horn'** between his eyes. And he came to the **RAM** that had **'Two Horns,'** which I had seen standing before the river, and ran unto him in the **fury of his power.** And I saw him come close unto the **RAM,** and he was moved with **choler** (rage) against him, and **smote the RAM,** and **brake his 'Two Horns:'** and there was no power in the **RAM** to stand before him, but he **cast him down to the ground,** and **stamped on him**: and there was none that could deliver the **RAM** out of his hand."

THE FOUR HORNS

"Therefore the **HE-GOAT** waxed very great: and when he was strong, the **'GREAT HORN'** (the 'Notable Horn,' verse 5) **was broken**; and for it came up **FOUR NOTABLE ONES** (Horns) toward the **'Four Winds of Heaven.'"**

THE LITTLE HORN

"And out of one of them came forth a **LITTLE HORN,** which waxed exceeding great, toward the **South** (Egypt), and toward the **East** (Babylonia), and toward the **Pleasant Land** (Palestine). And it waxed great, even to the **'Host of Heaven;'** and it cast down some of the **'Host,'** and of the **'Stars'** to the ground, and stamped upon them. Yea, he magnified himself even to the **'PRINCE OF THE HOST'** (Christ), and by him (the Little Horn) the **'Daily Sacrifice'** was taken away, and the Place of His (Christ's) Sanctuary was cast down. And a Host was given him against the **'Daily Sacrifice'** by reason of transgression, and it (the Little Horn) cast down the truth to the ground; and it practiced and prospered." Verses 3-12.

AN ANGELIC CONVERSATION

While Daniel was pondering over the meaning of the "Vision" of the "Ram and He-Goat," he overheard a conversation between two "Saints" or "Holy Ones"—

"Then I heard one Saint speaking, and another Saint said unto that certain Saint which spake, **How long shall be the Vision concerning the 'DAILY SACRIFICE,'** and **the 'TRANSGRESSION OF DESOLATION,'** to give both the **'Sanctuary'** and the **'Host'** to be **trodden under foot?** And he (the first Saint) said unto me (Daniel), unto **TWO THOUSAND AND THREE HUNDRED DAYS;** then shall the Sanctuary be cleansed." Verses 13-14.

Before we proceed any further let us try to clear up the meaning of the **"Two Thousand and Three Hundred Days."** The Hebrew expression is not **"days,"** but **"evening-mornings,"** that is 2300 evening-morning **sacrifices,** which proves that actual days of twenty-four hours are intended. The question the second saint asked of the first was, "How long shall be the Vision concerning the **'Daily Sacrifice,'** and the **'Transgression of Desolation,'** to give both the Sanctuary and the Host to be trodden under foot?" This question was prompted by the previous statement, that the "Little Horn" would take away the **"Daily Sacrifice,"** and that the **"Place of His Sanctuary"** (the Temple) would be cast down, or desolated. The answer to the question was—"Unto **two thousand and three hundred days."** Now as these days are literal days, and date from the time when the "Daily Sacrifice" shall be taken away by the "Little Horn" (the Antichrist), which is in the **"Middle"** of Daniel's "Seventieth Week" (Dan. 9:27), then these 2300 days begin in the **"Middle of the Week,"** and as the "Week" is seven years long, half the "Week" would be three and one-half years, or forty-two months of thirty days each, or 1260 days. This would make the 2300 days overrun the last half of the Week 1040 days, or two years, ten months, and twenty days. And as the "Sanctuary" is not to be cleansed, or the "Daily Sacrifice" renewed until then, it would appear as if the Temple services are not to be re-established until Ezekiel's Temple has been built. Exek. 41:1—43:27.

While Daniel was pondering on the meaning of his Vision, he was startled by an apparition that had the appearance of a man.

THE INTERPRETER

"And it came to pass when I, even I Daniel, had seen the 'Vision,' and sought for the meaning, then, behold, there stood before me as the **appearance of a man.** And I heard a man's voice between the banks of the Ulai (probably from a cloud over the river), which called and said, **GABRIEL,** make this man to **UNDERSTAND THE 'VISION.'"** Verses 15-16.

Everything was done to make Daniel **UNDERSTAND** the Vision. The "Interpreter" was no earthly being but the Angel Gabriel. What he told Daniel must have been perfectly clear to him, and will be to us if we put ourselves in Daniel's place. What had troubled Daniel in his Vision of the "Four Wild Beasts" was the **"Little Horn,"** and now in this Vision of the "Ram and He-Goat" is another "Little Horn." Are they one and the same or are they different? Or was this Vision given to throw additional light upon the "Little Horn" as to the place of his origin? We must not forget that God led Daniel step by step. Each succeeding Vision was to throw additional light upon the Visions that went before.

> "So he (Gabriel) came near where I stood: and when he came, I was afraid, and fell upon my face (as every sinful man will in the presence of a Holy being): but he said unto me, **UNDERSTAND,** O son of man: for at the **'TIME OF THE END'** shall be the Vision. Now as he was speaking with me, I was in a deep sleep on my face toward the ground (Daniel swooned): but he touched me, and set me upright. And he said, Behold, I will make thee know what shall be **'IN THE LAST END OF THE INDIGNATION'** (The Great Tribulation): for at the time appointed **'THE END'** shall be." Verses 17-19.

Now notice, and this is the **"KEY"** to the Vision, that the Vision has to do with the **"TIME OF THE END."** The **"TIME OF THE END"** is a definite statement of Scripture, and has reference to the **"END"** of the **"Times of the Gentiles."** The Vision then had no bearing upon the times in which Daniel lived, and so, after it had been explained to him, he was told to **"shut it up,"** for it would not be fulfilled for **"many days"** (verse 26), that is, until the **"TIME OF THE END."** So the **"END TIME"** of this Vision is the same as the **"END TIME"** of all the "Dreams" and "Visions" in the Book.

THE INTERPRETATION

"The **RAM** which thou sawest having **'Two Horns'** are the **Kings** (Kingdoms) of **Media** and **Persia.** And the **ROUGH GOAT** is the King (Kingdom) of **Grecia**: and the **'Great Horn'** that is between his eyes is the **First King.** Now that (the Great Horn) being broken, whereas **FOUR** (Horns) stood up for it (in the place of it), **FOUR KINGDOMS shall stand up out of the nation,** but not in his (the Great Horn) power. And in the **LATTER TIME** of their Kingdom (the Four Kingdoms into which the Grecian Empire was divided at Alexander the Great's death), **when the transgressors are come to the full,** a King of **'FIERCE COUNTENANCE,'** and understanding **'dark sentences,'** shall stand up. And his power shall be **mighty,** but not by his **own power** (by Satanic power): and he shall **destroy wonderfully,** and **shall prosper,** and **practice,** and shall **destroy the mighty and Holy People** (the Jews). And through his policy also he shall cause **craft to prosper in his hand**; and he shall **magnify himself in his heart,** and by peace shall destroy many: he shall also **stand up against the 'Prince of Princes'** (Christ); but he shall be **BROKEN WITHOUT HAND."** Verses 20-25.

While Daniel knew from the "Dream Image" of Nebuchadnezzar (B. C. 603) that there were to be "Four World-wide Empires" that were to succeed each other, symbolized by the Gold, Silver, Brass, and Iron, of the Image (Dan. 2: 36-40), he was not told their names, except the first, Babylon. Neither in his "Vision" of the "Four Wild Beasts" (chapter 7), given sixty-two years later (B. C. 541), were the names of the Kingdoms that were to succeed the Babylon given. But in this Vision of the "Ram and He-Goat" there were revealed the names of the Kingdoms represented by the "Silver" and "Brass" of the

"Image," and their corresponding Beasts, the "Bear" and "Leopard." This information had been withheld until the time had come for the "Fall of the Babylonian Empire," and was given to Daniel at this time that he might know that the Medes and Persians, that were then besieging the city, represented the "Arms and Breast" of the Image, and therefore that the Fall of Babylon was at hand. This knowledge doubtless helped Daniel to interpret the "Handwriting on the Wall."

In Daniel's Vision of the "Four Wild Beasts," Medo-Persia and Greece are represented by a **"Bear"** and a **"Leopard;"** in this Vision they are also represented by Beasts, a "Ram" and a "He-Goat." The change in the Beasts is to further identify the Empires by their "Heraldic Devices." The Emblem of Persia was a **"RAM."** Coins have been discovered which display a "Ram's Head" on one side, and a Ram recumbent on the other. We also read of a Persian king riding in front of his army wearing "a Golden Figure of a 'Ram's Head' set with gems, instead of a diadem." In the Zendavesta, Ized Behram, the guardian spirit of Persia, appears like a Ram, with cloven feet, and sharp-pointed horns. The national Emblem of Macedonia (Greece) was a **"GOAT,"** and is found on the coins of that country, the ancient capital of which was called **Aegae,** or the **"GOAT CITY,"** while the adjacent waters were called the Aegean, or **"GOAT-SEA."** Hence the son of Alexander the Great by Roxana was called Aegus, the **"Son of a goat."**

To Daniel the "Ram" and the "He-Goat" corresponded to the "Bear" and the "Leopard" of the "Four Wild Beasts" Vision, and the "Arms and Breast of Silver," and the "Abdomen of Brass" of the "Image," he saw that the Empires that these represented were Medo-Persia and Greece. This correspondence was further confirmed as Daniel more closely compared the Beasts of his two Visions. The higher **"Shoulder"** of the "Bear" corresponded to the higher **"Horn"** of the "Ram" (Persia). And the **"Three Ribs"** in the mouth of the "Bear," which stood, as we have seen, for the three Kingdoms of Lydia, Babylon, and Egypt, that formed a "Triple Alliance" to check the Medo-Persian power, but were destroyed by it, corresponded to the action of the "Ram" that pushed **"Westward"** toward Lydia; **"Northward"** toward Babylon; and **"Southward"** toward Egypt.

When Daniel compared the "Leopard" and the "He-Goat" he saw that the **"Four Heads"** of the "Leopard" corresponded to the **"Four Horns"** that came up in the place of the "Great Horn" on the head of the "He-Goat." So far all was clear to Daniel. But what was meant by the **"LITTLE HORN"** that came up on one of the "Four Horns" of the "He-Goat" was to him a mystery. He had seen nothing to correspond to it on the "Leopard," and there was no Beast in this Vision to compare with the "Fourth Wild Beast" of the previous Vision, on whose head were "Ten Horns," amid which a **LITTLE HORN** sprang up. What relation did these "Little Horns" have to each other, if any? Now as to this "Little Horn" we can do no guessing. We must take the interpretation of the Angel Gabriel.

We are told by Gabriel that the **"Great Horn"** that was between the eyes of the "He-Goat" represented the **"First King"** (of Greece). Now this King, as all historians know, was **ALEXANDER THE GREAT** (B. C. 356-323, the son of Philip of Macedon), who became King of Greece when but twenty years of age, B. C. 336. Two years later (B. C. 334), in goat-like fashion, he leaped the Hellespont, and with an army of 30,000 infantry and 5000 cavalry he defeated a Persian force on the banks of the Granicus. By a swift advance eastward he, in the following year, B. C. 333, defeated at Issus a Persian army of 600,000 men, commanded by the Persian King, Darius. After minor conquests in Phoenicia and Egypt he returned to Syria, where on the banks of the Tigris River he defeated an enormous army led by Darius. This is known as the Battle of Arbela, B. C. 331. From B. C. 330 to 327, Alexander was engaged in subjugating the outlying provinces of the Persian Empire. Later he returned to Babylon, where, at the climax of his glory, he died of marsh fever and intemperance in June, B. C. 323, in his thirty-third year.

After the death of Alexander there was dissension as to who should be his successor, which ended, as the prophecy foretold, in four of his Generals dividing the territory of the Empire among themselves.

GASSANDER took Macedonia and the Western part.

LYSIMACHUS took Thrace and the Northern part.

SELEUCUS took Syria and the Eastern part.

PTOLEMY took Egypt and the Southern part.

The "Four Horns" may therefore be named **"Macedonia," "Thrace," "Syria,"** and **"Egypt."** These "Four Kingdoms" were in time absorbed by the "Fourth World Wide Empire," the Roman. The last to lose its identity was Egypt in B. C. 30. Thus we see that while there were to be but **FOUR** "World Wide Empires," the "Babylonian," "Medo-Persian," "Grecian," and "Roman," during the "Times of the Gentiles," yet they were not to succeed each other **without a break.** This was not shown on the "Image," nor in the Vision of the "Four Wild Beasts," but is first revealed in the Vision of the "He-Goat." The "break" or **"GAP"** between the "Grecian" and "Roman" Empires is covered by the "Four Minor Kingdoms" of "Macedonia," "Thrace," "Syria," and "Egypt." Here is history proving prophecy.

Having explained the meaning of the "Ram" and the "He-Goat," and of the "Four Horns" that came up in the place of the "Great Horn," the Angel Gabriel proceeds to an explanation of the **"LITTLE HORN"** that came up out of one of the "Four Horns." If the Vision had been given to us without an interpretation, we naturally would have supposed that the "Little Horn" indicated some "Monarch" that arose out of one of the "Four Kingdoms" **soon after their establishment,** such as Antiochus Epiphanes, who in some respects answers the description in verses 9-12. But Gabriel tells us in verse 23, that he is not to rise **"until the LATTER TIME of their Kingdom, when the transgressors are come to the full."** Here is a distinction between the **"FORMER"** and **"LATTER"** time of the "Four Kingdoms" into which Alexander's Empire was divided, which prophetically declares that those "Four Kingdoms" are to be **resuscitated** and become "Four" of the "Ten Kingdoms" into which the Revived Roman Empire shall be divided, for God is able to revive **dead nations** as well as dead men. As proof of this **Greece** is a sovereign State today, and **Egypt** is again coming into power, and in the upheaval of nations no one can foretell how soon **Thrace** and **Syria** shall again appear as independent Kingdoms.

It will not do to say that by the "Latter Time of their Kingdom" is meant the "Latter Time" of the "Four Kingdoms" before they were swallowed up by the Roman Empire, for they were not all swallowed up at the same time. Egypt was the last in B. C. 30. Neither will it do to say that by the "Little Horn" Antiochus Epiphanes is meant. Antiochus did not live in the "Latter Time" of those Kingdoms. He was the eighth out of twenty-six kings that ruled over Syria, and he died in B. C. 164, or 134 years before the last of the "Four Kingdoms" disappeared. As Antiochus was one of the twenty-six kings who constituted the **"Syrian Horn,"** he could not be that **"Horn"** and **also the "LITTLE HORN" that sprang out of it.** The "Little Horn" waxed **exceedingly great,** but Antiochus never did. It is true that he desecrated the Temple at Jerusalem, but the Maccabees rebelled, and in B. C. 165 restored its worship. When Jesus spoke of the "Abomination of Desolation" spoken of by Daniel the Prophet (Matt. 24:15), He did not refer to it as a thing of the past, but as something still future, therefore it was not something connected with the career of Antiochus, for he had been dead nearly 200 years. Antiochus never stood up against the **"Prince of Princes"** (Christ), for he died 160 years before Christ was born. Neither was he **"broken without hand,"** for he died a natural death at Tabae (Persia) in B. C. 164. It will not do to say that verses 9-12 refer to Antiochus, and verses 23-25 to the Antichrist, for verses 23-25 are the interpretation of verses 9-12, and therefore the **same person** must be meant. Therefore if verses 23-25 refer to some **future** person, verses 9-12 cannot refer to Antiochus. From this we see that there is a **"GAP"** that takes in the space between the **"Former"** and **"Latter Time"** of the "Four Kingdoms" into which Alexander's Empire was divided, and which corresponds with the **"GAP"** between Daniel's Sixty-ninth and Seventieth Week as revealed to Daniel in the next chapter.

THE LITTLE HORN

In comparing the descriptions of the "Little Horn" the mistake is made of supposing that they should agree as to details, etc., whereas they are progressive, each successive description adding new details to the preceding one. Thus the picture is filled out until the "Portrait" of the "Little Horn" (Antichrist) is complete. In chapter seven Daniel describes the "Little Horn" as plucking up three of the "Ten Horns," and having eyes like the eyes of a **man,** and a mouth **speaking great things.** The "Bystander" (a Holy One) who interprets the Vision repeats that the "Little Horn" will subdue "Three Kings," and adds—"He shall speak great words **against the Most High,** and shall **wear out the Saints of the Most High,** and think to **change Times and Laws**: and they shall be given into his hand until a **Time and Times and the Dividing of Time."**

Daniel describes the "Little Horn" of chapter eight as, **"Waxing exceedingly great,** toward the **South,** and toward the **East,** and toward the **Pleasant Land** (Palestine). And it waxed great, even to the Host of Heaven; and it **cast down** some of the Host and of the Stars to the ground, and **stamped upon them.** Yea, he magnified himself even to the **'Prince of the Host,'** and by him the **Daily Sacrifice was taken away,** and the place of His (Christ's) Sanctuary was cast down. And an host was given him against the Daily Sacrifice by reason of transgression, and it (the Little Horn) cast down the truth to the ground; and it **practiced,** and **prospered."** Verses 9-12. The Angel Gabriel in interpreting this "Little Horn" says—"A King of **'Fierce Countenance,'** and understanding **'dark sentences,'** shall stand up. And his power shall be **mighty,** but **not by his own power** (it shall be superhuman): and he shall **destroy wonderfully,** and shall **prosper,** and **practice,** and **shall destroy the mighty and the Holy People** (the Jews). And through his **policy** also he shall cause **craft** (all kinds of business) **to prosper in his hand:** and he shall **magnify himself** in his heart, and by peace shall destroy many: he shall also **stand up against the 'PRINCE OF PRINCES'** (Christ): but he shall be **BROKEN WITHOUT HAND."** Verses 23-25.

But these two descriptions from chapters seven and eight do not complete the picture of the "Little Horn." So we will anticipate and turn to the description of

THE WILFUL KING

in chapter 11:36-39, which fills out the picture—"And the **KING** (of the North) shall do according to **his will;** and he shall **exalt himself** and **magnify himself above every god,** and shall speak marvelous things **against the 'God of Gods,'** and shall prosper till the **'INDIGNATION'** (The Great Tribulation) **be accomplished,** for that that is determined, shall be done. Neither shall he regard the **God of his fathers,** nor the

desire of women, nor regard **any god; for he shall magnify himself above all.** But in his estate shall he honor the **'God of Forces;'** and a god whom his fathers **knew not** shall he honor with **gold** and **silver,** and with **precious stones,** and **pleasant things.** Thus shall he do in the most strong holds with a **strange god,** whom he shall **acknowledge and increase with glory;** and he shall cause them to rule over many, and shall divide the land for gain." This completes the picture of the "Little Horn" as far as it was revealed to Daniel.

From what has thus far been revealed **it** is clear that the "Little Horn" is to rise amid the "Ten Horns" of the "Fourth Wild Beast" or in the Roman Empire, and that of those "Ten Horns" or Kingdoms, **four** shall be the "Four Kingdoms" into which Alexander's Empire was divided, or Macedonia (Greece), Thrace (Asia Minor), Syria (Assyria), and Egypt, and that out of one of these four the "Little Horn" (Antichrist) shall rise. Which one will be revealed to us later as Syria. See "The Wilful King," chapter 11:36-45. We are told that this King of "Fierce Countenance" shall understand **"dark sentences,"** that is, he will be a Revealer of Secret Things, which will add to the mystery of his power. He will also stand up against the **"PRINCE OF PRINCES"** (Christ). That will bring his transgression **to the full,** and he shall be **BROKEN WITHOUT HAND.** The meaning of this is disclosed in 2 Thess. 2:8, where we are told that the Antichrist (that Wicked) shall be consumed with the Spirit of the Lord's mouth, and shall be destroyed by the brightness of His Second Coming. See the Battle of Armageddon. Rev. 19:11-20.

Having received the Vision, Daniel was told to **"shut it up,"** for its fulfilment would not be for **many days.** Not until the "Latter Time" of the "Four Kingdoms," which is still future. Then Daniel fainted and was sick certain days. The revelation of what was to befall his people in the "Latter Days" was too much for him, and made his heart sick. He says, "I was astonished at the Vision, but none understood (it)." The word "it" is not in the original. What Daniel meant was, that no one understood why he was sick, for he had "shut up the Vision," that is, he had told no one about it, and therefore they did not know the cause of his illness. But Daniel's disturbed state of mind did not prevent his attending to the affairs of State, for he says—"I rose up, and did the King's business." Verse 27.

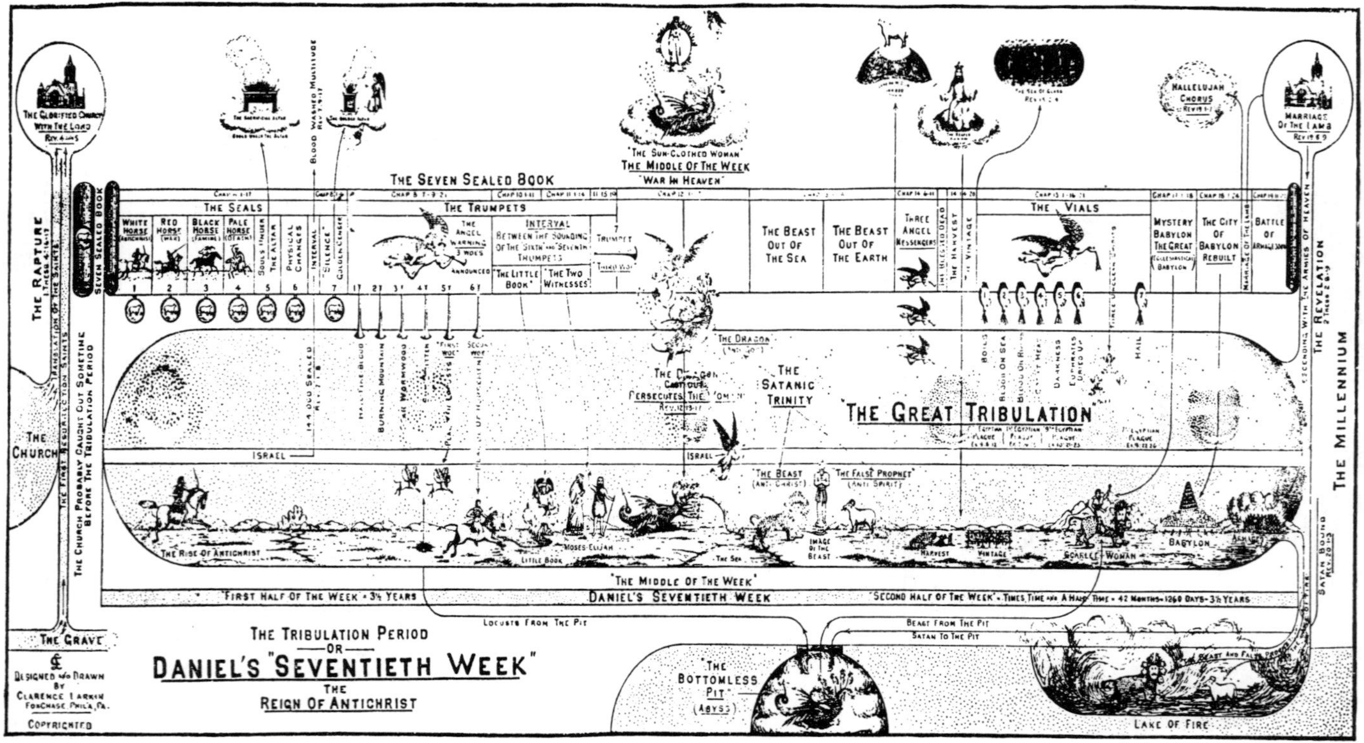
THE RAPTURE
1 THESS 4:16-17
TRANSLATION OF THE SAINTS
THE FIRST RESURRECTION SAINTS
THE CHURCH PROBABLY CAUGHT OUT SOMETIME BEFORE THE TRIBULATION PERIOD
THE GLORIFIED CHURCH WITH THE LORD
REV. 4:4-5
THE CHURCH
THE GRAVE
SEVEN SEALED BOOK
THE SEVEN SEALED BOOK
THE SEALS
WHITE HORSE (ANTICHRIST)
RED HORSE (WAR)
BLACK HORSE (FAMINE)
PALE HORSE (DEATH)
SOULS UNDER THE ALTAR
PHYSICAL CHANGES
INTERVAL
"SILENCE"
GOLDEN CENSER
BLOOD WASHED MULTITUDE
REV 7:9-17
144 000 SEALED
ISRAEL
THE TRUMPETS
THE ANGEL WARNING 3 WOES ANNOUNCED
HAIL-FIRE-BLOOD
BURNING MOUNTAIN
WORMWOOD
"FIRST WOE"
"SECOND WOE"
INTERVAL
BETWEEN THE SOUNDING OF THE SIXTH AND SEVENTH TRUMPETS
"THE LITTLE BOOK"
"THE TWO WITNESSES"
7 TRUMPET
THIRD WOE
"THE SUN-CLOTHED WOMAN"
THE MIDDLE OF THE WEEK
"WAR IN HEAVEN"
THE DRAGON
THE DRAGON CAST OUT PERSECUTES THE WOMAN
REV. 12:13-17
THE SATANIC TRINITY
THE BEAST OUT OF THE SEA
THE BEAST OUT OF THE EARTH
"THE BEAST" (ANTI-CHRIST)
"THE FALSE PROPHET" (ANTI SPIRIT)
IMAGE OF THE BEAST
THREE ANGEL MESSENGERS
THE BLESSED DEAD
THE HARVEST
THE VINTAGE
THE VIALS
BOILS
BLOOD ON SEA
DARKNESS
EUPHRATES DRIED UP
HAIL
"THE GREAT TRIBULATION"
MYSTERY BABYLON THE GREAT (ECCLESIASTICAL) BABYLON
THE CITY OF BABYLON REBUILT
MARRIAGE OF THE LAMB
BATTLE OF ARMAGEDDON
HALLELUJAH CHORUS
MARRIAGE OF THE LAMB
REV 19:6-9
DESCENDING WITH THE ARMIES OF HEAVEN
THE REVELATION
2 THESS 2:8-9
THE MILLENNIUM
SATAN BOUND
REV. 20:1-3
THE RISE OF ANTICHRIST
LITTLE BOOK
MOSES-ELIJAH
THE SEA
HARVEST
VINTAGE
SCARLET WOMAN
BABYLON
"THE MIDDLE OF THE WEEK"
"FIRST HALF OF THE WEEK" = 3½ YEARS
DANIEL'S SEVENTIETH WEEK
"SECOND HALF OF THE WEEK" = TIMES, TIME AND A HALF TIME = 42 MONTHS = 1260 DAYS = 3½ YEARS
LOCUSTS FROM THE PIT
BEAST FROM THE PIT
SATAN TO THE PIT
"THE BOTTOMLESS PIT" (ABYSS)
BEAST AND FALSE PROPHET
LAKE OF FIRE
THE TRIBULATION PERIOD
—OR—
DANIEL'S "SEVENTIETH WEEK"
THE
REIGN OF ANTICHRIST
DESIGNED AND DRAWN BY CLARENCE LARKIN FOX CHASE PHILA., PA.
COPYRIGHTED

CHAPTER NINE

The Seventy Weeks

THE TIME OF THE VISION

"In the **FIRST YEAR** of Darius the son of Ahasuerus, of the seed of the Medes, which was made king over the realm of the Chaldeans; in the **FIRST YEAR** of his reign I Daniel understood by books the number of the years, whereof the word of the Lord came to Jeremiah the Prophet, that he would accomplish **SEVENTY YEARS** in the desolations of Jerusalem." Verses 1-2.

The date of the chapter is important. The Prophet tells us that it was in the **FIRST YEAR** of the reign of Darius the Median over Babylon, which was B. C. 538. The time was critical, and Daniel's mind was in a state of perplexity and confusion. He had understood the Visions of the "Four Wild Beasts," and the "Ram and He-Goat," which foretold of a prolonged period of "Dispersion" for his people, but while he believed what had been revealed to him, he found it hard to reconcile with what he **understood "THE BOOKS,"** the writings of Moses and the Prophets, to teach as to the Captivity of his people, the Jews. From the Book of Jeremiah, Daniel understood that the Babylonian Captivity was to last but seventy years.

"And this whole land shall be a desolation, and an astonishment; and these nations (Judah and the surrounding nations) shall serve the King of Babylon **SEVENTY YEARS."** Jer. 25:11.

The "False Prophets" contradicted this, and encouraged the people to believe that the Captivity would be of short duration. To counteract this the Prophet Jeremiah wrote to the Captives at Babylon to settle down for a long stay, saying,

"Thus saith the Lord of Hosts, the God of Israel. . . . Build ye houses, and dwell in them; and plant gardens, and eat the fruit of them; take ye wives, and beget sons and daughters; and take wives for your sons, and give your daughters to husbands, that they may bear sons and daughters; that ye may be increased there and not diminished. And seek the peace of the city whither I have caused you to be carried away captives, and pray unto the Lord for it: for in the peace thereof shall ye have peace. . . . For thus saith the Lord, That after **SEVENTY YEARS** be accomplished at Babylon I will visit you, and perform my good word toward you, in causing you to **return to this place** (Jerusalem)." Jer. 29:4-10.

From this we see that Jeremiah was recognized as a Divinely inspired Prophet, and that Daniel, while himself a Prophet, was a **STUDENT OF PROPHECY**, and that he not only **read** the Word of God, but also **BELIEVED** it. Like Daniel, we should **"Search the Scriptures"** and find out what they have to say as to the times in which we live, and then believe what they say.

Now Daniel knew that as the Captivity began when he was carried a captive to Babylon in B. C. 606, that sixty-eight years of the seventy had already expired. He also knew that the man whom the Prophet Isaiah foretold would issue the edict for the return of the Jews, Cyrus, had taken Babylon as prophesied. Isa. 44:28. To him therefore the Captivity should end in a couple of years. How was he to reconcile this with his Visions that **FOUR** "World Wide Empires" were to come and go before the Children of Israel were to be restored to their "National Existence." Only one had come and gone, the Babylonian, leaving only two years for the passing of the other three. This was the cause of his perplexity. He had to learn that Israel's seventy years' sojourn in Babylon was a **TYPE** of a longer Dispersion, that was to last seven times as long. The Vision of the **"SEVENTY WEEKS"** that we are about to study was given to Daniel for this purpose. In the meantime Daniel gave himself to prayer, because he had read in the writings of Moses (Lev. 26:40-45; Deu. 30:1-10) that if Israel as a nation repented and turned to God, He would hear their cry and restore them to their own land.

DANIEL'S PRAYER

Daniel's prayer is one of the most sublime in the Bible, and is a model of **confession, supplication,** and **intercession,** in which Daniel, the most spotless character outside of Christ, associates himself as a sinner with his people. It was in this year that Daniel was cast into the "Lions' Den" for praying to his God, and it may have been that during that testing period, as he knelt at the time of the "Evening Oblation" (3 P. M.), verse 21, that Daniel made this prayer, and saw this Vision of the "Seventy Weeks." If so, we can understand how it strengthened him to face the "Lions' Den." As a preparation for the prayer Daniel fasted, and clothed himself in sackcloth and ashes, a token of humility. Verse 3.

THE CONFESSION

"And I prayed unto the Lord my God, and made **MY CONFESSION,** and said, O Lord, the great and dreadful God, keeping the covenant and mercy to them that love Him, and to them that keep His commandments; **WE** have **sinned,** and have **committed iniquity,** and have done **wickedly,** and have **rebelled,** even by departing from Thy precepts and from Thy judgments: neither have we hearkened unto Thy servants the Prophets, which spake in Thy name to our kings, our princes, and our fathers, and to all the people of the land. O Lord, righteousness belongeth unto Thee, but unto us confusion of faces, as at this day; to the men of Judah, and to the inhabitants of Jerusalem, and unto all Israel, that are near, and that are far off, through all the countries whither Thou hast driven them, because of their trespass that they have trespassed against Thee. O Lord, to us belongeth confusion of face, to our kings, to our princes, and to our fathers, because we have **sinned against Thee.** To the Lord our God belong mercies and forgiveness, though we have rebelled against Him; neither have we obeyed the Voice of the Lord our God, to walk in His Laws, which He set before us by His servants the Prophets. Yea, all Israel have transgressed Thy Law, even by departing, that they might not obey Thy voice; therefore the curse is poured upon us, and the oath that is written in the Law of Moses the servant of God, because we have **sinned against Him.** And He hath confirmed His words, which He spake against us, and against our Judges that judged us, by bringing upon us a great evil: for under the whole heaven hath not been done as hath been done upon Jerusalem. As it is written in the Law of Moses, all this evil is come upon us: yet made we not our prayer before the Lord our God, that we might turn from our iniquities, and understand Thy truth. Therefore hath the Lord watched upon the evil, and brought it upon us: for the Lord our God is righteous in all His works which He doeth: for we obeyed not His voice. And now, O Lord our God, that hast brought Thy People forth out of the Land of Egypt with a mighty hand, and hast gotten Thee renown, as at this day: **WE have sinned, WE have done wickedly."** Verses 4-15.

THE SUPPLICATION

"O Lord, according to all Thy Righteousness, I beseech Thee, let Thine anger and Thy fury be turned away from Thy city Jerusalem, Thy Holy Mountain: because for **OUR** sins, and for the **iniquities of our fathers,** Jerusalem and Thy People (the Jews) are become a reproach to all that are about us. Now therefore, O our God, hear the prayer of Thy servant, and his **supplications,** and cause Thy face to shine upon Thy Sanctuary that is desolate, for the **LORD'S SAKE.** O my God, incline Thine ear, and hear; open Thine eyes, and behold our desolations, and the City which is called by **THY NAME**: for we do not present **OUR supplications before Thee for OUR righteousnesses,** but for **THY GREAT MERCIES.** O Lord, **HEAR;** O Lord, **FORGIVE;** O Lord, **HEARKEN AND DO; defer not, for Thine own sake, O my God**: for **Thy City** and **Thy People are called by THY NAME."** Verses 16-19.

In his Prayer Daniel associates himself with sinning Israel. He does not say—"Behold, **the people** have sinned," but **"WE" have sinned,** and **committed iniquity,** and **done wickedly,** and have **rebelled,** and **departed** from Thy precepts and judgments. There is no covering up of the shameful facts. To **"US"** belongs **confusion of face.** And he confesses that all the evil that had befallen them was because they had broken the "Law of Moses." He does not base his supplication upon any righteousness that he or Israel had done, but upon God's deliverance of Israel from Egyptian bondage, and that the renown of that would be lost if God should now permit them to perish. He also pleaded that the Lord would deliver them for the sake of Jerusalem, His Holy Mountain, that the Sanctuary, then desolate, might be rebuilt. It was the "Glory of the Lord" he had in view, and not their worthiness.

THE INTERRUPTED PRAYER

"And whiles I was speaking, and praying, and confessing my sin and the sin of my people Israel, and presenting my supplication before the Lord my God for the Holy Mountain of God; yea, whiles I was speaking in prayer, even the man

Gabriel, whom I had seen in the Vision at the beginning, being caused to fly swiftly, touched me about the time of the **'Evening Oblation'** (3 P. M.). And he informed me, and talked with me, and said, O Daniel, I am now come forth to give thee skill and understanding. At the beginning of thy supplications the commandment came forth, and I am come to shew thee; for thou art **GREATLY BELOVED**: therefore understand the matter, and consider the Vision." Verses 20-23.

It is not often that God breaks in upon our prayers, but He did in this instance. This is the **INTERRUPTED PRAYER** of the Bible. The time of the "Interruption" was that of the "Evening Oblation" in the Temple, which was 3 P. M. There was no Temple in Babylon, and the one at Jerusalem had been destroyed, but Daniel, as he had been taught in his youth, observed the set times of the Temple services. This throws a "side-light" upon his religious habits. Special note is made of the **swiftness** of the man Gabriel. That between the commencement of Daniel's prayer, and its conclusion Gabriel had flown from Heaven to Babylon. The margin translates **"swift,"** with **"weariness,"** as if the flight was of such a great distance as to produce weariness. While Gabriel is an **angel,** Daniel speaks of him as a **man,** because angels when they appear to human beings always assume the form of a man. Gen. 18:1-2. The reason Gabriel gave for coming to Daniel was, that he was **GREATLY BELOVED IN HEAVEN.** Think of celestial beings, the highest in the Universe—the Father, the Son, the Holy Spirit, and the angels—having such high regard and esteem for a mortal man here upon the earth, as to deputize an angel of the rank of Gabriel to tell him so.

It would appear from the words—"Gabriel, whom I had seen in the Vision **at the beginning"** (verse 21), as if Daniel had a Vision at the beginning of his prayer that is not recorded. For there does not appear in the preceding Vision anything that was **not ex-**

plained to Daniel. If there was a Vision that is not recorded, we may surmise what it was from the character of the revelation of the "Seventy Weeks." It must have been a Vision connected in some way with the "Seventy Years" of the Babylonian Captivity, that led Daniel to pray as he did. And Gabriel was sent to show him that the "Seventy Years" were only a **"type"** of a longer period that would be **seven times** as long. The time therefore of the chronological disclosure of the "Seventy Weeks" was very appropriate. It was as definite a forecast of the 490 years of "Dispersion" that still remained for Israel, as was the seventy years of Captivity then closing. Daniel adds—"He (Gabriel) informed me, and talked with me, and said, O Daniel, I am now come forth to give thee **skill and understanding."** How blessed to have an angel, or the Holy Spirit, to instruct us in God's Plan and Purpose as to this world's affairs.

THE SEVENTY WEEKS

Dan. 9:24-27

Verse 24. **"SEVENTY WEEKS** are determined (marked off) upon **THY** (Daniel's) **PEOPLE** (the Jews) and upon **THY** (Daniel's) **HOLY CITY** (Jerusalem), to **finish the transgression,** and to make an **end of sins,** and to make **reconciliation for iniquity,** and to **bring in everlasting righteousness,** and to **seal up the vision and prophecy,** and to **anoint the most Holy.**

Verse 25. "Know therefore and understand, that from the going forth of the commandment to **'restore and to build Jerusalem'** unto the **'MESSIAH THE PRINCE'** shall be **SEVEN WEEKS,** and **THREESCORE AND TWO WEEKS:** the street shall be built again, and the wall, even in troublous times.

Verse 26. "And **AFTER 'Threescore and Two Weeks'** shall **MESSIAH** (Christ, the Anointed One) be **'CUT OFF,'** but **not for Himself:** and the **people** (Romans) of the **'PRINCE THAT SHALL COME'** shall destroy the City (Jerusalem) and the Sanctuary (the Temple); and the end thereof shall be with a flood, and unto the end of the war desolations are determined.

Verse 27. "And he (the **'Prince that shall come'—Antichrist)** shall confirm the Covenant with many for **ONE WEEK** (the last or Seventieth Week): and in the **MIDST** of the Week he (Antichrist) shall cause **the sacrifice and the oblation to cease,** and for the overspreading of abominations he (Antichrist) shall make it (the Temple) desolate, even until the consummation, and that determined shall be poured upon the desolate (Desolator)."

This Vision of the "Seventy Weeks" is the most important revelation, in many ways, made in the Scriptures. It is not only an interpretation of "Prophetic Chronology," but it is the **"Key"** that unlocks the "Scriptures of Truth." It also discloses another important fact that the "Seventy Weeks" only cover the period when the Jews are **DWELLING IN THEIR OWN LAND,** and does not cover the present period of their "Dispersion," but takes up their history again when they return to their own land, thus covering the time from the going forth of the decree to **"restore and rebuild Jerusalem"** until the **"Second Coming of Christ."**

THE PURPOSE OF THE SEVENTY WEEKS

We are told in verse 24 that the purpose of the "Seventy Weeks" is "six-fold"—

I. TO FINISH THE TRANSGRESSION.

II. TO MAKE AN END OF SIN.

III. TO MAKE RECONCILIATION FOR INIQUITY.

IV. TO BRING IN EVERLASTING RIGHTEOUSNESS.

V. TO SEAL UP THE VISION AND PROPHECY.

VI. TO ANOINT THE MOST HOLY.

I. TO FINISH THE TRANSGRESSION

We are told that these "Six Things" concern **only Daniel's PEOPLE** (the Jews), and the **HOLY CITY** (Jerusalem). This is very important. It discloses the fact that the "Seventy Weeks" have nothing to do with the **"Gentiles"** or the **"Church,"** but only with the **JEWS** and **JERUSALEM.** While the "Messiah the Prince" (Christ) when He was **"CUT OFF"** (Crucified), as described in verse 26, made an **"End of Sin"** (Heb. 10:12), and **"Reconciliation for Iniquity"** (Rom. 5:6-10), that was for the whole world. But the Atonement of Christ for the whole world is not in view here. It is the "putting away" or "finishing" of the **"Transgression"** of one class of persons—**THE JEWS.** That their "Transgression" is not yet finished is evident from the fact that they are still in disfavor with God. It will not be finished until they **as a Nation** repent and turn to God.

II. TO MAKE AN END OF SIN

Here again it is the "Sin" of Israel that is meant. The margin reads **"Seal up Sin."** That is, restrain it, as when a criminal is "locked up" and the door sealed. We read that the time will come when God "shall turn away ungodliness from Jacob, and take away from Israel all their sins." But this will not be until the **"DELIVERER"** (Christ at His Second Coming) comes. Rom. 11:26-27.

III. TO MAKE RECONCILIATION FOR INIQUITY

Here again it is the "Iniquity" of Israel that is meant. The word "iniquity" means **wickedness, unrighteous-**

ness, etc. It is written in Isa. 53:6—"The Lord hath laid on **HIM** (Christ) the **iniquity of us all."** This is blessedly true. But it has no application to the Jews **as a people** in this Dispensation. If a Jew desires to be saved by the Blood of Christ he must renounce his nationality and become a member of the "Body of Christ" (the Church), in which there is neither Jew nor Gentile. Gal. 3:26-28. Col. 3:10-11. But when the "Body of Christ" is complete, and "caught out," then the Jews, not as individuals but **as a Nation,** shall look upon Him Whom they pierced (Rev. 1:7) at His Second Coming, and a **"nation,"** the **JEWISH NATION,** shall be **born** (converted) **IN A DAY.** Isa. 66:8. "In **'That Day'** (the Day of the Lord) there shall be a **'Fountain'** opened to the **'HOUSE OF DAVID' (Israel)** and to the **inhabitants** of **JERUSALEM** for **sin** and **uncleanness."** Zech. 13:1.

IV. TO BRING IN EVERLASTING RIGHTEOUSNESS

There can be no "Everlasting Righteousness" until the "Millennial Kingdom" of Christ is set up, and it cannot be set up until the "Transgressions of Israel" have come to an end, and their "sins" sealed up. Then shall the Lord make a "New Covenant" with the "House of Israel."

> "But this shall be the **COVENANT** that I will make with the **'House of Israel;' AFTER THOSE DAYS** (the days of their present Dispersion), saith the Lord, I will put 'My Law' in their inward parts, and write it in their hearts; and I will be their God, and they shall be 'My People.' And they shall teach no more every man his neighbor, and every man his brother, saying, **Know the Lord:** for they shall **ALL KNOW ME,** from the least of them unto the greatest of them, saith the Lord: for I will **forgive their iniquity, and I will remember their sin no more."** Jer. 31:33-34.

V. TO SEAL UP THE VISION AND PROPHECY

While **"Vision"** and **"Prophecy"** appear to be sealed up at present to the Jews, it is only temporary.

> "For I would not, brethren, that ye should be ignorant of this Mystery, lest ye should be wise in your own conceits; that **'blindness in part'** is happened to Israel, **UNTIL THE FULNESS OF THE GENTILES BE COME IN."** Rom. 11:25.

When the "Transgression" of Israel has ceased, and they have uninterrupted communion with God, there will no longer be any need for "Vision" or "Prophet."

> "Love never faileth: but whether there be Prophecies, they shall fail (cease) . . . For we know in part, and we prophesy in part. But when that which is **PERFECT IS COME,** then that which is in part **shall be done away."** 1 Cor. 13:8-10.

It is a noteworthy fact that "Vision" and "Prophecy" have been confined to the Jewish race, and when all the "Visions" and "Prophecies" have been fulfilled, and there is no further use for them, they will be **"sealed up"** for preservation.

VI. TO ANOINT THE MOST HOLY

Some claim that by the "Most Holy" Christ is meant, and that this anointing of the "Most Holy" was fulfilled when He was anointed with the Holy Spirit at His Baptism. But the "Most Holy" is a **PLACE, not a person.** The reference is doubtless to the "Most Holy Place" of the new "Millennial Temple" as described in Ezek. 41:1—42:20, whose erection is still future. The first appearance of the "Shekinah Glory" of God was at the Exodus, when the Lord went before the Children of Israel in a "Pillar of Cloud" by day, and a "Pillar of Fire" by night. Ex. 13:21-22. Later when the "Tabernacle" was erected the "Shekinah Glory" took possession of the "Most Holy Place," and dwelt between the Cherubim on the "Ark of the Covenant." Ex. 40:34-35. Ex. 25:10-22. Num. 7:89. When the Temple of Solomon was dedicated the "Shekinah Cloud" filled the "Holy Place" so that the Priests could not stand to minister. 1 Kings 8:10-11. The Prophet Ezekiel tells us that he saw the "Shekinah Glory" of God reluctantly leave "The House" (The Temple), Ezek. 9:3, and later the City (Jerusalem), Ezek. 11:23, to return to Heaven. And in his Vision of the "Millennial Temple" Ezekiel sees the "Shekinah Glory" return from the East. Ezek. 43:1-6. From this we see that when the "Millennial Temple" is built the "Shekinah Glory" of the Lord will return and anoint the "Most Holy Place." Thus the "Time Space" between the "Departure" and "Return" of the "Shekinah Glory" marks the duration of the "Times of the Gentiles."

Now as the "Six-fold" purpose of the "Seventy Weeks" is all still **future,** the "Seventy Weeks" did not end with the "First" Coming of Christ, as some claim, but reach on down to His "Second" Coming.

THE SEVENTY WEEKS

Literally these words should read **"SEVENTY SEVENS."** The word **"WEEK"** is retained because we have no exact equivalent for the Hebrew original, which signifies a period of **"Seven."** Whether those "sevens" are days, weeks, or years, is to be determined by the context. It is a noteworthy fact that both the "Natural World" and the "Spirit World" are built on the **"Law of Sevens,"** thus proving that they have a common origin. In the Natural World we read that God rested on the "Seventh Day." And all through the Scriptures the number "Seven" is a basic number. There is the "Week of **DAYS,"** the "Week of **WEEKS,"** the "Week of **MONTHS,"** the "Week of **YEARS,"** the "Week of **WEEKS OF YEARS,"** the "Week of **MILLENNIUMS,"** and the "Week of **AGES,"** seven in all. The last book of the Bible, the book of Revelation, which is the book of **"Consummation,"** has seven divisions,

1. **The Seven Churches.**
2. **The Seven Seals.**
3. **The Seven Trumpets.**
4. **The Seven Personages.**
5. **The Seven Vials.**
6. **The Seven Dooms.**
7. **The Seven New Things.**

The number "Seven" is the **PERFECT** number. It is composed of the "Divine Number"—**THREE,** Father, Son, and Holy Spirit; and the "World Number"—**FOUR,** Spring, Summer, Autumn, and Winter.

PROPHETICAL CHRONOLOGY

Now if nature and the Scriptures are based on the "Law of Sevens," does it not seem reasonable that there is a "Time Element" that enters into all God's plans, and that He has a system of **"Prophetical Chronology"** by which He makes known His "Plans and Purposes" as to the Ages and Dispensations? That this is so is clear from Christ's reply to His Disciples when they asked Him—"Lord, wilt Thou at this time restore again the Kingdom of Israel?" and He said—"It is not for you to know the **'TIMES'** or the **'SEASONS,'** which the Father hath put in His own power." Acts 1:6-7. From this we see that there are **"Times"** and **"Seasons"** in God's plans for the Ages. And we know that—"When the **'FULNESS OF THE TIME' was come,** God sent forth His Son." Gal. 4:4. In other words everything moves on "Schedule Time" in the Universe. And as we have seen from fulfilled prophecy that nothing has failed to be fulfilled **on time,** so we can confidently believe that all that the Scriptures foretell of the future will likewise come to pass to the very minute.

In "Prophetical Chronology" we come across such divisions of time as "hours," "days," "weeks," "months," "years," "time, times, and an half." It is evident that these divisions of time, in order to be intelligible, must all be interpreted on the same **scale.** What scale is it? God has given us the **"Key"** in His Word. In Num. 14:34 we read—

> "After the number of the **DAYS** in which ye searched the land, even **FORTY DAYS,**
>
> **EACH DAY FOR A YEAR,**
>
> shall ye bear your iniquities, even **FORTY YEARS."**

Now we know that this judgment was literally fulfilled, for the Children of Israel wandered in the Wilderness forty years, a **YEAR** for every **day** that the spies searched out the land of Canaan. See also Ezek. 4:6. From this we see that the "Divine Scale" of "Prophetical Chronology" is, **A DAY STANDS FOR A YEAR.**

Apply now this "Scale" to the "Seventy Weeks," and we find that in 70 weeks we have 490 days, or on the "Year Day Scale" 490 years. We are told in verse 25—"That from the going forth of the commandment to restore and to build Jerusalem unto the Messiah the Prince shall be **'seven weeks,'** and **'threescore and two weeks,'** " that is $7 + 62 = 69$ weeks, or on the "Year Day Scale" **483 YEARS.** If we take as the beginning of this period the edict of Cyrus, B. C. 536, and its end the birth of Christ, B. C. 4, we have the length of the period as 532 years, which is 49 years too much. Right here it will be well to note that we are not sure as to the chronology of the above period. The Old Testament stops with Malachi, 400 years before Christ, and we have to depend upon profane writers such as Ptolemy for the chronology of those times, and some think that he makes the time too long, having given too much time to the kings of Persia. It is not generally known that if it were not for the Bible we would not know how long the human race has been on the earth. The genealogical tables giving the length of life of the patriarchs up to the Exodus, and then of the Judges and Kings of Israel and Judah on down to the Babylonian Captivity, bring us down to B. C. 606, and from there we have to depend on profane history. When we study profane history and try to find the origin of such nations as Egypt, Assyria, Babylon, Medo-Persia, Greece, and Rome, we find them enveloped in the mists of Mythology. They seemed not, until a late date, to have seen the importance of keeping any chronological records, and the method some adopted of keeping the record by dynasties, or from some event in their history, is confusing. The fact is they all date from Babel, or the "Confusion of Tongues" (Gen. 11:1-9), and the traditions they have of Creation and the Flood are proof of this rather than the reverse.

The reliability of Biblical Chronology as recorded in the Old Testament is seen when we understand God's purpose in it was to trace the **"Line of Descent"** from Adam to Christ. While the records are incomplete in some cases, as not giving the birth date, or where the reign of father and son overlap, the number of years involved are trifling in comparison with the sum total. This is seen when we compare the total number of years from Adam to Christ as given by the following leading Bible Chronologists:

Archbishop Ussher	B. C. 4004
Henry F. Clinton	B. C. 4138
Martin Anstey	B. C. 4124

Here there is only a difference of 134 years in 4000 The length of time then that man has existed on the earth is B. C. 4004+ A. D. 1924.* or 5928 years. With this understanding of the difficulty of securing, with absolute certainty, chronological data, let us return to the "Seventy Weeks."

---

*The year the author was called Home.

THE STARTING POINT OF THE SEVENTY WEEKS

The first thing to do in studying the Period of the "Seventy Weeks" is to find the date of its commencement. Here there is a conflict of opinion. There are four "Decrees" as to the restoration of Jerusalem and the Temple, after the Babylonian Captivity.

FIRST DECREE

The "First Decree" was given by Cyrus in B. C. 536.

> "Now in the first year of Cyrus king of Persia, that the word of the Lord **by the mouth of Jeremiah might be fulfilled,** the Lord stirred up the spirit of Cyrus king of Persia, that he made a Proclamation throughout all his kingdom, and put it also in writing, saying, Thus saith Cyrus king of Persia, The Lord God of Heaven hath given me all the Kingdoms of the earth; and He hath charged me to **BUILD HIM AN HOUSE** at Jerusalem, which is in Judah. Who is there among you of all His people? His God be with him, and let him go up to Jerusalem, which is in Judah, and **BUILD THE HOUSE OF THE LORD GOD OF ISRAEL** (He is the God), which is in Jerusalem. And whosoever remaineth in any place where he sojourneth, let the men of his place help him with silver, and with gold, and with goods, and with beasts, beside the freewill offering for the **HOUSE OF GOD** that is in Jerusalem." Ezra 1:1-4.

This proclamation of Cyrus is confirmed in 2 Chron. 36:22-23. But a careful reading of it reveals the fact that nothing is said in it about **"restoring and rebuilding Jerusalem,"** all that is mentioned is the **"House of the Lord,"** or the **TEMPLE.** But some claim that it must be interpreted by the passage in Isa. 44:28, where the Lord says of Cyrus, 176 years before he came to the throne—

> "He is My Shepherd, and shall perform all my pleasure: even saying to **JERUSALEM, Thou shalt be built**; and to the **TEMPLE, Thy foundation shall be laid."** Isa. 44:28.

It would be interesting to know what prompted the heathen King, Cyrus, to utter his decree. Did Daniel call his attention to the prophecy of Jeremiah (Jer. 25:11-14), that the Jews were to be captives in Babylon for seventy years, and that the time was up, and did he ask for their freedom, or did he call the King's attention to Isa. 44:28, which the Holy Spirit used to move Cyrus to free the Jews from their Captivity and send them back to rebuild the Temple, even restoring the gold and silver vessels that Nebuchadnezzar had taken from the Temple? Whatever prompted Cyrus to issue his "Decree," we are told that as the result of it 50,000 captives returned to Jerusalem (Ezra 2:64-65), that they set up an altar and renewed their sacrificial offerings and feasts, and proceeded to rebuild the Temple, but the work dragged because of adversaries. Is this a fulfilment of Gabriel's words to Daniel? As Cyrus limited himself in his commandment to the **rebuilding of the Temple,** and said nothing about the restoration and rebuilding of Jerusalem, are we to infer that he included that, or in the 176 years between Isaiah's prophecy and the issuance of Cyrus' decree, had the Lord changed His mind and limited the work of Cyrus to the mere rebuilding of the Temple? It would seem as if we should limit ourselves to the words of Cyrus himself, that the Lord charged him to simply build Him an **"HOUSE"** in Jerusalem.

SECOND DECREE

The "Second Decree" was that of Darius, B. C. 519. It is recorded in Ezra 6:1-12. In Ezra 5:1-17 we read how those who were trying to rebuild the Temple were interfered with in their work on the score that they had no authority for it, so they made an appeal to Darius to make a search in the king's treasure house in Babylon, which he did. The search revealed the Decree of Cyrus; and Darius' Decree is simply a **reaffirmation** of the Decree of Cyrus with penalties attached. It is worthy of note that Darius' Decree has reference to the Temple only, nothing is said about restoring and rebuilding the City, thus confirming the limitation of Cyrus' decree to the Temple.

THIRD DECREE

The "Third Decree" was that of Artaxerxes, king of Persia, in B. C. 458. It was simply a letter giving to Ezra permission to go up to Jerusalem and take with him some of the Priests and Levites, with authority to collect gold and silver to purchase bullocks, rams, and lambs for offerings in the Temple, and if necessary to draw on the King's Treasurers to the extent of "an hundred talents of silver, and to an hundred measures of wheat, and to an hundred baths of wine, and to an hundred baths of oil, and salt without prescribing how much." Ezra 7:11-22. There is nothing in this "Decree" that had anything to do with **restoring or rebuilding of Jerusalem.** It was simply a **"letter"** given to a Scribe who had prepared his heart to seek the Law of the Lord, and who wished to see that Law carried out in the service of the House of the Lord.

FOURTH DECREE

This was the Decree of Artaxerxes Longimanus, given in B. C. 445, in the twentieth year of his reign, and is recorded in Neh. 2:1-8. It was given to Nehemiah, the King's "Cupbearer," a very high official of the Persian Court, and one of the King's trusted servants; and was permission to return to Jerusalem and **"BUILD"** it. It was a political and not a religious mission, as is evident from the opposition of outsiders, such as Sanballat and Tobiah, who felt that the rebuilding of the walls and the fortifying of the City was a rebellious act. While the walls were repaired in fifty-two days, it took Nehemiah twelve years to rebuild and restore the City, and re-establish the Law, thus fulfilling the prophecy — "The street shall be built again, and the wall, even in **troublous times.**" Verse 25. The purpose of Nehemiah's mission was the restoration of Jerusalem as a political capital, and the re-establishment of the Jewish Nation. While the words of the Decree are not given, the character of Nehemiah's work, that of **restoration,** is proof of its nature. That the "letters" given Nehemiah by the King were in the form of a Decree is evident, otherwise Nehemiah would have had no authority to do what he did. As there is no other Decree authorizing such restoration, therefore this one of Artaxerxes Longimanus must be the one meant by Gabriel.

Let us look at it in another way. If we take the "First Decree," that of Cyrus, B. C. 536, as the starting point of the "Seventy Weeks," then the 7 + 62 Weeks, or 483 years on the "Year Day Scale" to "Messiah the Prince," ran out in B. C. 53, or 49 years **before** the "Birth of Christ," B. C. 4. If we take the "Second Decree," that of Darius, B. C. 519, the 483 years ran out in B. C. 36, or 32 years **before** the "Birth of Christ." Now if our present chronology is correct we cannot take either of the first two "Decrees" as a starting point, unless we admit that there is a **"time-space"** of 49 or 32 years between the "7 Weeks" and the "62 Weeks," which the prophecy will permit, in fact implies, by the division of the "69 Weeks" into "7 Weeks" and "62 Weeks."

Decree of Cyrus B. C. 536	7 Weeks / 49 Years	(49 Years)	62 Weeks / 434 Years	Birth of Christ B. C. 4

If we take the "Third Decree," that of Artaxerxes, B. C. 458, the 483 years **carry us over to A. D. 25, or**

29 years **after** the "Birth of Christ." Christ being born B. C. 4. If we take the "Fourth Decree," that of Artaxerxes Longimanus, B. C. 445, the 483 years carry us over to A. D. 38, or 8 years after the "Crucifixion of Christ" in A. D. 30. From this we see that we must either allow a "Time-Space" between the "7 Weeks" and the "62 Weeks," or we must use some other method of calculation.

THE TERMINUS OF THE "SIXTY-NINE WEEKS"

But there is another factor that enters into the problem. We have considered the four possible **"starting points"** of the "Seventy Weeks," how about their **"ending?"** What does the statement—**"Unto Messiah the Prince"** mean? We know that "Messiah the Prince" means Christ, but to what particular period or event in His life does the prophecy point? To His Birth, His Baptism, or His "Triumphal Entry?" These cover a period of 33 years and affect our reckoning. Let us look at them. Was the **"BIRTH"** of Christ the **"Terminus"** of the Sixty-nine Weeks?" Naturally we would suppose it was. If Gabriel was sent to Daniel to announce the "Seventy Weeks," what more suitable person could there be than he to announce the expiration of the "69 Weeks," and the **Birth** of "Messiah the Prince." So we find that when the **"Fulness of Time"** (Gal. 4:4) of the "Seventy Weeks" had come for the appearance of "Messiah the Prince," Gabriel appeared to Mary and said—

> "Fear not, Mary: for thou hast found favor with God. And, behold, thou shalt conceive in thy womb, and bring forth a son, and shalt call His name **JESUS.** He shall be great, and shall be called the 'Son of the Highest:' and the Lord God shall give unto Him the Throne of His father David: and He shall reign over the House of Jacob forever: and of His Kingdom there shall be **no end."** Luke 1:30-33.

While Gabriel did not announce to Mary, or the angels, that Jesus was the "Messiah the Prince," he did announce that He was to have the Throne of His father David, and therefore he was born as a **"Prince"** of the "House of David." While the "Wise Men" (Matt. 2:1-2) and Pilate (John 18:33-39) called him a King, and He was so crucified, He is still a **"Prince,"** for a Prince is a King in the making, and Jesus has not as yet been crowned and received His Kingdom, for He is now a "High Priest," and will not be a King until He receives the Kingdom from the Father. Dan. 7:13-14. There was a wonderful suitableness therefore in Jesus being called "Messiah the **PRINCE"** when He came the first time, for if Gabriel had said, **"Unto Messiah the KING,"** the "69 Weeks" would have reached to His "Second Coming" as **KING.** But as Jesus did not become publicly known at His birth it becomes a question whether that event fulfils the prophecy.

The first public event in Jesus' life was His Baptism, when, at the age of thirty, He had the twofold witness of the Father and the Holy Spirit to His Deity. Matt. 3:13-17. The Father saying—"This is My beloved Son in whom I am well pleased," and the Holy Spirit, in the form of a dove, anointing Him. Luke 4:16-19. Now the word "Messiah" means the **"Anointed One,"** and so the date of Christ's Baptism might have been the time of the expiration of the "Sixty-nine Weeks," for at that time He entered upon His Public Ministry and proclaimed that the "Kingdom of Heaven" was **"at hand,"** but the offer of the Kingdom was rejected, and from that time Jesus' ministry took on a different form. So the "Baptism" of Jesus could not have been the **"Terminus"** of the "69 Weeks" because Jesus avoided all public recognition of His claim as Messiah, even charging His Disciples again and again that they should not make Him known.

The third event in Christ's life that might be considered as the **"Terminus"** of the "Sixty-nine Weeks" was the "Triumphal Entry" of Christ into Jerusalem on "Palm Sunday," April 2, A. D. 30, a few days before His Crucifixion, and recorded in all four Gospels. Knowing that He was soon to be **"cut-off"** (Crucified), Dan. 9:26, and that His **MESSIAHSHIP** must be publicly recognized before that event, Jesus Himself took steps toward the fulfilment of Zech 9:9.

> "Rejoice greatly, O daughter of Zion; shout, O daughter of Jerusalem: because thy **KING** cometh unto thee: He is just, and having salvation; lowly, and **riding upon an ass, and upon a colt the foal of an ass."**

We are told in John 12:13, that the people who went out to meet Him as He descended the Mount of Olives, cried—**"Hosanna: Blessed is the 'KING OF ISRAEL' that cometh in the name of the Lord."** Why was this public proclamation of the **"Kingship"** of Jesus? The fact that Jesus at that time not only consented, but **took steps to bring about His "Triumphal Entry"** by commanding His Disciples to bring a **"certain ass,"** whose location He pointed out to them (Matt. 21:1-3), and declared, when He was asked to rebuke His Disciples (Luke 19:39-40), that if they should hold their peace the **stones would immediately cry out;** the fact, I say, that Jesus not only **consented** to be called **"KING,"** but **aided in bringing it about,** is proof that the "Triumphal Entry" had some prophetical significance, and what greater significance could it have had than that of proclaiming the **end of the "Sixty-nine Weeks,"** and the **coming of "MESSIAH THE PRINCE?"** There was no reason why the prophecies of Dan. 9:25 and Zech. 9:9 should not be fulfilled in the **same event,** the **"TRIUMPHAL ENTRY,"** for those who thus accepted Jesus as **"King,"** in that act accepted Him as **"MESSIAH THE PRINCE."** When Jesus came the first time He rode, meek and lowly, into Jerusalem on an **"ass;"** when **He comes to Jerusalem** the second time it will be on a

"WHITE HORSE" accompanied by the armies of Heaven. Rev. 19:11-16. It seems logical therefore that we should accept His "Triumphal Entry" as the date of the **"Terminus"** of the "Sixty-nine Weeks," rather than either that of His "Birth" or "Baptism."

Having reached the conclusion that the **"STARTING POINT"** of the "69 Weeks" was the "Decree" of Artaxerxes Longimanus, given March 14th, B. C. 445, and the **"TERMINUS"** the "Triumphal Entry" of Jesus into Jerusalem on "Palm Sunday," April 2, A. D. 30, it remains to be seen if the "69 Weeks" cover the "Time-Space" between these dates. But before we proceed it would be well to note that there is a difference of opinion as to the date of Christ's birth and death. He was not born A. D. 1, for He was born before the death of Herod (Matt. 2:1-23), and Herod died the latter part of B. C. 4. Then we read that when Christ was Baptized He was **"about thirty years of age"** (Luke 3:23), which would make the date of His Baptism the **latter part of A. D. 26.** And as His Public Ministry lasted three and one-half years, that would carry Him over until the **spring** of A. D. 30, when He was Crucified at the time of "The Passover," which that year fell on Friday, April 7, making the "Triumphal Entry" fall on the preceding Sunday, April 2, A. D. 30.

Thus far we have figured on the **Julian,** or Astronomical year of 365¼ days, but there are other years. There is the **Solar** year of 365 days, the **Calendar** year of 360 days, and the **Lunar** year of 354 days. Which of these years does God use in the Scriptures? We find the answer in the account of the Flood in Gen. 7:11-24; 8:3-4. There we are told that the 5 months, from the 17th day of the second month until the 17th day of the seventh month, are reckoned as 150 days, or 30 days to a month, or 360 days to a year. So we see that in "Prophetical Chronology" we are to use a "Calendar" year of 360 days. Having discovered that God's measures of "Prophetic Time" are **"A DAY FOR A YEAR,"** and **"THIRTY DAYS TO A**

MONTH," let us now apply them to the "Seventy Weeks" of Daniel.

According to ordinary chronology the 475 years from B. C. 445 to A. D. 30 inclusive are "Solar" years of 365 days each. Now counting the years **between** these two dates (444 + 29 = 473 years), and counting B. C. 1 and A. D. 1 as 2 years,

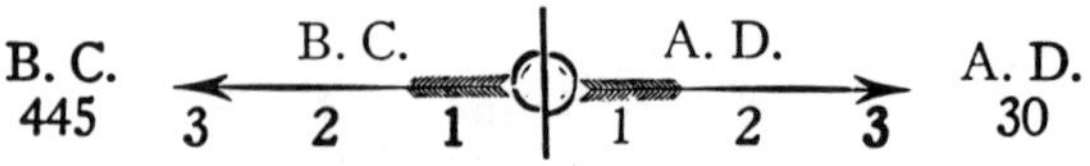

we have 473 "Solar" years. Multiply these by 365 (the number of days in a "Solar" year) and we have 172,645 days, to which add the number of days inclusive from March 14 to December 31, B. C. 445 = 293 days, and the number of days from January 1 to April 2, A. D. 30 = 92 days, we have 172,645 + 293 + 92 = 173,030 days. To which add 116 days for "leap years," and we have 173,146 days. Divide these by 360, the number of days in a "Prophetic Year," and we have 481 years, less 14 days, or within 2 years and 14 days of 483 years, the number of "Year Days" in "69 Weeks."

This reckoning does not agree with that of Sir Robert Anderson in his book, "Daniel in the Critic's Den," page 134. Sir Robert claims that Jesus' "Triumphal Entry" was made on Sunday, April 6, A. D. 32. He fixes the date on the statement of Luke (Luke 3: 1-3), that John the Baptist began his ministry in the fifteenth year of the reign of Tiberius Caesar, which was A. D. 29, **if profane history is correct.** Now as Jesus was baptized during the first year of John's ministry, then He must have been baptized in A. D. 29. And Sir Robert by limiting Jesus' ministry to three years, makes the date of the "Triumphal Entry" to be Sunday, April 6, A. D. 32. This conflicts with the previous statement of the writer that Jesus was born in B. C. 4, because He was born before the death of Herod (Matt. 2: 1-23), and Herod died the latter part of that year. Now Luke **tells us that Jesus was "about thirty**

years of age" when He was Baptized (Luke 3:23), and if He was born in B. C. 4, and John the Baptist began his ministry in A. D. 29, Jesus was 33 years old when He was Baptized, and if His Ministry lasted for 3½ years, He was 36½ years old when He was crucified. The whole thing hinges on whether Herod died in B. C. 4, or Tiberius Caesar began his reign in A. D. 14.

We quote below the figures of Sir Robert:

"From B. C. 455 to A. D. 32 is 476 years (he counts B. C. 1 and A. D. 1 as one year) = 173,740 days (476 × 365) + 116 days for leap years. And from 14th March to 6th April (reckoned inclusively according to Jewish practice) is 24 days. But 173,740 + 116 + 24 = 173,880. And 69 × 7 × 360 = 173.880." Thus he claims that the "69 Weeks" were exactly fulfilled to the day. But Sir Robert counts the years B. C. 445 and A. D. 32 as **full years,** when he ought only to count from March 14 to December 31 of B. C. 445, and from January 1 to April 6 of A. D. 32. That would leave only 474 **full years** in between B. C. 445 and A. D. 32, counting B. C. 1 and A. D. 1 as one year. Figuring this out, we have 474 × 365 = 173,010 + 293 days from March 14 to December 31, B. C. 445, + 96 days from January 1 to April 6, A. D. 30. + 116 days for leap years (173,010 + 293 + 96 + 116) equals 173,515. Divide this by 360 and we have 482 years less 5 days, or 1 year and 5 days short of the 483 years.

The first of these calculations (that of the writer) is 2 years and 14 days short of 483 years, while that of the second (Sir Robert Anderson's) is 1 year and 5 days short. How are we to explain this shortage? The only way we can explain it is that there is an error in profane chronology, of a year or two, between B. C. 445 and A. D. 30 or 32. If such an error is discovered, and it amounts to more than a year or two, that would not invalidate the calculation, but could readily be explained on the supposition that there is a

"Time-Space" between the "7 Weeks" and the "62 Weeks." The fact is, that the difference in time, in either of the above calculations, is so small as to amount to a demonstration that the "69 Weeks" cover the time between the Edict of Artaxerxes Longimanus, B. C. 445, and the "Triumphal Entry" of Jesus into Jerusalem.

We see from this that if the "Students of Prophecy" of Christ's day had been on the alert, and had understood Daniel's Prophecy of the "Seventy Weeks," they would have been looking for Him, and would have known to a certainty whether He was the Messiah or not. What a rebuke is all this to those teachers and preachers of today who make light of the prophetical statements of the "Word of God." The "Second Coming" of Christ will find them just as much unprepared to receive Him as the Jews were to receive Him at His First Coming. It was just as the man "clothed in linen," who stood on the river bank, said to Daniel—**"None of the wicked shall understand; but the Wise Shall Understand."** Dan. 12:10. That is, the scripturally and spiritually wise.

THE GREAT PARENTHESIS

Having shown that 69 of the "70 Weeks" ran their course with the "Triumphal Entry" of Christ into Jerusalem, the next question is, does the "70th Week" **immediately** follow the "69th" or is there a "Time-Space" between them? A "Time-Space" that takes in the whole of the present Dispensation. There are some who claim that there is no "Time-Space." Some of these claim that the "69th Week" ended at the Birth of Christ, and the Middle of the "70th" at His Crucifixion, when He was **"cut off,"** and that the remainder of the "70th Week" is now in the process of fulfilment. The fallacy of this is seen in that it divides the "70th Week" into two unequal parts, one of 33½ years, from the Birth of Christ until His Crucifixion, the other of 1900 or more years, when the "70th

Week" can be no longer than each of the "69 Weeks," which we have seen were 7 years.

Some of those who claim that there is no "Time-Space" between the "69th" and "70th Week" affirm that it would be contrary to other Scripture to put a **"Gap"** between them, and they quote the "Seventy Years" of the Babylonian Captivity, which lasted for exactly 70 years without a break. They also mention the 430 years' sojourning of Abraham's descendants in Egypt (Gen. 15:13; Ex. 12:40; Gal. 3:17), which was fulfilled to a day (Ex. 12:41-42), and the 40 years' wandering in the Wilderness of the Children of Israel (Num. 14:34), which was literally fulfilled without a break. But they forget that there were no "Time Divisions" in those prophecies, while in this prophecy of the "Seventy Weeks" there are three (7 + 62 + 1), and each period has its own particular work to do. The fact that each period is mentioned separately is an intimation, if not direct proof, that in the mind of God there was to be a **"break,"** if not a **"GAP,"** between them.

"If this be true," you ask, "what filled in the 'Gap' between the '7 Weeks' and the '62 Weeks?'" While there is no statement as to what happened between the "7 Weeks" and the "62 Weeks," as there is as to what happened between the "69th" and "70th" Week (which was the Crucifixion of Christ and the Destruction of Jerusalem), it is clear from the fact that they are mentioned separately, that the "7 Weeks" lead up to some event that marks a "Time Space," which might have been only a day or a year. Now we know that the "7 Weeks," or 49 years, give the time it took to rebuild the Temple, and re-establish the Temple form of worship, and that they cover the time exactly between the Decree of Artaxerxes, B. C. 445, and the close of Hebrew prophecy and of the Old Testament Scriptures, B. C. 396. This leaves the "62 Weeks" to cover the **"Time of Silence"** from the close of the Old Testament, B. C. 396, to Christ's "Triumphal Entry" into Jerusalem, A. D. 30.

Verse 26 tells us what is going to happen **between** the "69th" and "70th Week." **First,** that "Messiah the Prince" (Christ) should be **"cut-off"** (Crucified). **Second,** that Jerusalem and the Temple were to be destroyed by the Romans. **Third,** that after their destruction there would be a long period covered by wars, etc. It was of this last period that Jesus said—"Jerusalem shall be trodden down of the Gentiles, until the 'Times of the Gentiles' be fulfilled" (Luke 21:24), and as the "Times of the Gentiles" are **still running,** we see that verse 26 cannot be a description of the "70th Week" **immediately following** the "69th," for it covers a period now nearly 1900 years long, while the "70th Week" is to cover only **SEVEN YEARS.**

Those who claim that the "69th Week" ended and the "70th" began when Jesus appeared at the Jordan to be Baptized, and that the 3½ years of His Public Ministry were the "First Half" of the "70th Week," and that His Crucifixion was the "Middle of the Week," when by His death on the Cross He caused **"the Sacrifice and the Oblation to cease,"** meaning that He then caused all "bloody sacrifices" to cease, forget that the "bloody sacrifices" of the Temple did not cease at the Crucifixion, nor were they put away by Christ. They did not cease until the destruction of the Temple by the Romans 40 years later.

THE OLIVET DISCOURSE

Matt. 24:1-35. Mark 13:1-31. Luke 21:5-33.

When Jesus uttered His "Olivet Discourse" the "69 Weeks" were already **BEHIND** Him, and He stood within two days of the **"AFTER"** when He was to be **"CUT-OFF"** (Crucified). Dan. 9:26. And as in that "Discourse" He foretold the destruction of Jerusalem, and how it was to be trodden under foot of the Gentiles **until the "Times of the Gentiles" be fulfilled** (and they are still running), **After Which** He would return, we see that the "70th Week" could not appear **until**

the END of this Dispensation, and therefore there is a "**GAP**" of 1900 or more years between the "69th" and "70th Week." The "Olivet Discourse" then is the "**Key**" to the interpretation of Dan. 9:26-27.

But we have still further confirmatory evidence in the Book of Revelation, written A. D. 96, twenty-six years after the destruction of Jerusalem. We must not forget that the Book of Revelation, while written by the Apostle John, is the **"Revelation of JESUS CHRIST"** (Rev. 1:1), and therefore is a "Revelation" made by Him **AFTER HIS ASCENSION,** and is not only confirmatory of His "Olivet Discourse," but gives **in detail** what is to happen during "Daniel's Seventieth Week." The Book of Revelation is written in chronological order.* In chapters 2 and 3, in the "Messages to the Churches" there is a "Prophetic Outline" of the Christian Church during the present Dispensation. In chapter 4 the Church is **"caught out,"** and passes through the **"OPEN DOOR"** (verse 1) into Heaven. This is the "Rapture" of the Church as described in 1 Thess. 4:13-18. And from the 5th chapter to the 19th inclusive, we have a description of the whole of "Daniel's Seventieth Week," which covers the **"End Time"** of this Dispensation.

From this we see that "Daniel's Seventieth Week" (Dan. 9:24-27), Jesus' "Olivet Discourse" (Matt. 24:1-35), and John's "Seals, Trumpets and Vials" (Rev. 6:1 to 18:24), cover the **SAME** period, and are Jewish and have no reference to the Christian Church. Daniel draws the outline in his "Seventieth Week," Jesus roughs in the picture in His "Olivet Discourse," and John fills in the details in the "Book of Revelation." What Daniel condenses in one verse, John enlarges to thirteen chapters.

---

*See the writer's book on Revelation.

DANIEL'S SEVENTIETH WEEK, CHRIST'S OLIVET DISCOURSE, AND THE BOOK OF REVELATION COMPARED

DANIEL'S SEVENTIETH WEEK

Dan. 9:27

FIRST HALF	MIDDLE	LAST HALF
(3½ Years) The "Prince that shall come" (Antichrist) makes a 7-year "Covenant" with the Jews	The Covenant Broken —— Sacrifices and Oblations Cease	(3½ Years A Period of Desolations

THE SECOND ADVENT

CHRIST'S OLIVET DISCOURSE

Matt. 24:1-31

FIRST HALF	MIDDLE	LAST HALF
Wars Famines Pestilences Earthquakes False Christs These are the Beginning of Sorrows	The Appearance of the "Abomination of Desolation" Spoken of by Daniel	A Period of Tribulation such as there has never been before
Matt. 24:4-14	Matt. 24:15-19	Matt. 24:20-22

THE SECOND ADVENT

Matt. 24:29-31

THE BOOK OF REVELATION

Rev. 5:1—19:21

FIRST HALF	MIDDLE	LAST HALF
(3½ Years)	The Dragon Cast Out on to the Earth and Incarnates Himself in Antichrist	(3½ Years)
The Seals and Trumpets		The Vials —— The Great Tribulation
Rev. 5:1-11-19	Rev. 12:1-17	Rev. 13:1—18:24

THE SECOND ADVENT

Rev. 19:1-21

We must not forget that the Book of Daniel treats of the **"TIMES OF THE GENTILES,"** and that therefore its **"Visions"** should cover the whole sweep of "Gentile Times." Take the "Dream Vision" of Nebuchadnezzar. It covers the whole "Time of the Gentiles," and the "Golden Headed Image" he saw was not to be destroyed until Christ sets up His "Stone Kingdom" at His Second Coming. The "Beast Visions" of Daniel also carry us down until the **"END,"** when the **"Little Horn"** (Antichrist) is destroyed at the Second Coming of Christ. Is the "Vision" of the "Seventy Weeks" an exception to these? Does it only extend to the "First Coming" of Christ, and end with the destruction of Jerusalem? Does it not follow that it must cover the **whole period of the "Times of the Gentiles,"** like the others, to be in harmony with the purpose of the "Vision," which was to inform Daniel what was to happen to his people (the Jews), and the Holy City (Jerusalem), until the transgressions of the Jews are finished, and their transgressions are not yet finished, else why are they scattered all over the world, and Jerusalem still trodden down of the Gentiles?

From this we see that the "Seventy Weeks" are distinctively **"JEWISH,"** and are **"cut out"** from the whole course of the "Times of the Gentiles." Neither have they any reference or application to the "Christian Church." We must not forget that the "Christian Church" was not revealed in the Old Testament. This is why Daniel jumps from the "cutting off" (Crucifixion) of Christ, and the destruction of Jerusalem (verse 26), to the confirming of a Covenant by Antichrist (verse 27), which is still future. The fact then that the "Christian Church," which comes in between the "Crucifixion" and the revealing of the "Prince that shall come" (Antichrist), had no place in a prophecy concerning **Daniel's People and City,** makes it **imperative** that there should be a **"GAP"** or **"PARENTHESIS"** between the "69th" and "70th Week," a "Gap" as wide as this "Church Dispensation" shall last.

THE SEVENTY WEEKS OF SCRIPTURE

It is most interesting, and not generally known to Bible students, that there is not only one "Seventy Week" period in the Scriptures but **four,** and that these four begin with the birth of Abraham, and follow each other, without a break, until the Second Coming of Christ, and are connected with the Jews only, and give us the "Prophetic Chronology" of that nation, and prove that God in the Scriptures only reckons time when the Jews are in His favor, for there is no revelation of the length of the "Times of the Gentiles," or of the Church Period, in the Scriptures, for if there were we might be able to find out the time of the Lord's return.

THE FIRST SEVENTY WEEKS

In Gen. 12: 1-4 we read: that Abraham was seventy-five years old when he received the **"Promise."** And in Gal. 3: 17, Paul tells us that the "Covenant," or "Promise," was not annulled by the "Law" (the Law given on Mt. Sinai), which was given 430 years later. This would make the length of time from the birth of Abraham to the Exodus, 75 + 430 = 505 years. But during that time, from the conception of Ishmael, Gen. 16: 16, to the birth of Isaac, Gen. 21: 5, a period of about 15 years, Ishmael was a usurper, and the time should not be reckoned. So when we subtract those 15 years from the 505 years we have remaining 490 years, or our first "Seventy Weeks" of years, which run from the birth of Abraham, B. C. 2111, to the Exodus, B. C. 1606. While these dates are not those of Archbishop Ussher given in our Bibles, which dates are only approximately true, we find that counting back from Christ, on the basis of these four "Seventies," that the above dates are established.

THE SECOND SEVENTY WEEKS

In 1 Kings 6: 1 we are told that it was **480** years from the Exodus to the fourth year of Solomon's reign, when he began to build the Temple. But in Acts 13: 18-21, Paul tells us in his sermon at Antioch that God for 40 years suffered the manners of Israel in the Wilderness; then, after the dividing of the land, for **about** 450 years (say 448 years), He gave them Judges (which it would appear included Joshua and the Elders that outlived him) until Samuel the Prophet, who acted as Judge about 20 years. Then follows the reign of King Saul, 40 years; the reign of King David, 40 years; and up to the fourth year of Solomon's reign, which makes from the Exodus to the building of the Temple 591 years. Here there is a difference between the statement in Acts, and the one in 1 Kings, of 111 years. How are we to account for it? It is accounted for by not reckoning the time during that period that the Children of Israel were out of favor with God. From the Exodus to the building of the Temple the Children of Israel were in **SERVITUDE** six times, as follows—

		Years
1.	To **MESOPOTAMIA.** Judges 3:8	8
2.	To the **MOABITES.** Judges 3:12-14	18
3.	To the **CANAANITES.** Judges 4:2-3	20
4.	To the **MIDIANITES.** Judges 6:1	7
5.	To the **PHILISTINES AND AMMONITES.** Judges 10:7-8	18
6.	To the **PHILISTINES.** Judges 13:1	40
	Total	111

Subtract these 111 years of **"Servitude"** from Paul's statement in Acts of the 591 years, and you have 480 years the time mentioned in Kings, which clearly shows that the writer in Kings deducted the "Years of Servitude" from the time from the Exodus to the building of the Temple, thus recognizing the fact that God does not count time for the Children of Israel when they are in servitude to other nations.

Now we know that the Temple was not finished until 7 years later (1 Kings 6:38), and as it probably took Hiram 3 years longer to cast the brazen pillars and make the brazen vessels for the service of the Temple (1 Kings 7:13-51), we have 10 years, which added to the 480 years makes 490 years from the Exodus to the "Dedication of the Temple" (1 Kings 8:1-66), according to the Jewish way of reckoning time, but the actual time was 480 years plus the 111 of "Servitude," or 591 years, making the date of the "Dedication of the Temple" B. C. 1005.*

---

*See Chart of "The Seventy Weeks of Scriptures."

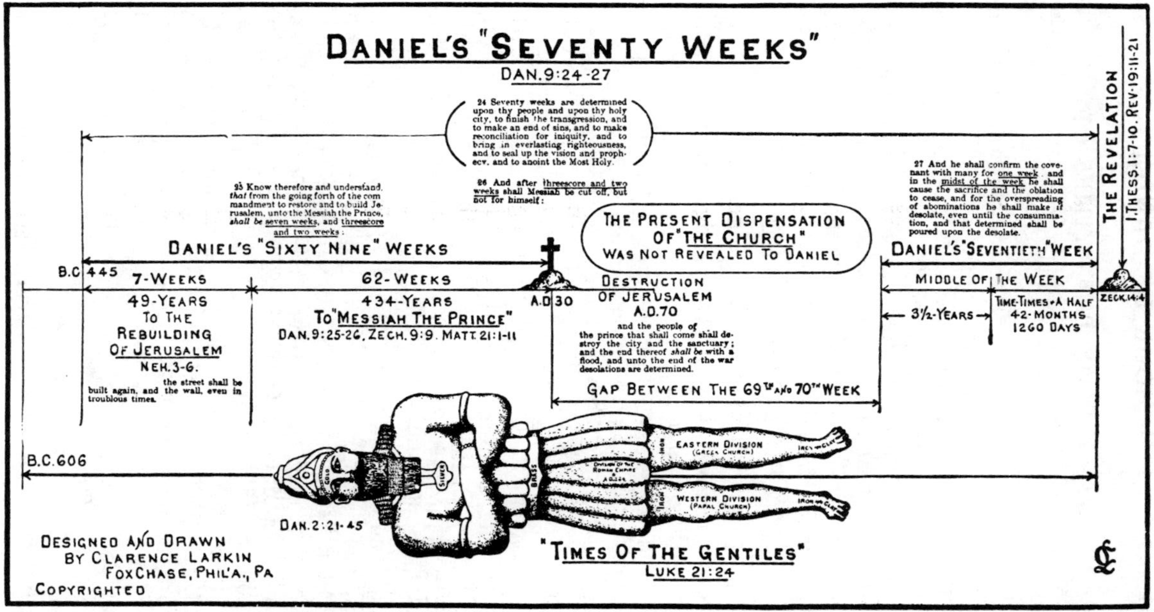
DANIEL'S "SEVENTY WEEKS"
DAN. 9:24-27
24 Seventy weeks are determined upon thy people and upon thy holy city, to finish the transgression, and to make an end of sins, and to make reconciliation for iniquity, and to bring in everlasting righteousness, and to seal up the vision and prophecy, and to anoint the Most Holy.
26 And after threescore and two weeks shall Messiah be cut off, but not for himself:
25 Know therefore and understand, that from the going forth of the commandment to restore and to build Jerusalem, unto the Messiah the Prince, shall be seven weeks, and threescore and two weeks:
27 And he shall confirm the covenant with many for one week: and in the midst of the week he shall cause the sacrifice and the oblation to cease, and for the overspreading of abominations he shall make it desolate, even until the consummation, and that determined shall be poured upon the desolate.
THE REVELATION
I.THESS.1:7-10. REV.19:11-21
DANIEL'S "SIXTY NINE" WEEKS
THE PRESENT DISPENSATION OF "THE CHURCH" WAS NOT REVEALED TO DANIEL
DANIEL'S "SEVENTIETH" WEEK
B.C 445
7-WEEKS
62-WEEKS
49-YEARS TO THE REBUILDING OF JERUSALEM
NEH. 3-6.
the street shall be built again, and the wall, even in troublous times.
434-YEARS TO "MESSIAH THE PRINCE"
DAN. 9:25-26, ZECH. 9:9. MATT. 21:1-11
A.D 30
DESTRUCTION OF JERUSALEM A.D. 70
and the people of the prince that shall come shall destroy the city and the sanctuary; and the end thereof shall be with a flood, and unto the end of the war desolations are determined.
MIDDLE OF THE WEEK
3½-YEARS
TIME-TIMES & A HALF
42-MONTHS
1260 DAYS
ZECK. 14:4
GAP BETWEEN THE 69TH AND 70TH WEEK
B.C. 606
GOLD
SILVER
BRASS
IRON
EASTERN DIVISION (GREEK CHURCH)
WESTERN DIVISION (PAPAL CHURCH)
DAN. 2:21-45
"TIMES OF THE GENTILES"
LUKE 21:24
DESIGNED AND DRAWN BY CLARENCE LARKIN FOXCHASE, PHIL'A., PA
COPYRIGHTED

LENGTH OF THE "TIMES OF THE GENTILES"

Right here it might be well to correct the erroneous method of calculating the length of the "Times of the Gentiles." It has already been stated that there is no revelation of the length of the "Times of the Gentiles," or of the "Church Period," in the Scriptures. But some claim that there is, and base their claim on Lev. 26:18-21, 24-28, where Moses foretold, and four times repeated it, that if the Children of Israel disobeyed God, He would punish them **"Seven Times"** for their sins, and that Jesus referred to these **"Seven Times"** when He spoke of the **"TIMES** of the Gentiles," and that He meant by a **"TIME,"** a **"Prophetical Time,"** which they claim is a year of 360 days, each day standing for a year, thus making a **"Time"** equal to 360 years, and **"Seven Times"** equal to 2520 years. If this be true, and "Seven Times" is the length of the "Times of the Gentiles," then the length of the "Times of the Gentiles" is 2520 years, and as they began in B. C. 606, they ran out in A. D. 1914, which we know is not true, for the "Times of the Gentiles" are still running, with no end in sight. We have already seen that a "Time" is not 360 years but only **one** year, and "Seven Times" would be but seven years. And if we should admit that the "Times of the Gentiles" are 2520 years long, they would not be years of 365¼ days but "Prophetic Years" of 360 days, and we would have to reduce the 2520 years from 365¼ days per year to 360 days as follows: 2520 × 365¼ = 920.430 ÷ 360 = 2556¾ years, which is 36¾ years over 2520. So if the 2520 years of 365¼ years ran out in A. D. 1914, the 2520 years of 360 days ran out 36¾ years before, or in A. D. 1878. As the "Times of the Gentiles" are still running, this proves that they are more than 2520 years long, and that their length is not given. The fact is the "Seven Times" of Lev. 26:18-28 have no reference to the "Times of the Gentiles" at all, but refer to the "Six Servitudes" during the time of the Judges, and to the "Babylonian Captivity," which makes the seventh. The present "Dispersion" of the Jews does not count, for it is neither a "Servitude" nor a "Captivity." So we see that the "Children of Israel" have been already punished **"Seven Times,"** and that Lev. 26: 18-28 has been fulfilled.

THE THIRD SEVENTY WEEKS

By counting the years from the "Dedication of the Temple," B. C. 1005, to the Edict of Artaxerxes to restore and rebuild Jerusalem, B. C. 445, we find they are 560, but when we deduct the 70 years of the "Babylonian Captivity" we have left 490 years, making our "Third Seventy Years," and proving our contention that God does not count time prophetically when the Jews are out of favor. This is also further proof that the "Seventy Weeks" begin with the "Decree" of Artaxerxes Longimanus, B. C. 445.

THE FOURTH SEVENTY YEARS

We have now reached the period covered by Daniel's "Seventy Weeks." We have seen that "69 Weeks," or 483 years on the "Year Day Scale," of those "Seventy Weeks" elapsed with the "Triumphal Entry" of Jesus into Jerusalem in A. D. 30. While Jerusalem was not destroyed and the Jews scattered until A. D. 70, their doom was sealed when Christ was crucified. The remaining 40 years were merely years of probation, like the 40 years in the Wilderness, and cannot be counted as years of favor. So far then 483 years of the 490 of Daniel's "Seventy Weeks" have expired. There is **"One Week,"** or seven years, yet to be fulfilled. For nearly 1900 years the Jews have been scattered over the earth. They have never been assimilated by the nations. They have never lost their identity or national peculiarities. And we have the unique spectacle of a people without a king, government, or land, retaining their national existence, and a land, Palestine, that seems to be under a curse, awaiting the return of its legal owners. Why is this? Is it not a fulfilment of the prophecy of Hosea 3:4?

> "The Children of Israel shall abide **MANY DAYS** without a King, and without a Prince, and without a Sacrifice, and without an Image (they are no longer idolators), and without an Ephod, and without Teraphim."

And the prophet adds in the next verse—

> **"AFTERWARD** shall the Children of Israel **RETURN,** and seek their God, and David their king; and shall fear the Lord and His goodness in the **LATTER DAYS."**

Here is the secret of their preservation. They are being kept that they may **RETURN IN THE LATTER DAYS.** We see from this that **"God has NOT CAST AWAY HIS PEOPLE"** (the Jews—Rom. 11:1-2), that **"blindness IN PART** is happened to Israel, **UNTIL the 'Fulness of the Gentiles'** (the Church) **be come in"** (Rom. 11:25), and that the Jews are to be nationally restored to their own land. Jer. 30:10-11; 16:14-15; 24:6. Isa. 11:11-12; 43:5-7. Amos 9:14-15.

For the time being the Jews are out of favor with God, and God's **"Time-piece,"** as far as the Jews are concerned, stopped at the end of the "69th Week" of Daniel's "Seventy Weeks," when they crucified the Lord. Acts 2:22-23. We are living in the "Gap" between the "69th" and "70th Week," and the "70th Week" cannot begin until God begins to deal again with Israel. From this study of the four "Seventy Week" periods, from the birth of Abraham, B. C. 2111, to the present time, A. D. 1924,* we find that 4035 years have elapsed; but when we deduct the number of years that Abraham and his descendants have been out of favor with God, which amounts to 2090 years (15 + 111 + 70 + 1894 = 2090), we find that God's people, the Children of Israel, have been under discipline **over half the time.**

*The year the author was called Home.

THE GAP

In the "Gap" between the "69th" and "70th Week," we are told in verse 26 that four things would occur.

I. **That Messiah should be "cut-off," but not for Himself.**

II. **That the City (Jerusalem) and the Sanctuary (the Temple) would be destroyed.**

III. **That a "Prince" would come of the same nationality as the People who should destroy the City and the Sanctuary.**

IV. **That Palestine would be desolated until the Consummation, that is, until the "Seventy Weeks" have ended in the Second Coming of Christ, who shall destroy the "Desolator"—the Antichrist.**

Let us look at these four things more in detail.

I. THAT MESSIAH SHOULD BE "CUT-OFF," BUT NOT FOR HIMSELF.

Jesus did not die for Himself, He died for others. He died that He might bear our sins on the "Tree." 1 Pet. 2:24. The margin reads—**"and shall have nothing."** It was announced to Mary by the Angel Gabriel, that her son Jesus should have the **"Throne"** of his father David. Luke 1:30-33. But instead of receiving the Kingdom, which John the Baptist, Jesus, and His Disciples proclaimed as **"at hand,"** Jesus was rejected as the Messiah and **"cut-off" without anything.** Instead of sitting on the Throne of His father David, and reigning in peace over the whole earth, He was Crucified between two thieves, and had none of the earthly dignities and glories to which, as Israel's promised Messiah, He was entitled. He received no Crown, except the "Crown of Thorns," no Throne, no Kingdom. Thus was foretold by Daniel the Crucifixion of Christ, and the postponement of the Kingdom.

II. THAT THE CITY (JERUSALEM) AND THE SANCTUARY (THE TEMPLE) WOULD BE DESTROYED.

It is clear that as soon as the Jews rejected Jesus as their King, that He refused to any longer recognize them as a nation. The day after His "Triumphal Entry" Jesus visited the Temple and drove out the "Money Changers," declaring **"MY** House shall be called the **'House of Prayer,'** but ye have made it a **'Den of Thieves.'"** Matt. 21 : 13. From that time Jesus no longer recognized the Temple as "God's House," but said of it—**"YOUR** House is left unto you desolate," that is, God-forsaken. Matt. 23 : 38. On the evening of the following day, as Jesus sat on the Mount of Olives, overlooking the City over which He had wept, He foretold its destruction, saying of it and its inhabitants—

> "And they shall fall by the edge of the sword, and shall be led away captive into all nations: and Jerusalem shall be trodden down of the Gentiles, **UNTIL the 'Times of the Gentiles' be fulfilled."** Luke 21 : 24.

Now we know that this came to pass in A. D. 70, just as Jesus foretold. Jerusalem has never since been a Jewish city. It has been besieged and rebuilt over twenty times, and been under the control of a number of foreign Governments, but the Jews for the most part have not been permitted to set their foot in it. There is a movement on foot, called "Zionism," to recover the possession of Palestine, but it will be of little avail, for it must remain desolate until the "Times of the Gentiles" are fulfilled, when God will restore it, without a penny of expense, to its original owners, the Children of Israel, and thus fulfil His Covenant with Abraham. Gen. 13 : 14-18. How do those who claim that the Book of Daniel was written by some pious Jew after the time of Antiochus Epiphanes

(B. C. 175-164), because they do not believe that it is possible to predict future events, account for the fact that the verse we are considering foretells two outstanding historical events as the "Crucifixion of Christ," and the "Destruction of Jerusalem," neither of which took place until over 190 years after the time they claim the Book of Daniel was written?

III. THAT A "PRINCE" WOULD COME OF THE SAME NATIONALITY AS THE PEOPLE WHO SHOULD DESTROY THE CITY AND THE SANCTUARY.

This "Prince" was not the "Messiah the Prince" of verse 25, for the "Prince to come" is to be a **"Roman,"** that is of the **"People"** who destroyed the City of Jerusalem, who were the Romans, but "Messiah the Prince" (Jesus) was not a Roman. Those who claim that by the "Prince that shall come," Titus, the leader of the Roman forces, was meant, and not some still future "Prince," declare, that as the "Prince" is to be a Roman, and there is no Roman nation today, therefore some past Roman Prince, such as Titus, must have been meant. But such claimants forget that the Roman Empire is to be revived, and a "Prince," the Antichrist, is to arise in it. The use of the words **"People"** and **"Prince That Shall Come"** show clearly that Titus was not that "Prince," for the words **"shall come"** are future in their application, and imply that the "Prince that shall come" was to come at a time **far removed** from the time of Titus and the destruction of Jerusalem. The same argument applies to Herod.

We must not forget that it was not necessary for the Angel Gabriel to specify to Daniel more in detail who the "Prince that was to come" was, or to give his name, for Daniel already knew. He knew that he would be the **"Little Horn"** that would rise among the "Ten Horns" on the head of the "Fourth Wild Beast."

Dan. *7:7-8, 23-27.* While Daniel knew what Empires the first three "Wild Beasts" stood for (Babylon, Medo-Persia and Greece), we are not sure that he knew that the "Fourth Wild Beast" stood for Rome. If he did, then he knew that the "People" that should destroy the City and the Sanctuary would be the Romans. We must not forget in the study of the Book of Daniel, that it has to do with the "Times of the Gentiles," and its purpose is to disclose in the **"Little Horn"** the last great **"Gentile Ruler"—THE ANTICHRIST.** Naturally, the Prophecy of the "Seventy Weeks" should include him, for the purpose of the Prophecy is to inform us as to the **"END TIME,"** and what shall come to pass in the **"LATTER DAYS."**

IV. THAT PALESTINE WOULD BE DESOLATED UNTIL THE CONSUMMATION, THAT IS, UNTIL THE "SEVENTY WEEKS" HAVE ENDED IN THE SECOND COMING OF CHRIST, WHO SHALL DESTROY THE "DESOLATOR"—THE ANTICHRIST.

The Land of Palestine when it was first occupied by the Children of Israel under Joshua was a land of "milk" and "honey," and of "all manner of fruits" (Deu. 8:7-9), and its soil brought forth "abundantly," and this continued as long as the Children of Israel kept its Sabbaths. But God had warned them that if they did not obey Him and turned aside to worship other gods He would shut up the heavens and the harvests would fail. Deu. 11:13-17. Palestine today has the same fertile soil it had in Joshua's time, but it lacks rain and irrigation. **It is under the curse.** God has withheld the **"early"** (October and November) and the **"latter"** rains (April and May), though they are now becoming more frequent, a sign that the lifting of the curse is near. This desolation of Palestine is what was foretold by Daniel in verse 26, and it is to continue until the Millennium, when

"The wilderness and the solitary place shall be glad for them; and the desert shall rejoice, and blossom as the rose." Isa. 35:1. "Instead of the thorn shall come up the fir-tree, and instead of the briar shall come up the myrtle tree." Isa. 55:13. "**THEN** shall the earth yield her increase." Psa. 67:6. "And the floors (threshing floors) shall be **full of wheat,** and the vats shall **overflow with wine and oil.** And I will **RESTORE** to you the years that the **locust hath eaten,** the **cankerworm** and the **caterpillar,** and the **palmerworm,** my great army which I sent among you. And ye shall **eat in plenty** and be **satisfied,** and praise the name of the Lord your God that hath dealt wondrously with you; and **MY PEOPLE** (the Jews) **SHALL NEVER BE ASHAMED.**" Joel 2:24-26.

Thus we see from these four things that were prophesied in verse 26 to occur **AFTER** the "69th Week," two of which have been fulfilled, one now in the process of fulfilment, and the third, the coming of the "Prince," still future, that there is a "Gap," covering the whole of this "Church Dispensation," between the "69th" and "70th Week."

THE SEVENTIETH WEEK

We now come to the last verse of the Prophecy, the 27th.

"And **'HE'** shall confirm the Covenant with many, for **'ONE WEEK:'** and in the **'MIDST OF THE WEEK'** he shall cause the **Sacrifice and the Oblation to cease,** and for the overspreading of abominations he shall make it desolate, even until the consummation, and that determined shall be poured upon the desolate."

The first question is, who is meant by the pronoun **"HE?"** Some claim that the pronoun "He" refers to "Messiah the Prince," or Christ, and that the "Covenant" is the "New Covenant" that Christ proclaimed when He instituted the Lord's Supper, saying as He handed to His Disciples the cup—"This is my blood of the 'New Testament' (Covenant), which is shed for many for the remission of sins." Matt. 26:28. But they forget that Christ's Covenant is an **"Everlasting Covenant"** (Heb. 13:20), while this "Covenant" is broken in the "Midst of the Week," or at the end of three and one-half years. The pronoun "He" then cannot refer to Christ, but must refer to the last person mentioned in the preceding verse, who is the "Prince that shall come," or the Antichrist.

We know from other Scriptures that the Jews are to be gathered back to their own land and become a "Nation" again. Jer. 30:10-11. Amos 9:14-15. Jer. 16:14-15. Isa. 43:5-7. When the time comes for this there will have gathered back to Palestine a great number of Jews, whose desire will be to repossess the land, build a Temple in which they can revive their sacrificial form of worship, and re-establish the Jewish State. They will not be able to do this without outside assistance, and at the **"Psychological Moment"** the Antichrist will appear on the scene and enter into a Covenant with them, that the Prophet Isaiah calls—

"A COVENANT WITH DEATH AND AN AGREEMENT WITH HELL."

Isa. 28:15, 18.

Notice that this "Covenant" will be made with **"many,"** not with all, for God will have His "Reserves," like the 7000 of Israel (1 Kings 19:18) and the 144,000 of Rev. 7:2-10, who will not bow the knee to Antichrist. Christ refers to this time in His Parable of

THE UNCLEAN SPIRIT.

"When the **'Unclean Spirit'** is gone out of a man, he walketh through dry places, seeking rest, and findeth none. Then he saith, I will return into my house from whence I came out; and when he is come, he findeth it **empty, swept,** and **garnished.** Then goeth he, and taketh with himself seven other spirits more wicked than himself, and they enter in and dwell there: and the last state of that man is worse than the first. Even so shall it be also unto **THIS WICKED GENERATION."** Matt. 12:43-45.

It is clear from the words—**"This Wicked Generation,"** that Christ applied the parable to the Jews; and not merely the Jews of His own time, but to all time, for the word "generation" means **"race,"** and not merely a period of time.

It is a matter of history that the Jews were delivered of the "Unclean Spirit of Idolatry" by their "Babylonian Captivity," and they are free from it today, their house being **"empty," "swept,"** and **"garnished,"** but the "Unclean Spirit" can still say of them—**"MY HOUSE."** The "Unclean Spirit of Idolatry" is yet to return to the Jews, and he will take with him **seven more spirits more wicked than himself.** This will happen when, in the "Midst of the Week," the Antichrist will break the Covenant, treat it as a **"scrap of paper,"** and cause the "Sacrifice and Oblation" to cease, and the "Abomination of Desolation" to stand in the Holy Place of the rebuilt Temple (Matt. 24:15), which "Abomination of Desolation" will be an **"Image of the BEAST,"** that the "False Prophet" will cause the followers of Antichrist to erect and worship under penalty of death. Rev. 13:14-15. This "Image" will be the Antitype of the "Golden Image" that Nebuchadnezzar commanded to be made and set up in the "Plain of Dura" in the Province of Babylon (Dan. 3:1-30), before which, at the sounding of musical instruments, the people were commanded to bow down and worship under penalty, for those who disobeyed, of being cast into a **"BURNING FIERY FURNACE."** Doubtless there will be many in the "Day of Antichrist" who will refuse to bow down and worship the "Image of the Beast," and who will not escape as did the "Three Hebrew Children," unless miraculously delivered by God, but will die by the "Guillotine." Rev. 20:4.

The word "Abomination" was a common term among the Hebrews for a "false god," and in the Old Testament means an "idol," and in one passage (1 Kings 11:5-7) we read how King Solomon, to please his heathen wives, built a "high place" for Chemosh, the "Abomination of Moab," in the hill that is before Jerusalem, and for Molech, the "Abomination of the Children of Ammon." The word rendered **"overspreading,"** literally means **"wings,"** which in the Scriptures suggests the idea of protection, as "Under His wings shalt thou trust." The meaning is that the Jews in that day shall seek protection under the **"Wing of the Abomination of Desolation,"** or the **"Idol Image"** of the **ANTICHRIST.** This will mean a **"SEVENFOLD"** return of the "Evil Spirit of Idolatry," so that their last state shall be worse than their first. And this shall continue until the "Consummation," that is until the "End of the Week," when Christ will return, and they shall look upon Him whom they pierced (Rev. 1:7) and turn from their idolatry, and the "Desolator" (Antichrist) shall be destroyed by the "brightness of His Coming." 2 Thess. 2:8. Rev. 19:20. From this we see that in those Antichristian days there will be set up in the rebuilt Temple the "Wings of Abomination" instead of the "Wings of the Cherubim."

It is at this time, after their **"national repentance,"** and they have received Christ as their **"Messiah the KING,"** that He will make a **"NEW COVENANT"** with them that shall never be broken.

"Behold, the days come (they are still future), saith the Lord, that I will make a **'NEW COVENANT'** with the **'House of Israel,'** and with the **'House of Judah:'** (the whole twelve Tribes) not according to the Covenant that I made with their fathers in the day that I took them by the hand to bring them out of the land of Egypt; which 'My Covenant' they brake, although I was a husband unto them, saith the Lord: but this shall be the 'Covenant' that I will make with the **'House of Israel;' AFTER THOSE DAYS** (the days of their present scattering), saith the Lord, **I will put my law in their inward parts, and write it in their hearts; and will be their God, and they shall be MY PEOPLE.** And they shall teach no more every man his neighbor, and every man his brother, saying, 'Know the Lord:' for they shall **all know me,** from the least of them unto the greatest of them, saith the Lord: for I will **forgive their iniquity,** and will **remember their sin NO MORE."** Jer. 31:31-34.

The writer of Hebrews quotes the above passage (Heb. 8:7-13) and declares the promise of the "New Covenant" is for the Jews, and not for the Church, though the Church has a share in it; and that the time when this New Covenant shall be made with the Jews will be when their **sins and iniquities have been put away.** Which corresponds to Dan. 9:24, or at the **end** of the "Seventy Weeks," which is further proof that the "Seventy Weeks" have not as yet reached their end.

The Scripture of Truth

CHAPTERS TEN, ELEVEN, TWELVE

The last three chapters of the Book of Daniel belong together, and there should be no chapter divisions. The three chapters for clearness may be divided into three parts.

PART ONE

The Relation of Supernatural Beings to the Earth
Chap. 10: 1—11: 1

PART TWO

The Pre-written History of the Kings of the North and the South
Chap. 11: 2-35

PART THREE

The "Time of the End"
Chap. 11: 36—12: 13

PART ONE

The Relation of Supernatural Beings to the Earth

Chap. 10:1—11:1

THE TIME OF THE VISION

> "In the **THIRD YEAR of Cyrus King of Persia** a thing was **revealed** unto Daniel, whose name was Belteshazzar; and the thing was true, but the time appointed was long: and he understood the thing, and had understanding of the Vision." Chap. 10:1.

This, Daniel's last Vision, came to him in the "Third Year" of the reign of King Cyrus, which was B. C. 533. Daniel at this time was over ninety years of age, and probably was no longer active in public affairs, as we are told in chapter 1:21, that he continued only unto the first year of King Cyrus. Why Daniel did not return three years before with those who took advantage of King Cyrus' Decree, we are not told. Ezra 1:1-11. It may have been his age, but more likely because God had some further revelations to give him, and restrained the Prophet from going.

Relieved from the burden of public affairs, Daniel doubtless spent his time in inquiring as to the success of those who had returned to Jerusalem in building up the walls and restoring the Temple. He doubtless was disappointed in the number that returned, only 42,360. Ezra 2:64. The great majority of the priests and chief of the people preferred the houses which they had built, and the gardens which they had planted, in Babylonia, to the desolation of their home-land. How numerous were those who remained we may learn from the Book of Esther. Possibly, too, he had been informed that the Samaritans, irritated by the refusal of the Jews to accept their help and alliance, were hindering the work by every means in their power, and were about to seek an injunction from the Persian Court. Ezra 4:1-6. Thus disheartened by the fact that so many of his people were not interested in the restoration of Jerusalem and the Temple, and that those who returned were a "feeble folk," dispirited, and harassed on every side by their enemies, is it any wonder that the Prophet fasted and mourned.

> "In those days I Daniel was **mourning THREE FULL WEEKS.** I ate no pleasant bread, neither came flesh or wine in my mouth, neither did I anoint myself at all, till **three whole weeks were fulfilled."** Chap. 10:2-3.

This does not mean that he did not eat or drink anything, but that he refrained from all dainties, and restricted his fare to the simplest articles of diet. And this he did for twenty-one days, and doubtless would have continued to do, if an angelic being had not come to his relief.

THE VISION OF THE SON OF MAN

> "And in the four and twentieth day of the First Month, as I was by the side of the great river, which is Hiddekel (Tigris); then I lifted up mine eyes, and looked, and behold a **CERTAIN MAN** clothed in linen, whose **LOINS were girded with fine gold of Uphaz:** His **BODY** also **was like the beryl,** and His **FACE as the appearance of lightning,** and His **EYES as lamps of fire,** and His **ARMS** and His **FEET like in color to polished brass,** and the **VOICE** of His words **like the voice of a multitude."** Chap. 10:4-6.

Who was this **"CERTAIN MAN?"** He was no other than the **"LORD OF GLORY."** If the Lord appeared to Abraham (Gen. 18:1-8), and to Moses at the Burning Bush (Ex. 3:1-6, 13-14), why not to Daniel? To find out who is meant, all we have to do is to turn over to the Book of Revelation, and compare the description there of the **"SON OF MAN"** as He appeared to John on the Isle of Patmos, to see that the descriptions are of the **same person.**

"And I turned to see the voice that spake with me. And being turned, I saw seven Golden Candlesticks (Lamp-stands); and in the midst of the seven Candlesticks one like unto the **SON OF MAN,** clothed with a garment down to the foot, and girt about the paps (breast) with a **GOLDEN GIRDLE.** His **HEAD** and His **HAIRS** were **white like wool, as white as snow;** and His **EYES** were as a **flame of fire;** and His **FEET like unto fine brass,** as if they burned in a furnace; and His **VOICE** as the **sound of many waters."** Rev. 1:12-15.

Daniel had been told, in the Vision of the "Seventy Weeks," that the "Messiah" when He came would be **"CUT-OFF"** (Crucified). What more reasonable then than that the "Messiah" should appear to him at this time, when he was filled with perplexity and anxiety. Daniel saw the Lord before His "Incarnation" and John beheld Him after His "Ascension," but in both instances His appearance was the same. The effect of the "Visions" of Daniel and John upon themselves was the same. Daniel says—**"There remained no strength in me: for my comeliness was turned in me into corruption, . . . then was I in a deep sleep on my face, and my face toward the ground."** Verses 8-9. That is, Daniel fainted. John says—"When I saw Him, **I fell at His feet as dead."** Rev. 1:17. John also fainted. Thus the similarity of the effect of the "Visions" of Daniel and John upon them is proof that the **"Certain Man"** that Daniel saw was no other than the **LORD OF GLORY.**

And I Daniel **alone** saw the Vision: **for the men that were with me saw not the Vision; but a great quaking fell upon them, so that they fled to hide themselves.** Therefore I was left alone, and saw this 'Great Vision,' and there remained no strength in me: for my comeliness was turned in me into corruption, and I retained no strength. Yet **heard I the 'VOICE OF HIS WORDS:'** and when I heard the 'Voice of His Words,' then was I in a deep sleep on my face, and my face toward the ground." Chap. 10:7-9.

That the "Certain Man" Daniel saw was the "Lord of Glory," and not Michael the Archangel, as some claim, is clear from a comparison of Daniel's experience as given above, and the experience of Saul of Tarsus when the Lord appeared to him on the way to Damascus. Acts 9:1-9.

THE HEAVENLY MESSENGER

"And, behold, a **hand touched me,** which set me upon my knees and upon the palms of my hands. And he (the Heavenly Messenger) said unto me, O Daniel, a man **GREATLY BELOVED,** understand the words that I speak unto thee, and stand upright: for unto thee am I now sent. And when he had spoken this word unto me, I stood **trembling.**" Chap. 10:10-11.

From this we see that the Lord of Glory was not alone in this Vision. He was accompanied by a "Heavenly Messenger," who was no other than the Angel Gabriel. This we know from the words and conduct of the Angel. All we have to do is to compare this "Vision" with that of the "Ram and He-Goat" seen by Daniel six years before. Dan. 8:15-19. In it we were told that as Daniel was standing by the river Ulai there stood between the banks of the river, supported possibly by a cloud, the **"appearance of a man."** While Daniel did not at that time describe him, he doubtless was the same person as the **"Certain Man"** of this Vision, the Lord of Glory. Daniel heard this **"man"** call the Angel Gabriel and command him to interpret Daniel's Vision. And Daniel, who had **fallen** into a faint, as in this instance, was aroused by Gabriel and instructed. Then in the "Vision of the Seventy Weeks," while Daniel was speaking, and praying, and confessing the sins of his people, Gabriel was sent to him again. This time he saluted Daniel as the one **"GREATLY BELOVED."** And in this "Vision" we are now considering the "Heavenly Messenger" **twice** uses the same salutation. Verses 11 and 19. Surely he could have been no other than Gabriel. As further proof that it was Gabriel and not the "Certain Man" that touched Daniel is the fact that the one who touched Daniel had to call on Michael, one of the Chief Princes, to free him from the grip of the "Prince of Persia," a thing the Lord of Glory would not have had to do, for He would have smitten him with the "Two-edged Sword of His Mouth." Rev. 1:16; 19:15. It is clear from the language of the one who touched and assisted Daniel to his feet, that he was a servant, a subordinate, and not the Lord of Glory.

THE PRINCE OF PERSIA

> "Then said he unto me, Fear not, Daniel: for from the first day that thou didst set thine heart to understand, and to chasten thyself before thy God, thy words were heard, and I am come for thy words (sake R. V.). But the **'Prince of the Kingdom of Persia' withstood me one and twenty days:** but, lo, **MICHAEL,** one of the Chief Princes, came to help me; and I remained there with the Kings of Persia." Chap. 10:12-13.

The words—**"I remained"** are translated in the margin of the Revised Versions—**"I was not needed."** Later Gabriel said he would return to fight with the "Prince of Persia."

The first words that Gabriel spoke to Daniel were an explanation of his delay in answering Daniel's prayer. He said that he had been detained for twenty-one days, the same length of time Daniel had been praying, by the "Prince of Persia," and if Michael, the

Archangel (Jude 9) had not come to his rescue he would have been there still. Here the veil is lifted, and we are shown something of the workings of the **"UNSEEN WORLD,"** and of the connection between the "Spirit World" and the affairs of men and nations on the earth. This "Prince of Persia" was not Cyrus the King of Persia. No one for a moment would think that a mere human being like Cyrus could withstand a **supernatural being** like Gabriel, with a message from God, for twenty-one days. The Scriptures clearly teach that there is a

"KINGDOM OF DARKNESS"

over which Satan reigns as **KING** (Matt. 12:24-30), and that his Kingdom is composed of **"PRINCIPALITIES," "POWERS," "AGE RULERS OF DARKNESS,"** and **"WICKED SPIRITS."** All this is revealed in Eph. 6:12, where Paul says—"We wrestle not against **FLESH** and **BLOOD** (human beings), but against **PRINCIPALITIES,** against **POWERS,** against the **RULERS OF THE DARKNESS OF THIS WORLD** (Age), against **SPIRITUAL WICKEDNESS** in High Places (the Heavenlies)." Satan is the **"PRINCE OF THE POWERS OF THE AIR"** (Eph. 2:2), and the **"GOD OF THIS WORLD" (Age).** Eph. 2:2. It was no false claim he made when he offered to give to Jesus the "Kingdoms of this World, and the Glory of them." Matt. 4:8-9.

From this we see that Satan has his Kingdom organized in a wonderful manner. It is divided into Kingdoms and Principalities. These divisions correspond with the Kingdom divisions of our earth. If Satan has a "Prince of Persia" and a "Prince of Grecia," why not a Prince for every nation? Satan has his limitations. He is not omnipresent, neither is he omnipotent or omniscient. He has to depend upon his agents. And so great and powerful are his "Princes" that it takes a supernatural being, like Michael the Archangel, to overcome them. That Michael is a match for even

Satan himself is seen in two recorded instances in the Scriptures. In Jude 9 we are told that Michael contended with Satan as to the body of Moses, and while victorious, he had to treat him respectfully, for Satan is a great and "Mighty Potentate." And in Rev. 12:1-9 we are told that there is to be "War in Heaven" and that Michael and his angels shall prevail over Satan and his angels, and they shall be cast out of the Heavenlies on to the earth.* We know from Chap. 12:1, that Michael is the "Guardian Angel" that standeth for the "Children of Israel." The purpose of the "Prince of Persia" in detaining Gabriel was because his Master—Satan, was hostile to the Jews, and did not want his plans revealed to Daniel. This is seen in the purpose of Gabriel's visit as outlined in the next verse.

THE PURPOSE OF GABRIEL'S VISIT

> "Now I am come to make thee **understand what shall befall Thy People** (the Jews) **in the 'LATTER DAYS:'** for yet the Vision is for **MANY DAYS.**" Chap. 10:14.

This is a very important statement, and gives us the **"Key"** to the interpretation of the remainder of the book. But before Gabriel reveals what is to befall Daniel's People in the "Latter Days," there is a **"Prelude"** which describes in detail the wars of the **"Ptolemies"** and **"Seleucidae,"** two of the "Four Kingdoms" into which Alexander the Great's Empire was divided, and which are spoken of as the wars of the **"King of the North"** and the **"King of the South,"** and carry us down to the end of the reign of Antiochus Epiphanes, B. C. 164. This "Prelude" ends with Chap. 11:31, and verses 32-35 cover the whole period from the time of the Maccabees, B. C. 166, down to the **"TIME OF THE END,"** and verse 36 introduces us

---

*See the writer's book on "The Spirit World."

to the **"Wilful King"—ANTICHRIST,** and from there to the end of the Book we have an account of what shall befall Daniel's People in the **"LATTER DAYS."**

THE PROPHET STRENGTHENED

"And when he (Gabriel) had spoken such words unto me, I set my face toward the ground, and I became dumb. And, behold, one like the similitude of the sons of men **touched my lips**: then I opened my mouth, and spake, and said unto him that stood before me, O my lord, by the Vision my sorrows are turned upon me, and I have retained no strength. For how can the servant of this my lord talk with this my lord? for as for me, straightway there remained no strength in me, neither is there breath left in me." Chap. 10:15-17.

When Daniel realized the import of Gabriel's words he was dumb, until one like the "similitude of the sons of men" touched his lips. Then he opened his mouth and spake. This reminds us of the Seraphim that touched Isaiah's lips with a coal of fire from off the altar. Isa. 6:6-7. While Daniel addresses this angelic being as "lord," the word does not begin with a capital "L," which shows that he was not the Lord of Glory. After the Seraphim had restored Daniel's speech, Gabriel again approached him and strengthened him.

"Then there came **again** and touched me one like the appearance of a man (all angels appeared as men), and he strengthened me, and said, O man **GREATLY BELOVED,** fear not: peace be unto thee; be strong, yea, be strong. And when he had spoken unto me, I was strengthened, and said, Let my lord speak; for thou hast strengthened me. Then said he, Knowest thou wherefore I come unto thee? and now will I return to fight with the **'Prince of Persia:'** and when I am gone forth, lo, the **'Prince of Grecia'** shall come.

But I will shew thee that which is noted in the **'SCRIPTURE OF TRUTH:'** and there is none that holdeth with me in these things but **MICHAEL your Prince.** Also I in the first year ot Darius the Mede, even I, stood to confirm and to strengthen him." Chap. 10: 18—11: 1.

The angelic being that here **again** touched Daniel was the same angelic being that touched him in verse 10. For he uses the same salutation, **"Greatly Beloved,"** and declares that he is about to **return** to fight the "Prince of Persia," and that he and Michael are co-workers against the Satanic powers, for it was through the co-operation of Michael that the Fall of Babylon was brought about in the first year of Darius the Mede.

PART TWO

The Pre-written History of the Kings of the North and the South

Chap. 11 : 2-35

THE SCRIPTURE OF TRUTH

In this chapter we have what Gabriel calls the **"Scripture of Truth."** It is a **PRE-WRITTEN HISTORY** of the wars of the **Ptolemies of Egypt,** "the Kings of the South;" and the **Seleucidae of Syria,** "the Kings of the North." Here we have history so accurately foretold and **"written in advance,"** that the Critics claim that the Book of Daniel could not have been written as early as is claimed (B. C. 533), but that it must have been written after the wars of the Ptolemies and Seleucidae were over, or about B. C. 160, for it would have been impossible for Daniel, or any other person, to have so accurately described these wars **before they occurred.** But it is right here that the Scriptures and the Critics part. The Scriptures claim that they have been inspired by the Holy Spirit (2 Tim. 3 : 15-17), and that **"Holy Men of God spake as they were moved by the HOLY SPIRIT."** 2 Pet. 1 : 19-21. Prophecy then is **HISTORY WRITTEN IN ADVANCE.** And the "Spirit of God" can write History **beforehand** as well as **afterward.** The catching phrase "History Unveiling Prophecy" should be reversed to read "Prophecy Foretelling History." Historical interpretation of Prophecy always works mischief, for it leads to **"forced interpretation"** of historical events. The relation of History to Prophecy is not that of interpretation, but of verification. This makes Prophecy a **"LIGHT IN A DARK PLACE."** 2 Pet. 1 : 19. That is, Prophecy illuminates the future by forecasting it.

The detailed accuracy of the Prophecy is most marvellous. The Prophecy is not clothed in figures and symbols, as in the previous Visions. In fact it is not a Vision, but a description in **literal** language of historical events concerning Daniel's people and the Holy Land, from Daniel's time down to the Second Coming of Christ. For the sake of clearness we will take the Prophecy up verse by verse, or where necessary several verses together. The Prophecy begins with the second verse of chapter eleven.

> **VERSE 2—"And now I will shew thee the Truth** (Scripture of Truth. Chap. 10:21). **Behold, there shall stand up yet three kings in Persia; and the fourth shall be far richer than they all: and by his strength through his riches he shall stir up all against the realm of Grecia."**

Since the Prophecy was given in the third year of Cyrus (Chap. 10:1. B. C. 533), the three kings that were to "stand up yet," that is, "after him," were Ahasuerus, Artaxerxes, and Darius (Ezra 4:1-24), known in history as Cambyses (B. C. 529-522), Pseudo-Smerdis (B. C. 522-521), and Darius Hystaspes (B. C. 521-485). The **"fourth"** king was Xerxes (B. C. 485-465), the son of Darius Hystaspes, whose marvellous riches enabled him to put vast armies in the field. He stirred up Persia against Greece, which he invaded in B. C. 480, but failed to conquer it. Since prophecy touches only upon important events and characters, the remaining kings of Persia are omitted, and the prophecy jumps over nearly 150 years to the time of Alexander the Great. B. C. 336-323.

> **VERSES 3-4—"And a Mighty King shall stand up, that shall rule with great dominion, and do according to his will. And when he shall stand up, his Kingdom shall be broken, and shall be divided toward the 'Four Winds' of heaven; and not to his posterity, nor according to his dominion which he ruled: for his Kingdom shall be plucked up, even for others beside those."**

These verses take us back to the Vision of the

"Ram and He-Goat" (Dan. 8: 3-8, 20-22), and we recognize in the **"Mighty King,"** the "Notable Horn" of the "He-Goat" that was broken off, and in the "Four Horns" that came up in its place, the division of this "Mighty King's" Kingdom toward the "Four Winds." This "Mighty King" then was Alexander the Great, and the division of his Kingdom toward the "Four Winds" of heaven was the division of his Kingdom at his death among four of his Generals. Cassander took Macedonia and the Western part; Lysimachus took Thrace and the Northern part; Seleucus took Syria and the Eastern part; and Ptolemy took Egypt and the Southern part. None of Alexander the Great's posterity succeeded him, and within fifteen years his family was extinct.

VERSE 5—"And the 'King of the South' shall be strong, and one of his Princes; and he shall be strong above him, and have dominion; his dominion shall be a great dominion."

The Prophecy now narrows down to two of the four Kingdoms into which Alexander the Great's Empire was divided. And the reason is clear. Gabriel told Daniel that the Prophecy belonged to Daniel's **PEOPLE.** And as the **"Glorious Land"** (Palestine—verses 16, 41, 45) lay between Syria on the North and Egypt on the South, so the Prophecy narrows down to a description of the wars between the "Kings of the North" and the "Kings of the South," whose marching ground and battlefield would be the **"Glorious Land,"** where for centuries (B. C. 320 to A. D. ?) Daniel's People would be ground between the Upper and Lower Millstones. Because of the suffering that these wars would bring to Daniel's People, and the desolation they would cause the country, God revealed these wars to Daniel that he might see that it would be **"many days"** (chap. 10: 14) before his People would ever become a nation again.

Of the Four Kingdoms into which Alexander's Empire was divided, the Kingdom of Egypt was the first to appear. It was founded by Ptolemy Soter, one of Alexander's generals. Another of Alexander's generals, Seleucus Nicator, was appointed vicegerent of Babylonia, but was driven out by Antigonus and fled to Egypt, where he was favorably received by Ptolemy and made one of his Princes. With Ptolemy's assistance he recovered his province and enlarged it, until it extended to the Indus and included Syria, as well as Assyria, and so he became stronger than Ptolemy, and his dominion became a great dominion.

VERSE 6—"And in the end of years they shall join themselves together; for the King's daughter of the South shall come to the King of the North to make an agreement: but she shall not retain the power of the arm; neither shall he stand, nor his arm: but she shall be given up, and they that brought her (her attendants), **and he that begat her** (Margin—whom she brought forth), **and he that strengthened her in these times."**

There was peace between Egypt and Syria during the reigns of Ptolemy Soter and Seleucus Nicator. But, at length, Ptolemy Soter abdicated in favor of his son Ptolemy Philadelphus, whose half brother Magas had married a daughter of Antiochus Soter, who had succeeded Seleucus Nicator as King of Syria. This marriage led to war between Egypt and Syria. For Magas induced his father-in-law, Antiochus Soter, to declare war against Egypt. Antiochus Soter was succeeded by Antiochus Theus, who continued to war with Ptolemy. At length, **"at the end of years,"** Ptolemy offered Antiochus Theus, as a bribe for peace, his daughter Berenice with a large dower, on condition that the Syrian King should declare his former marriage to Laodice void, and her two sons illegitimate. This iniquitous compact was carried out. But when Ptolemy Philadelphus died, his daughter Berenice could no longer **"retain the power of her arm,"** for Antiochus Theus put her away, and took back his former wife Laodice. But neither did he himself

"stand," for Laodice, distrusting his motives, and eager to secure the crown for her own son, poisoned her husband, and so opened the succession to Seleucus Callinicus. Then Laodice persuaded Seleucus to have Berenice assassinated, and her child, who by the articles of her marriage had been made heir to the throne, was also killed, as well as all those who **"strentghened her in those times."**

VERSES 7-8—"But out of a branch of her (Berenice) **roots** (her parents) **shall one stand up in his estate, which shall come with an army, and shall enter into the fortress of the King of the North, and shall deal against them, and shall prevail. And shall also carry captives into Egypt their gods, with their princes, and with their precious vessels of silver and gold; and he shall continue more years than the King of the North."**

Out of a **"branch of her roots"** means an offspring of Berenice's parents, and refers to her brother, Ptolemy Euergetus, who succeeded his father Ptolemy Philadelphus. And who, indignant at the treatment of his sister, hastily marched into Syria with a large army, and, although he arrived too late to save Berenice and her son, took revenge by putting Laodice to death, captured Seleucia, the fortress of the King of the North, and would have possessed himself of the whole of the Kingdom had he not been recalled by an insurrection in Egypt. But he did not return empty handed. Not only did he carry back many princes, but spoil to the value of 40,000 talents of silver, and 2500 precious vessels and "idol-images" of the gods. Among these "images" were many that Cambyses had formerly taken from Egypt and carried into Persia. These were replaced in the Temples of Egypt with great ceremony, and it was in gratitude for their restoration that the Egyptian priests bestowed upon Ptolemy his surname of Euergetes, or Benefactor.

VERSES 9-10—"So the King of the South shall come into his Kingdom, and shall return into his

own land. But his sons shall be stirred up, and shall assemble a multitude of great forces: and one shall certainly come, and overflow, and pass through: then shall he return, and be stirred up, even to his fortress."

The Revised Version translates these two verses differently. But their meaning is clear if read thus—"So the King of the South shall come into his (the King of the North) Kingdom and shall return into his own land (Egypt)." Which we have seen he did. **"But his sons,"** not the sons of the King of the South, but the sons of the King of the North, **"shall be stirred up"** by the invasion of the King of the South, **"and shall assemble a multitude of great forces, etc."** Now we know that this is what actually occurred. The sons of Seleucus Callinicus, Seleucus Ceraunus, and Antiochus, afterwards surnamed Magnus (the Great), assembled large armies. Seleucus Ceraunus succeeded his father. He assembled a large army to recover his father's dominions, but being a weak and pusillanimous Prince, and unable to discipline his army, he was poisoned by two of his generals after an inglorious reign of two or three years. He was succeeded by his brother Antiochus, who assembled a large army and took the field in person. He is the **"one"** in the text who should **"overflow"** and **"pass through."** He directed his energies against the "King of the South," Ptolemy Philopater, who had succeeded his father, Ptolemy Euergetes. He seized Tyre and Ptolemais, overflowed and passed through Palestine, and marched against Gaza, the fortress of the King of the South, the limit set by the Prophecy. This was in B. C. 218.

VERSES 11-12—"And the King of the South shall be moved with choler (rage), and shall come forth and fight with him, even with the King of the North: and he (the King of the North) **shall set forth a great multitude** (army) **: but the multitude shall be given into his** (the King of the South) **hand. And when he hath taken away the**

multitude, his heart shall be lifted up; and he shall cast down many ten thousands: but he shall not be strengthened by it."

The voluptuous and dissolute King of the South, Ptolemy Philopater, was thoroughly aroused by the invasion of his realm by the King of the North, Antiochus. He assembled a great army, and defeated the large and well-appointed army of Antiochus, at Raphia, not far from Gaza, B. C. 217. Ptolemy's **"heart was lifted up"** by his success, and he might have followed up his victory and seized the Kingdom of Antiochus, but he was too anxious to return to his sensual pleasures, and so lost his opportunity of gaining supremacy, and thus he was **"not strengthened"** by his great victory.

VERSE 13—"For the King of the North shall return, and shall set forth a multitude greater than the former, and shall certainly come AFTER CERTAIN YEARS with a great army and with much riches."

The peace concluded between Ptolemy Philopater and Antiochus lasted thirteen years. In the meantime Antiochus strengthened himself in his Kingdom. And when his armies were numerous and well equipped, and flushed with many victories, and his treasury filled with spoils, having learned of the death of Ptolemy Philopater, and that he had been succeeded by his infant son Ptolemy Epiphanes, Antiochus, feeling the time was ripe, marched against Egypt with a **"great army and much riches,"** expecting an easy victory. How he succeeded we shall presently see, for new complications entered into the affairs of the two Kingdoms, and new actors were introduced upon the stage of history. In studying the history of these two Kingdoms and their Kings, we must not forget that while the Kingdoms remain the same, the "King of the North" and the "King of the South" change, though their official title does not.

VERSE 14—"And in those times there shall many stand up against the King of the South: also the robbers of thy people (the Jews) **shall exalt themselves to establish the Vision; but they shall fall."**

Among the **"many"** that stood up against the infant King of the South was Philip, King of Macedon, who entered into a league with Antiochus to divide the Kingdom of Ptolemy Epiphanes between them. Egypt itself was also a **"seething pot"** of sedition. And there were "wicked Jews" in Palestine who hoped to gain the favor of Antiochus. They were called **"robbers"** because by their conduct they made it hard for their brethren, and thus **"established the Vision,"** or prophecy of suffering for Daniel's people during those times. Antiochus turned against these "robber Jews" and thus caused them **"to fall."** This verse was fulfilled in the wars of Antiochus that followed.

VERSES 15-19—"So the King of the North shall come, and cast up a mount (breastwork) **and take the most fenced cities: and the arms** (army) **of the South shall not withstand, neither his** (the King of the South) **chosen people, neither shall there be any strength to withstand. But he** (the King of the North) **that cometh against him shall do according to his own will, and none shall stand before him: and he shall stand in the Glorious Land** (Palestine), **which by his hand shall be consumed. He shall also set his face to enter with the strength of his whole Kingdom, and upright ones with him; thus shall he do: and he shall give him** (the King of the South) **the 'daughter of women,' corrupting her: but she shall not stand on his** (the King of the North) **side, neither be for him. After this shall he turn his face unto the isles, and shall take many: but a Prince for his own behalf shall cause the reproach offered by him to cease; without his own reproach he shall cause it to turn**

upon him. Then he shall turn his face toward the fort of his own land: but he shall stumble and fall, and not be found."

These verses are taken together because they cover the remainder of the wars of Antiochus the Great, the King of the North. In considering them we must not forget that the "Glorious Land" was under the dominion of the King of the South, at this time Ptolemy Epiphanes. Therefore to reach Egypt it was necessary for Antiochus to first conquer the "Glorious Land." Upon his entrance into the land he encountered Scopas, the General of Ptolemy's army, and compelled him to seek refuge in the strongly fortified city of Sidon, which he besieged. Desperate attempts were made by the Egyptians to relieve the city, but all failed, and Sidon was compelled to surrender. Then Antiochus was able to do **"according to his own will, and none were able to stand before him."** So he took possession of the "Glorious Land."

Then he **"set his face"** to enter Egypt with the whole strength of his Kingdom. But he was compelled to change his plans. The Egyptian regency had sought the help of the Romans, then rising in power, and their assistance had been promised. So Antiochus decided to resort to diplomacy. He proposed that his daughter Cleopatra be espoused to the infant king Ptolemy Epiphanes, then seven years old. Cleopatra herself was very young, and it was because she was of tender years, and still under the care of her mother and a nurse, that she was called the **"daughter of women."** The marriage was consummated some five years later. The words **"corrupting her"** refer to Antiochus' scheme to get her to play into his hands, rather than into the hands of her husband. But the plan failed. Cleopatra not only took sides with her husband, but even joined him in sending congratulations to the Romans on their victories over her father.

To avenge himself against the Romans, Antiochus fitted out a fleet of 300 vessels and assailed the coasts and isles of Asia Minor. He was defeated at Magnesia, B. C. 190, by Scipio Asiaticus, the Prince mentioned in the prophecy. He then turned his face homeward. At Antioch he sent ambassadors to sue for peace. The terms were hard. He was not only to relinquish Europe, but Asia on the European side of the Taurus, and pay 2550 talents down, and 1000 talents annually for the next twelve years. A few months later, while traversing his Eastern Provinces to raise this tribute money, he attempted to plunder the Temple of Bel in Elymais, but the people rose and slew him. So he **"stumbled and fell and was found no more."**

VERSE 20—"Then shall stand up in his estate a raiser of taxes in the Glory of the Kingdom: but within a few days he shall be destroyed, neither in anger, nor in battle."

Antiochus the Great was succeeded by his eldest son, Seleucus Philopater. He was compelled to be a **"raiser of taxes"** to pay the heavy tribute imposed on his father. He seems to have reigned about twelve years. Toward the end of that time, being hard pressed for money, he sent his Treasurer, Heliodorus, to Jerusalem, called in the above Scripture the **"Glory of the Kingdom,"** to confiscate the treasures of the Temple. Shortly afterward, **"within few days,"** he was mysteriously poisoned. So he died **"neither in anger, nor in battle."**

ANTIOCHUS EPIPHANES

B. C. 175-164

VERSES 21-31—"And in his estate (place) shall stand up a VILE PERSON, to whom they shall not give the honor of the Kingdom: but he shall come in peaceably, and obtain the Kingdom by flatteries. And with the arms of a flood shall they be overflown from before him, and shall be broken;

yea, also the 'Prince of the Covenant.' And after the League made with him he shall work deceitfully: for he shall come up, and shall become strong with a small people. He shall enter peaceably even upon the fattest places of the Province; and he shall do that which his fathers have not done, nor his father's fathers; he shall scatter among them the prey, and spoil, and riches: yea, and he shall forecast his devices against the strongholds, even for a time.

"And he shall stir up his power and his courage against the King of the South with a great army; and the King of the South shall be stirred up to battle with a very great and mighty army; but he shall not stand; for they shall forecast devices against him. Yea, they that feed of the portion of his meat shall destroy him, and his army shall overflow: and many shall fall down slain. And both these Kings' hearts shall be to do mischief, and they shall speak LIES at one table; but it shall not prosper: for yet the end shall be at the time appointed. Then shall he return into his land with great riches; and his heart shall be against the HOLY COVENANT; and he shall do exploits, and return to his own land.

"At the time appointed he shall return, and come toward the South; but it shall not be as the former, or as the latter. For the ships of Chittim (the Romans) shall come against him: therefore he shall be grieved, and return, and have indignation against the HOLY COVENANT: so shall he do; he shall even return, and have intelligence with them that forsake the HOLY COVENANT. And arms shall stand on his part, and they shall pollute the SANCTUARY OF STRENGTH, and shall take away the DAILY SACRIFICE, and they shall place the ABOMINATION THAT MAKETH DESOLATE."

The next King of the North was **Antiochus Epiphanes,** spoken of in the text as a **"VILE PERSON."**

He was the younger son of Antiochus the Great. He was given up to the most degraded and unnatural passions, was unscrupulous, cruel, and of a savage nature, but did not lack courage and ability. The **"honor of the Kingdom"** was not given to him, because his nephew, Demetrius, was the rightful heir. He was aided by Eumenes, King of Pergamum, and his brother Attalus. With their help his enemies, as the **"arms of a flood,"** were swept away, and the **"Prince of the Covenant,"** the Jewish High Priest Onias III, was deposed. He broke the **"League"** he made with King Eumenes and his brother, Attalus, when he persuaded the Romans to recognize him, and meanwhile he was working **"deceitfully,"** letting on that he had but a small following. But he soon became **"strong with a small people,"** and entered **"peaceably into the fattest places of the Province."** Unlike his predecessors, he was profuse and extravagant in his gifts, and **"scattered the spoil"** of his conquests among his friends, all the time **"forecasting his devices against the strongholds"** of Egypt, three of which, Pelusium, Naucratis, and Memphis, he later occupied, but failed to take Alexandria. This he did, **"even for a time,"** but was finally checked by the Romans.

When he was ready to invade Egypt, he marched against it with a very great army, and was met by an equally great army, which, after great losses, dissolved, and Ptolemy Philometer fell into the hands of Antiochus, probably betrayed by those that **"fed of the portion of his meat."** His brother Physcon was proclaimed King in his stead. Antiochus received Ptolemy Philometer with much consideration, concluded a peace with him on favorable terms, and then, on pretense of taking his part against his brother Physcon, laid siege to Alexandria, but without success. In the meantime, Philometer suspicious of Antiochus, and scheming for himself, made overtures to Physcon, on the basis of a joint sovereignty, and was received into Alexandria. Both brothers then declared against Antiochus. So the prophecy was fulfilled—**"these kings'** (Antiochus and Philometer) **hearts shall be to do mischief** (against each other), **and they shall speak LIES** (to each other) **at one table."**

Antiochus then returned toward Syria, loaded with the rich spoils of Egypt. On the march he heard, that, owing to a false report of his death, Jason, who had been deprived of his High Priestly Office, had made an attack upon Jerusalem, and had endeavored to recover his Office by force. Choosing to regard this as a revolt of the Jews, especially when he found that the news of his supposed death caused great joy among them, he assailed Jerusalem, slew 40,000 of the inhabitants, sold as many more as slaves, and plundered the Temple, carrying off treasure to the value of 1800 Talents. And, after thus venting his anger against the **"Holy Covenant"** (the Temple), he continued his march to Antioch. 2 Macc. 5: 11-21.

In the spring of B. C. 168, Antiochus again led his troops to Egypt in order to subjugate the two brothers, Ptolemy Philometer and Ptolemy Physcon. But the same success no longer awaited him, for the Ptolemies had appealed to Rome. Along the well-known route the Syrian King passed, no one daring to arrest his progress, until he was within four miles of Alexandria. A Roman fleet lay at anchor in the bay, and presently Antiochus was met by Popilius Laenas, who put into his hand a missive from the Roman Senate commanding him to leave the friends of the Roman people unmolested, and to be content with his own Kingdom. Having read it, Antiochus remarked that he would call his advisers and consult with them as to what was to be done. Whereupon Popilius drew a circle around him in the sand with his staff, and said—"Before you step out of that circle give such an answer as I may report to the Senate." The King was cowed, and replied—"If it so please the Senate, we will depart."

Antiochus then withdrew his army from Egypt and vented his fury upon the Jews of the "Glorious Land," in the fearful massacres, persecutions, and pollutions of the Temple, described in the first chapter of the first Book of Maccabees. In doing this he repaired the massive walls and towers of the Citadel of David, and garrisoned them with Syrian soldiers. He commanded that all his subjects should be one people, with one religion, and with the same laws. And, in order to enforce this upon the Jews, their Sanctuary was profaned, the offerings and sacrifices prohibited, and an **"Idol-Altar"** built over the "Altar of Jehovah," upon which swine's flesh was sacrificed, presumably to an Image placed over it. This was the **"Abomination that maketh desolate,"** spoken of in the text, but not the **"Abomination of Desolation"** spoken of by Christ in Matt. 24:15. That is still future. It is mentioned in Dan. 12:11, and will be the fulfilment of the **"Overspreading of Desolations"** of Dan. 9:27. Antiochus' stringent measures for the Hellenization of Judea caused the Maccabean revolt. In the meantime he had gone with an army into Persia, gaining many victories everywhere. Later he was forced to retire to Babylon. Heartbroken at the news of the Maccabean revolt in Palestine, he died a natural death at Tabae in B. C. 164.

It is very important right here to note that all that has been recorded from verse 21 to 31, inclusive, has reference to **Antiochus Epiphanes,** and not to the Antichrist, or any other person, and was **literally and completely fulfilled by him as foretold.** So there is absolutely nothing in these verses **left for the future.** There is no intimation that Antiochus Epiphanes is even to be regarded as a type of Antichrist. They are distinct historical personages, each dealt with in his own place, and though they resemble each other in some respects, on account of their conduct, and their treatment of the Jewish race, yet they must not be confounded with each other.

This Prophetic and Pre-Written historical account, recorded in verses 2-31, of the wars of the Persian and Grecian Empires, and more in detail of the Syrian and Egyptian Divisions of the Grecian Empire, extending from B. C. 536 to B. C. 164, a period of 372 years, is the most marvellous **"Prophetic Foreview"** in the whole Bible, because it goes into **details that only the Omniscience of God could reveal.** It is therefore one of the strongest confirmatory evidences to the Inspiration of the Word of God found within its pages.

THE PERIOD BETWEEN ANTIOCHUS EPIPHANES AND "MESSIAH THE PRINCE"

B. C. 164–A. D. 30

VERSES 32-33, "And such as do wickedly against the Covenant shall he corrupt by flatteries: but the people **that do know their God shall be strong,** and do **EXPLOITS.** And they that understand among the people shall instruct many."

The behavior of the Jews under the oppression of Antiochus Epiphanes is shown in verse 32. Some of them did **"wickedly,"** and **forsook the "Covenant," and the religion of their fathers, and worshipped idols,** and were led into this by **"flatteries."** But there were some who **"knew their God,"** that He was able to deliver, and so they were made **"strong,"** and did **"EXPLOITS."** This refers to Mattathias, an aged Priest, and his sons, known as the **MACCABEES,** who, from B. C. 166 to B. C. 47, fought to restore the national life of Israel. Mattathias, driven to desperation by the outrages of Antiochus, raised a revolt against him, and fled to the mountains with a number of followers, zealous for the faith of Israel. Two years later he died and was succeeded by his third son, Judas, known as "The Hammer," who by avoiding pitched battles, and by guerilla warfare, defeated and routed every Syrian army sent against him, and in B. C. 165 retook

Jerusalem, purified the Temple, and restored the daily sacrifice. He fell in battle in B. C. 160, and was succeeded by his younger brother Jonathan, a High Priest. During the leadership of Jonathan the Syrians were engaged in civil war, so Judea was left in peace, and Jonathan strengthened his position by making a treaty with the Romans and the Spartans. He was treacherously slain by a Syrian general in B. C. 143, and was succeeded by his brother Simon, the last remaining son of Mattathias. Simon and two of his sons were treacherously slain by his son-in-law in B. C. 135. His son John, known as John Hyrcanus, who escaped, succeeded him and had a long and prosperous reign. Others in the same line followed, with varying success, until the Maccabeans, falling into disfavor, were succeeded by the Idumaen, Antipater, in B. C. 47. After the murder of Antipater, B. C. 43, Marc Anthony visited Syria, and appointed two of Antipater's sons, Phasaelus and Herod, afterward known as "Herod the Great" (B. C. 37 to B. C. 4), to look after the Jews. Herod the Great was King when Christ was born in B. C. 4. Matt. 2: 1-15. From this we see that the Maccabees bridged the greater part of the period from Antiochus Epiphanes to the Birth of Christ.

During the latter part of this period a new class of spiritual leaders arose who **"understood"** the Prophetic Scriptures, and knew how to **"instruct"** the people. They were persons like Simeon and Anna, who waited for the "Consolation of Israel."

THE GAP BETWEEN "MESSIAH THE PRINCE" AND THE "TIME OF THE END"

A. D. 30 to A. D. ?

VERSES 33-35. "They shall **fall by the sword,** and **by flame, by captivity,** and **by spoil, MANY DAYS.** Now when they shall fall they shall be holpen (helped) with a little help: but many shall

> cleave to them with flatteries. And some of them of understanding shall fall, to try them, and to purge, and to make them white, even to the **TIME OF THE END**: because it is yet for a **TIME APPOINTED.**"

In the "fulness of time" Christ was born, and offered unto the Jews as their Messiah. But His claim was rejected, and He was Crucified ("cut-off"), and forty years later (A. D. 70) Jerusalem was destroyed by the Romans, and then began the fulfilment of the last half of verse 33, "they shall **fall by the sword,** and **by flame, by captivity,** and **by spoil, MANY DAYS.**" The **"Many Days"** are the days of this Dispensation Christ referred to them when He said—

> "They (the Jews) shall fall by the **edge of the sword,** and shall be **led away captive** into all nations, and Jerusalem shall be trodden down of the Gentiles, until the **'TIMES OF THE GENTILES'** be fulfilled." Luke 21:24.

All this is in process of fulfilment before our eyes. The Jews have been **"spoiled,"** that is, repeatedly robbed of their material possessions, for **"MANY DAYS."** Although they have **"fallen,"** they have not been exterminated, and from time to time they have been **"holpen** (helped) **with a little help."** They have been **"flattered"** and promised many things, but these promises have seldom, if ever, been fulfilled. Even now they are putting their trust in **ZIONISM,** and other schemes of men, for the rehabilitation of their own land, and their restoration to it. Some of their **"understanding ones,"** even in the time of Antichrist, will be deceived and **"fall."** But it will be for the purpose of **"purging"** (Ezek. 20:34-38), that is **"refining"** (Ezek. 22:19-22, Malachi 3:1-3, Zeck. 13:9) and purifying them and others by their example, even unto the **"TIME OF THE END."** Here we have the meaning and purpose of all the afflictions and persecutions of the Jews down the centuries, and even unto **THE END,** outlined in one verse.

The verses we have just considered cover the **"GAP"** between **"Messiah the Prince"** (A. D. 30) and the **"Time of the End"** (A. D. ?), and correspond with the "Gap" between Daniel's "69th" and "70th Week." Thus showing the consistency of all the "Visions" of Daniel, and proving that they relate only to Daniel's People (the Jews), and not to the Church, for in every instance the present Church Dispensation **is** conspicuous by its **omission.**

PART THREE

"The Time of the End"

Chaps. 11:36-12:13

"THE WILFUL KING"

VERSES 36-45—"And the **KING** shall do **according to his will**; and he shall **exalt himself,** and **magnify himself above every god,** and shall **speak marvellous things against the GOD of gods,** and shall prosper **till the INDIGNATION be accomplished**: for that that is determined shall be done. Neither shall he regard the **GOD of his fathers,** nor the **desire of women,** nor **regard any god**: for he shall magnify himself above all. But in His estate (in God's place) shall he honor the **'God of Forces:'** and a god **whom his fathers knew not** shall he honor with gold, and silver, and with precious stones and pleasant things. Thus shall he do in the most strongholds with a **strange god,** whom he shall acknowledge and increase with glory: and he shall cause them to rule over many, and shall divide the land for gain.

"And at the **'TIME OF THE END'** shall the King of the South push at him: and the King of the North (the Wilful King described above) shall come against him like a whirlwind, with chariots, and with horsemen, and with many ships; and he shall enter into the countries, and shall overflow and pass over. He shall enter also into the 'Glorious Land' (Palestine), and many countries shall be overthrown: but these shall escape out of his hand, even **EDOM,** and **MOAB,** and the chief of the children of **AMMON.** He shall stretch forth his hand also upon the countries: and the land of Egypt shall not escape. But he shall have power over the treasures of gold and of silver, and over **all the precious things of Egypt**: and the Libyans and the Ethiopians shall be at his steps.

"But tidings out of the **East** and out of the **North** shall trouble him: therefore he shall go forth with great fury to destroy, and utterly to make away many. And he shall plant the **'tabernacles of his palace'** between the Seas (the Mediterranean and Dead Seas) in the **'Glorious Holy Mountain;'** yet he shall **COME TO HIS END, AND NONE SHALL HELP HIM."**

The sudden and abrupt appearance of **"THE KING"** in verse 36 implies that he is one of whom we have **heard before,** and is not a new character, and therefore does not need to be again introduced. Notice that it does not say **"a"** King, but **"THE"** King. There are some who claim that there are **THREE** Kings introduced to us in the Book of Daniel. First, the **"LITTLE HORN"** of the "Fourth Wild Beast" (Dan. 7:8), or the last Roman Emperor. Second, the **"LITTLE HORN"** that came up on one of the "Four Horns" of the He-Goat (Dan. 8:9-12), that represented Antiochus Epiphanes. And third, the **"WILFUL KING"** of the chapter we are now considering, who represents the **"Antichrist."** If this be true, then there is no **"progressive revelation"** of the Antichrist in the Book of Daniel, as we have tried to show. That these three Personages, the two "Little Horns," and the "Wilful King," appear and reign at the **same time,** the **"TIME OF THE END;"** that they display the same **"Wilful disposition,"** and shall be **destroyed in the same manner,** implies that they are one and the **SAME PERSON.**

The fact that this **"Wilful King"** appears on the scene at the **close** of **"THE GAP"** between "Messiah the Prince" and the "Time of the End" (verses 33-35), and which corresponds, as we have seen, with the **"interval"** between the "69th" and "70th Week" of Daniel's "Seventy Weeks," **identifies** him with the **"PRINCE THAT SHALL COME"** of Dan. 9:26-27. And as the "Prince that shall come" shall be the last Roman Emperor, it identifies the "Wilful King" as the last Roman Emperor, and therefore the "Little Horn" of Daniel's "Fourth Wild Beast." Again in verse 40 this "Wilful King" is called the "King of the North." Some dispute this, claiming that the statement—"And at the 'Time of the End' shall the King of the South push at **him**: and the King of the North shall come against **him,"** that the pronoun **"him"** stands for the "Wilful King," and that the Kings of the "North" and "South" are **"colleagues"** banded together against him. But this is disproved by verses 42-43, where it says that the "King of the North" shall treat the "King of the South" as an **enemy** and shall spoil Egypt. What verse 40 means is, that at the "Time of the End," the "King of the South" shall push at **him** (the Wilful King): and the King of the North (the Wilful King) shall come against him (the King of the South). That is, the "King of the North" will return the attack of the "King of the South."

We know from our study of chapter 8, that the "Four Kingdoms" into which Alexander the Great's Empire was divided are to be revived, and that in the **"latter time of their kingdom"** a King of **"Fierce Countenance"** shall stand up. Dan. 8:21-23. Now one of those "Four Kingdoms" was **SYRIA,** known as the "Kingdom of the North," and as the "Little Horn" of chapter 8 appeared on the "Syrian Horn," then the King of **"Fierce Countenance"** of chapter 8 must be the "King of the North" of the revived "Syrian Kingdom," or the **"WILFUL KING,"** the "King of the North," of chapter 11. Here again we have proved that the "Little Horn" of chapter 7, the "Little Horn" of chapter 8, and the "Wilful King" are one and the same person.

Those who claim that the "Wilful King" is **"Antichrist,"** and not to be confounded with the last Roman Emperor, and that the **"Beast"** that comes up out of the **sea,** of Rev. 13:1-10, is the last Roman Emperor, while the **"Beast"** that comes up out of the **earth** (Rev. 13:11-18), and called three times the "False Prophet" (Rev. 16:13, 19:20, 20:10), is the **Antichrist,** forget that the "False Prophet" is **not a King.** His Office-work is to exalt the first Beast. So as he is **not a King,** and the "Wilful King" **is,** then if the "Wilful King" is **Antichrist,** the "False Prophet" cannot be, and vice versa.

The "Wilful King" shall do according to his **will.** He shall **"exalt"** and **"magnify HIMSELF above every god,"** and shall speak **"marvellous things"** against the **"GOD of Gods"** (Jehovah), and he shall prosper until the **"Indignation"** (The Great Tribulation) is accomplished, for that which God has **"determined"** for the **TIME OF THE END "shall be done."** He shall not regard the **"God of his fathers,"** the God of Abraham, Isaac, and Jacob. That means he will be a **JEW.** Neither shall he regard the **"desire of women."** If this means the desire of Jewish women to be the mother of the Messiah, and we must not forget that to the Jews the Messiah has not yet come, then he will not regard **THE SON,** and this characteristic of the Antichrist is foretold by the Apostle John, who says—"He is Antichrist, that **denieth the Father and the Son."** 1 John 2:22. But in His place (Jehovah's) he shall honor the **"God of Forces,"** or **"Fortresses."** That is, he shall depend on the **"god"** that can secure for him the Kingdoms of this world, and that is the **"God of this World** (Age)"—**SATAN,** who offered the "Kingdoms" of the world to Christ. Matt. 4:8-9. Christ refused them at the hand of Satan, for He knew that He would receive them at the hand of the Father (Dan. 7:13-14. Rev. 11:15). but the Antichrist will accept, for we read that—"the **DRAGON** (Satan) shall give him (the Beast) his **power,** and his **seat** (Throne). and **great authority."** Rev. 13:2. By the help of this **"strange god"** the "Wilful King" shall secure the **"strongholds"** (Fortresses), or the fortified cities, of the Ten Federated Kingdoms, and shall garrison them with Imperial troops on pretense of maintaining peace and concord. Thus he shall **"increase the glory"** of all who acknowledge him. and give them authority, and for **"graft"** (gain) he will divide the land.

At this time the "King of the South" reappears. Who he will be we do not know. But he will be one of the "Ten Federated Kings," for he is to appear after the "Four Kingdoms," into which Alexander's Empire was divided, shall reappear, and he will be some future King of Egypt who will oppose the claims and military success of the "Wilful King," the "King of the North." The "King of the North" will lose no time in opposing the "King of the South," and will swoop down on him like a **"whirlwind,"** with chariots, and horsemen, and a large navy, and shall overflow many countries. But Edom, Moab, and the land of Ammon shall escape. But the "Glorious Land" and Egypt shall not escape. He shall confiscate the treasures of Egypt, and the Libyans and Ethiopians shall fall at his feet.

But in the midst of his conquest of Egypt bad tidings shall come to him from the East, from Babylon, his Capital City, and from the North. These will fill him with rage, and he will depart from Egypt with **"great fury"** and will plant (pitch) the **"Tabernacles of his Palace;"** that is, the **"Royal Tents"** in which he dwelt while in the field, **"between the seas,"** the Mediterranean and Dead Seas, on the **"GLORIOUS HOLY MOUNTAIN."** And there, with none to help, he shall come to his end. See Zech 14.

MICHAEL THE PRINCE

> **VERSE, Chap. 12:1.** "And at **THAT TIME** shall **Michael** stand up, the **'Great Prince'** which standeth for the Children of thy (Daniel's) People."

Here again we see that there should be no chapter division, for there is no break in the subject treated. The twelfth chapter begins with the words, "And at **THAT TIME.**" What **TIME?** The time of the "Wilful King," which we have seen is the **"TIME OF THE END."** Dan. 11:40. At that time **Michael** shall stand up. Stand up for, and take the part of Daniel's People.

Who is Michael? He is mentioned three times in Daniel (Dan. 10:13, 21; 12:1), where he is called a "Prince" who stands for Daniel's People—the Jews. He is called in Jude 9 the Archangel. He has his angels, and in Rev. 12:7 he is seen in command of the "Angelic Army" of Heaven. His work seems to be to deliver God's people, particularly the Jews, from the power of Satan, and finally to oust him and his angels from the Heavenlies, and cast them down on to the earth. Rev. 12:7-9. He also has something to do with the resurrection of the dead, for he is associated with the "Resurrection" mentioned in Dan. 12:1-2, and he contested with the Devil the resurrection of Moses (Jude 9), and the **"voice"** of the Archangel that will be heard when the "Dead in Christ" shall rise (1 Thess. 4:16) will be the "voice" of Michael, for he is the only Archangel mentioned in the Scriptures.

THE GREAT TRIBULATION

> **VERSE 12:1**—"And there shall be a **'TIME OF TROUBLE,'** such as never was since there was a nation even to that same time: and at that time thy People shall be delivered, every one that shall be found written in the Book."

The Scriptures speak of a "Great Tribulation" that is coming on the earth. Christ in his "Olivet Discourse," uttered on the Mount of Olives on the Tuesday evening before His Crucifixion, said—

> "Then shall be **GREAT TRIBULATION** such as was not since the beginning of the world to this time, no, nor ever shall be. And except those days **should be shortened,** there should **no flesh** (human or animal) **be saved**: but for the **Elect's Sake** (the elect of Israel) those days **shall be shortened."**

That the "Great Tribulation" spoken of by Christ was not the terrible sufferings that befell the Jewish people at the time of the destruction of Jerusalem in A. D. 70 is clear. That was **local,** and fell upon the

Jews only, while the Tribulation that Christ foretold is to come upon **the whole world,** and is to be **immediately** followed by great **physical changes,** and the **return of the Son of Man in the clouds of heaven with power and great glory.**

> **"IMMEDIATELY after the Tribulation of those days** shall the **sun be darkened,** and the **moon shall not give her light,** and the **stars shall fall from heaven,** and the **Powers of the heaven** (the Principalities and Powers of Evil) **shall be shaken:** and then shall appear the Sign (a cloud) of the Son of Man in heaven: and then shall all the tribes of the earth mourn, and they shall see the **SON OF MAN COMING IN THE CLOUDS OF HEAVEN WITH POWER AND GREAT GLORY."** Matt. 24:29-30.

Now none of these things happened **immediately after** the Destruction of Jerusalem, nor have they happened **as yet.** It will not do to say that the **"physical changes,"** such as the darkening of the sun, etc., are figurative, and represent the downfall of rulers, governments and authorities from the Political Firmament, for such "physical changes" have happened before, and they will happen again. They happened in the days of Moses, when there was **"Darkness"** in Egypt for three days (Ex. 10:21-23), and they shall happen again when the **"Vials"** of the Book of Revelation are poured out, as they will be during the "Great Tribulation" (Rev. 16:1-21), for four of the **"Vial Plagues"** are repetitions of four of the Plagues of Egypt. And if they were literal so must the "Vial Plagues" be. Christ also said that at that time, the time of the "Great Tribulation," the **"Powers of the heaven shall be shaken."** Now these "Powers of the Heavenlies," the "Principalities and Powers of Evil," of which the Apostle Paul warns us (Eph. 6:12), have not **as yet** been shaken, but in the Middle of Daniel's "Seventieth Week," when the "Great Tribulation" begins, there will be "War in Heaven," and Satan, who is the **PRINCE** of these "Evil Powers of the Air," will, with them, not only be **shaken,** but **"shaken out"** of the Heavenlies onto the earth, and it will be his presence, incarnate in the Antichrist, that will cause the Great Tribulation. Once more, **immediately after** "The Great Tribulation" the **"Sign"** of the "Son of Man" will be seen in the heavens. That "Sign" is a **"cloud."** He ascended in a "cloud" and He is to return in the "clouds." Matt. 24:30. But as the "Son of Man" (Jesus) did not return **immediately after** the destruction of Jerusalem in A. D. 70, then the destruction of Jerusalem was not the "Great Tribulation" spoken of by Matthew.

But our Lord's Prophecy does not stand alone. It is backed up by other prophecies both in the Old and New Testaments. Turning to the Old Testament, we find that there were other Prophets beside Daniel who spoke of a "Time of Trouble" for Israel. Jeremiah called it the time of **"Jacob's Trouble,"** and compared its sufferings to the **"birth-pangs"** of a woman. Jer. 30:4-7. Ezekiel speaks of it as the time when Israel shall **"Pass under the Rod,"** Ezek. 20:34-38; and when God shall gather Israel into the midst of Jerusalem, and cast them into His **"Melting Pot,"** where they are to be refined as silver is refined. Ezek. 22:18-22. See also Zech. 13:9 and Malachi 3:1-3. While the Old Testament Prophets, and Christ, foretell of this "Time of Trouble," the Apostle John in the Book of Revelation (Rev. 12:1 to 19:21) gives us the details. From these references we see that the "Great Tribulation" will be a time of **JUDGMENT** for the Jews, through which, as a **"refining process,"** they will be made fit to again be God's chosen people. The "Great Tribulation" is not for the "perfecting" of the Saints. It has nothing to do with the Church. The Book of Revelation is written in chronological order, and the Church is "caught out" through the "Open Door" in chapter 4:1, before the "Tribulation Period" begins, and is not seen again until she reappears with Christ at His Second Coming as the "Lamb's Wife." Rev. 19:6-9. If the Church is to pass through the "Great Tribulation," then the Church should be **watching** for the Tribulation, and not **waiting** for His Son from Heaven. 1 Thess. 1:10. During Daniel's **"Time of Trouble"** all of Daniel's People whose names are written in the Book will be miraculously **"delivered."** These will be the **"godly remnant"** of the **"END TIME."**

A JEWISH RESURRECTION

VERSE 12:2—"And many of them that **sleep in the dust of the earth** shall awake, some to **everlasting life,** and some to **shame and everlasting contempt."**

The Scriptures speak of three kinds of resurrection. 1. **SPIRITUAL.** This refers to those who are **spiritually dead in "Trespasses and Sins."** Eph. 2:1-16; 5:14. Rom. 6:11. This is a **"Present Resurrection"** and is going on continually. Every time a soul is **"born again"** there is a passing from **"death"** unto **"life,"** this is a **"Spiritual Resurrection."** John 5:24. 2. **PHYSICAL.** This is of the **dead body.** The "Spirit" of man does not die, it goes back to God who gave it. All that goes into the grave is the **body,** and all that can come out of the grave is the **body.** The bodies of both the "Righteous" and the "Wicked" shall rise, but not at the same time. There will be a thousand years' difference. The "Righteous" shall rise to the **"Resurrection of LIFE"** before the Millennium, and the "Wicked" to the **"Resurrection of DAMNATION"** at the close of the Millennium. John 5:28-29.* 3. **NATIONAL.** This refers to Israel who are now **nationally dead** and buried in the "Graveyard of the Nations," but who are to be revived and restored to their own land. Jer. 16:14-15.

When the Children of Israel shall be restored to their own land the **whole "Twelve Tribes" will return.** Paul says—**"ALL** Israel shall be saved." Rom. 11:26. Ezekiel, in his Vision" of the **"Valley of Dry Bones,"**

*See the Chart on "The Resurrections" in the writer's book on "The Spirit World."

was told that the bones represented the **"Whole House of Israel."** Ezek. 37: 11. There are some who teach that what is here meant is, that previous to the Millennium God will resurrect all the descendants of Israel and put them back in the Land of Palestine, and they base it on the statement in Ezek. 37: 12—

> "Behold, O my People, I will open your **graves,** and cause you to **come up out of your graves,** and **bring you into the Land of Israel."**

Now such an interpretation cannot be true for several reasons. First, the Land of Palestine is not large enough to hold and sustain such a multitude, and secondly, this is not a description of a **physical** resurrection of **dead bodies,** but of a **"National Resurrection"** of a People. The cry of the **"bones"** (verse 11), where they say—"Our bones are dried, and our hope is lost: we are cut off for our parts," is not the cry of **individual dead** Israelites, but the cry of a **DEAD NATION** that has been "cut off" from its own land. It is the cry of a **Spiritually** and **Nationally dead People.** By the word **"graves"** we are not to understand **"literal graves,"** for the bones were **not in graves but scattered over the Valley.** Ezek. 37: 1-2. What the passage means is, that God is going to bring back His People Israel, who are **figuratively buried** in the **"Graveyard of the Nations,"** and place them again in their own land. This is clear from what follows—

> "I will open your **graves** (among the nations), and cause you to come up out of your graves (that is back from among the nations), and bring you into the **"Land of Israel."** Ezek. 37: 12, 21, 22.

Notice that nothing is said here of the opening of any graves in the **Land of Israel,** where the Patriarchs, Judges, Prophets and Kings of Israel were buried. This therefore could not be a **"General Resurrection"** of all the **DEAD OF ISRAEL,** but only of those who died in other lands. But the next two verses settle the question, for the Lord says—

"When I have opened your graves, O My People, and brought you up out of your graves (that is back in their own land), and shall put **MY SPIRIT** (Holy Spirit) **in you**, and ye **shall live** (Nationally) and I shall place you in your own Land (according to your Tribes, as described in Ezek. 48:1-29): **THEN** shall ye know that **I the Lord** have spoken it, and performed it." Ezek. 37:13-14.

This is in exact accord with other Scriptures that teach that Israel is to be gathered back into their own Land (Jer. 16:14-15. Isa. 43:5-7. Amos 9:14-15), where they are to pass through the **"Fiery Judgment"** of the **"Tribulation Period"** (Ezek. 20:34-38; 22:19-22. Zech. 13:9. Malachi 3:1-3), the sufferings of which will cause them to call on the Lord for deliverance, and He will pour out upon them the **"Spirit of Grace and Supplication"** (Zech. 12:10), and they shall **"Nationally Repent"** (Zech. 12:11-14), and be **"Converted"**—

"I will take you from among the Heathen (the Gentiles), and **gather you out of all countries**, and will **bring you into your own Land. THEN will I sprinkle clean water upon you**, and ye **shall be clean**: from all your filthiness, and from all your idols, will I cleanse you. A **New Heart** also will I give you, and a **New Spirit** will I put within you: and I will take away the **'Stony Heart'** out of your flesh, and I will give you an **'Heart of Flesh.'** And I will put **MY SPIRIT within you**, and cause you to **walk in My Statutes**, and ye **shall keep My Judgments, and do them.**" Ezek. 36:24-27.

Then will be fulfilled Isa. 66:8—

"Who hath **heard** such a thing? who hath **seen** such things? Shall the earth be made to bring forth in **ONE DAY?** or shall a **NATION be Born at Once?** for as soon as **ZION TRAVAILED** (the Tribulation was her **"birth pangs"**), she **BROUGHT FORTH HER CHILDREN.**"

Then a **"Nation,"** the **"Jewish Nation,"** shall be converted, or **"Re-born" IN A DAY.**

This interpretation of Ezekiel's Vision of the "Valley of Dry Bones" is confirmed by the "Object Lesson" of the **"Two Sticks"** that follow it. Ezek. 37 : 15-28. The Prophet was told to take a stick and write on it— "For **JUDAH** and for the **'Children of Israel'** his companions." Which means the "Two Tribes," Judah and Benjamin, known as **"Judah."** Then he was told to take another stick, and write on it—"For **JOSEPH,** the stick of **Ephraim."** Ephraim was the son of Joseph, for whom the "Ten Tribes" were sometimes called after Jeroboam's insurrection. When the Prophet had marked the "Sticks," he was told to join them together **"end to end,"** so as to make **ONE STICK,** which when He had done, the Lord said—

> "When the children of thy (Ezekiel's) people shall speak unto thee, saying, Wilt thou not shew us what thou meanest by these? . . . Say unto them. Thus saith the **Lord GOD;** Behold, I will take the 'Children of Israel' from among the heathen (Gentiles), whither they be gone, and will gather them on every side, and bring them into their **own Land,** and I will make them **ONE NATION in the Land** (Palestine) **upon the Mountains of Israel; and One King shall be King to them all: and they shall be no more 'Two Nations,' neither shall they be divided into 'Two Kingdoms' ANY MORE AT ALL."** Ezek. 37 : 18-22.

From this we see, that the **"WHOLE HOUSE OF ISRAEL,"** that is, the **Whole Twelve Tribes,** are to be gathered back to their own land, and redistricted upon it, according to the manner described in Ezek. 48. Then will be fulfilled the words of Jer. 3 : 18—

> "In those days the **'House of Judah'** shall walk with the **'House of Israel,'** and they shall come together out of the land of the **North** (the bulk of the Jews are in Russia) to the Land (Palestine)

that I have given for an inheritance unto your fathers."

Now we must not forget that in these "Scriptures of Truth" the Angel Gabriel was trying to make Daniel understand—"What shall befall his **PEOPLE** (the Jews) in the **LATTER DAYS"** (Dan. 10:14), or the **"TIME OF THE END."** Dan. 11:35; 12:4. Naturally therefore we should expect the Angel to have something to say about the **"National Resurrection"** of the Jewish Nation, and as it is to follow the **"Time of Trouble"** (Tribulation), how better could it be foretold than in the words of verse 12:2—"And many of them that sleep in the dust of the earth shall awake, some to everlasting life, and some to shame and everlasting contempt." If we claim that the words mean a **"physical resurrection of dead bodies"** we will find that the verse conflicts with the teaching of the New Testament as to the Resurrection. While, as we have seen, the New Testament teaches that there is to be an **OUT** Resurrection of the "Righteous" **before** the Millennium, and a thousand years before the "Wicked" rise, the verse we are considering declares, that while **many** (not all) shall rise, thus making it an **Out** Resurrection, some shall be to **"Everlasting Life,"** and some to **"Shame and Everlasting Contempt,"** thus making it a resurrection of a mixed character. Again the time of Daniel's Resurrection is **after** the **"Time of Trouble,"** while the New Testament declares that the **"First"** or **"OUT Resurrection"** of the Righteous **precedes** the Tribulation. But you say, there is to be a Resurrection of the "Righteous" **after,** or at the close, of the Tribulation, the Resurrection of the **"Tribulation Saints."** Rev. 20:4-6. This is true. But it is not a **mixed** Resurrection. It is only of those who died during the Tribulation, and who were beheaded for the **witness of Jesus,** and for the **word of God,** and who **did not worship the Beast.** In other words, a Resurrection of Righteous persons.

Some commentators try to get over the difficulty by paraphrasing the text. For instance, Tregelles translates the verse thus, "Many from among the sleepers of the dust of the earth shall awake; these shall be unto everlasting life, but those (the rest of the sleepers) shall be unto shame and everlasting contempt." But this is neither satisfactory or Scriptural, for it is only a separation into two classes of the **"many"** that rise, leaving the vast majority of the dead in the grave. While the words—**"sleep in the dust of the earth"** seem to imply physical death, and under ordinary circumstances would so mean, we must not forget that the verse refers to a condition of Daniel's people in their **"latter days."** Not a condition of **"death,"** but of **"National Existence."** If therefore we interpret the words **"sleep in the dust of the earth"** to mean the same as the words of Ezekiel—**"I will open your graves, and cause you to come up out of your graves"** (Ezek. 37:12), which we saw means a **"National Resurrection"** of the Jewish People of the **"End Time,"** the meaning of the verse is clear. That is, it means not a Physical or Spiritual, but a **"National"** Resurrection of the Jewish People **after** the Tribulation, and **before** the Millennium. That is where Christ in His Olivet Discourse puts it—

> **"Immediately after the Tribulation of those days** . . . shall appear the Sign of the Son of Man in heaven: and then shall all the tribes mourn (possibly the Twelve Tribes of Israel are meant), and they shall see the Son of Man coming in the clouds of heaven with power and great glory. And He shall send His angels with a great sound of a trumpet, and they shall **gather together His ELECT from the four winds, from one end of heaven** (the atmosphere of the earth) **to the other."** Matt. 24:29-31.

The **"Elect"** here are not those of the Church. They were caught out **before** the Tribulation. These are caught out **after** the Tribulation, and as the passage is Jewish, they must be the **"Elect"** of Israel. Notice it is not a **"catching up,"** but a **"gathering together."**

The scene is earthly. The Jews are looked upon at present as those that **"dwell in dust,"** but who are yet to **"awake and sing."** Isa. 26:19. The Apostle Paul says of them—"If the casting away of them (Israel) be the reconciling of the world, what shall the receiving (back) of them be but **LIFE FROM THE DEAD?"** Rom. 11:15. Israel, while lost, is not dead. The Prodigal Son, while lost, was called **"dead,"** but when he returned home his father said of him that he was **"alive again."** Luke 15:24. If we accept this interpretation of Israel's Resurrection, then the **"many"** that shall awake reveals the fact that not all the Jews in the world will return to Palestine, and that the **"some to Everlasting Life"** will be Righteous, while those to **"shame and Everlasting Contempt"** will be Unrighteous.

THE REWARD OF THE WISE

> **VERSE 12:3.** "And they (the Teachers) that be **wise** shall shine as the **'Brightness of the Firmament,'** and they that **turn many to righteousness** as the **Stars forever and ever."**

The marginal reading in the Revised Version for the word **"they"** is **"Teachers,"** and the passage should read—"And the **Teachers that be WISE,"** inferring that, as in our time, some will not be wise. We must not forget that the "Gospel of the Kingdom" shall be again preached, for it must be preached **in all the world** for a **witness unto all nations,** and then shall the **END COME** (the End of this Dispensation). Matt. 24:14. We must not forget that there are "Four Gospels" spoken of in the New Testament.

1. **The Gospel of the KINGDOM.**
2. **The Gospel of the GRACE OF GOD.**
3. **The GLORIOUS GOSPEL.**
4. **The EVERLASTING GOSPEL.**

The word "Gospel" means **"Good News."** The "Gospel of the Kingdom" is the "Good News" that God is going to set up a Kingdom of the earth over which David's Son, **JESUS,** shall reign. Luke 1:32-33. This Gospel was proclaimed by John the Baptist and Jesus and His Disciples, in the words—"Repent, for the Kingdom of Heaven is **at hand."** The call to repent was not to individuals but to the Nation. The Nation refused, rejected the King, and crucified Him. But before the King's death the "Gospel of the Kingdom," which up to that time had been preached **only in Palestine,** and not to **all the world,** was withdrawn. It is to be preached again after the Church has been "caught out," and then not only in Palestine but in the **whole world.** And as it is a call to Israel as a Nation to repent, and a proclamation that Christ is coming to set up the **"STONE"** (Dan. 2:34-35, 44-45) or Millennial Kingdom, the Kings of the earth, particularly Antichrist, will hate such a "Gospel" that proclaims the downfall of his Kingdom. This will account for Antichrist's hatred of the Jews, and his persecution of those who preach that Gospel.

Between the two preachings of the "Gospel of the Kingdom" we have the preaching of the **"Gospel of the Grace of God."** It is the proclamation of **Salvation** through faith in the **"Atoning Sacrifice"** of Christ on the Cross. The **"Glorious Gospel** is the Gospel of the **"Glorious Appearing,"** or **"Second Coming"** of our Lord and Saviour Jesus Christ. Titus 2:13. The **"Everlasting Gospel"** will be preached by an Angel just before the **"Vial Judgments"** are poured out on the earth, and it will be **"good news"** to all who are passing through the "Great Tribulation," because it declares that their sufferings will soon cease, and it will be **"bad news"** to Antichrist and his followers because it will proclaim that the **"hour of God's judgment"** for them has come. Rev. 14:6-7. **There is also "ANOTHER GOSPEL"** (Gal. 1:6-12, 2 Cor. 11:4), which is **not another,** and which Paul repudiated. **It is a perversion of the true Gospel, and has many se-**

ductive forms, and in the main teaches that **"FAITH"** is **NOT SUFFICIENT** to Salvation, nor able to keep and perfect, and so emphasizes **"GOOD WORKS."** Col. 2:18-23, Heb. 6:1; 9:14. The Apostle Paul pronounces a fearful **"Anathema"** upon its preachers and teachers. Gal. 1:8-9.

The **"wise"** teachers of the "End time" will be like the children of Issachar, "which were men that had **understanding of the Times."** 1 Chron. 12:32. They shall understand the Scriptures, and being mostly Jews, the Old Testament; particularly the prophecies relating to Israel. So prominent and noted will they be, they will shine as the brightness of the firmanent on a clear winter's night, and as "stars" in the "Prophetic Heavens," and like the great Prophets of old, Moses, Isaiah, Ezekiel and Daniel, they shall shine forever and ever. So true and clear and forceful will be their exposition of the Word of God, that it will convict the hearers and they shall turn many to righteousness.

THE SEALED BOOK

> **VERSE 12:4.** "But thou, O Daniel, shut up the words, and **SEAL THE BOOK,** even to the **'TIME OF THE END:'** many shall run to and fro (then), and **knowledge** (Prophetic Knowledge) shall be increased."

Notice the difference in the command to Daniel the Prophet, and John the Apostle. Daniel was told to **"SEAL UP"** the revelations given to him, while John was told to **"SEAL NOT"** the prophecies of the Book of Revelation. Rev. 22:10. And the reason is evident. When the Disciples came to Jesus and said—

> "Why speakest Thou unto them (the multitude, mostly Jews) in Parables? He answered and said unto them, Because it is given unto you (the Disciples) to know the **MYSTERIES of the Kingdom of Heaven,** but to them it is not given. . . . Therefore speak I to them in Parables: because they seeing see not; and hearing they hear not,

neither do they understand. And in them is fulfilled the Prophecy of Esaias (Isa. 6:9-12), which saith, By hearing ye shall hear, and shall not understand; and seeing ye shall see, and shall not perceive: for this people's (the Jews) heart is **waxed gross,** and their ears are **dull of hearing,** and their eyes **THEY have closed;** lest at any time they should see with their eyes, and hear with their ears, and should understand **with their heart,** and should **be converted,** and I should **heal them.**" Matt. 13:10-15.

From these words of Christ we learn that the Jews of His time were **"wilfully ignorant"** of the Prophetic Scriptures. They had ears to hear, but they did not understand, because they did not want to. And so, not to add to their sin, Christ had to unveil the **"Mysteries"** of the Kingdom of Heaven in Parables. And the reason was because the **"Veil of Unbelief"** was on their hearts. Of the Children of Israel, Paul says—

> "Their minds were **BLINDED:** for until this day remaineth the same **VEIL** untaken away in the **reading of the OLD TESTAMENT:** . . . Nevertheless when it (a man, R. V. margin) shall **TURN TO THE LORD,** the **'Veil' shall be taken away.**" 2 Cor. 3:14-16.

Therefore, as far as the Jews are concerned, the Book of Daniel is a **"sealed book."** But it is only sealed up to them until the **"Time of the End."** When that "Time" comes many of Daniel's People shall **"run to and fro,"** and their **"knowledge** (of the Book) **shall be increased,"** and they shall be comforted and sustained amid the sufferings and trials of that **"Time of Trouble."**

But the Book of Daniel is no longer sealed to the Christian believer. He has seen its prophecies being fulfilled in history. And now that the Book is being better understood, it is more and more studied, which is a sign of the near approach of the **"Time of the End."**

THE LENGTH OF THE "TIME OF THE END"

VERSES 12: 5-12—"Then I Daniel looked, and, behold, there stood other two, the one on this side of the bank of the River, and the other on that side of the bank of the River. And one said to the **'Man Clothed in Linen,'** which was upon the waters of the River, **How long shall it be to the END of these Wonders?**

"And I heard the **'Man Clothed in Linen,'** which was upon the waters of the River, when he held up his right hand and his left hand unto heaven, and sware by him that liveth forever that it shall be for a **TIME, TIMES, AND AN HALF;** and when he shall have accomplished to scatter the power of the Holy People, **all these things shall be FINISHED.**

"And I heard, but I understood not: then said I, O my Lord, what shall be the **end of these things?** And he said, Go thy way, Daniel: for the words are **closed up** and **sealed** till the **TIME OF THE END.** Many shall be purified, and made white, and tried; but the wicked shall do wickedly: and none of the wicked shall understand; but the **WISE shall understand.**

"And from the time that the **'Daily Sacrifice'** shall be taken away, and the **'Abomination that maketh Desolate set up,'** there shall be a **THOUSAND TWO HUNDRED AND NINETY DAYS.** Blessed is he that waiteth, and cometh to the **THOUSAND THREE HUNDRED AND FIVE AND THIRTY DAYS.**"

We must not forget that Daniel was still standing by the side of the River Hiddekel (Tigris), and that chapters 10 to 12 inclusive are one "Vision." Therefore the **"Man Clothed in Linen"** is the same mentioned in chapter 10: 5-6, and has been already described. But at this point in the "Vision" Daniel noticed two other angelic beings, one on each side of the River. One of them addressed the **"Man Clothed**

in Linen," supported in a cloud over the River, and asked—**"How long shall it be to the END of these Wonders?"** And the **"Man Clothed in Linen"** lifted up both hands and sware by the Almighty, that it should be for a **"TIME, TIMES, AND A HALF,"** or three and a half years.

Now there are two things in this answer, the **"Oath,"** and the **"Length of the Time,"** that remind us of Rev. 10:1-6. And as the Book of Revelation is the interpreter of the Book of Daniel we turn to the reference.

> "And I saw another **MIGHTY ANGEL** come down from Heaven, **clothed with a cloud**: and a **Rainbow was upon His head,** and **His face was as it were the sun,** and **His feet as pillars of Fire**: and He had in His hand a **'LITTLE BOOK' open**: and He set His **right foot** upon the **SEA,** and His **left foot** on the **EARTH,** and cried with a loud voice as when a **LION** roareth: and when He had cried **'SEVEN THUNDERS'** uttered their voices. And when the **'SEVEN THUNDERS'** had uttered their voices, I was about to write: and I heard a **'Voice from Heaven'** saying unto me, **SEAL UP those things which the 'SEVEN THUNDERS' uttered, and write them not.** And the **'ANGEL'** which I saw stand upon the sea and upon the earth lifted up His hand to Heaven, and **'sware'** by Him that **LIVETH FOREVER AND EVER,** Who created Heaven, and the things that therein are, and the earth, and the things that therein are, and the sea, and the things which are therein, that there should be **TIME NO LONGER** (delay no longer, R. V.)."

As the description of this **"MIGHTY ANGEL,"** in His appearance and actions, harmonizes with that of the **"MAN CLOTHED IN LINEN"** (Dan. 10:5-6; 12:6-7), they must be one and the same, or the Lord Jesus Christ. The description corresponds to that of Him as He stands in the midst of the "Lampstands" in Rev. 1:12-16, and we know that in the Old Testament He was called the **"ANGEL OF THE LORD"** (Ex. 3:2-18), and that the **"I AM"** of the Old Testament is the same as the **"I AM"** of the New Testament. John 6:35; 8:12; 10:9. Now as these closing chapters of Daniel deal with Israel, and as Christ was to them the **"ANGEL OF THE LORD,"** what more appropriate title could He have in chapters 6 to 19 of Revelation, that also deal mainly with Israel, than that of a **"MIGHTY ANGEL?"** The fact that He cried with a loud voice, as a **"Lion roareth,"** identifies Him as the **"LION OF THE TRIBE OF JUDAH."** Rev. 5:5.

This **"Mighty Angel,"** like the **"Man Clothed in Linen,"** swears by the Almighty, that there shall be **"TIME NO LONGER,"** or as the margin of the King James Version, and the Revised Version, translate it—**"DELAY NO LONGER."** And as the "Mighty Angel" uttered these words in the **"Middle"** of Daniel's **"Seventieth Week,"** there was only three and a half years to run or forty-two months (Rev. 13:5), which is the exact time given by the "Man Clothed in Linen," for forty-two months is equal to Daniel's **"TIME, TIMES, AND A HALF."** Verse 7. Thus we see that Daniel and Revelation agree as to the **LENGTH** of the **"Time of the End,"** and that it is given by the same Person, the Lord Jesus Christ.

While Daniel heard the answer, he did not understand the meaning, so he himself repeated the question, but no explanation was vouchsafed him, and he was told to go his way, for the words were **"closed up and sealed"** till the **"TIME OF THE END,"** when the **"WISE shall understand."** Then two other measures of time were revealed to Daniel, 1290 and 1335 days. These days were to date from the time when the **"Daily Sacrifice" was taken away,** and the **"Abomination of Desolation" set up,** which we know will be in the **"Middle"** of Daniel's **"Seventieth Week."** Dan. 9:27. Thus we have three measures of time given in Daniel, all dating from the **"Middle"** of his **"Seventieth Week."** First, the 2300 days of Dan. 8:13-14, and these two measures of 1290 and 1335 days. The termini of these three measures of time are respectively 1040, 30, and 75 days **beyond the "End"** of Daniel's "Seventieth Week." The 2300 days have to do with the cleansing of the Sanctuary, but we are not told what events the other two measures of time lead up to. But we do know that after the return of the Lord at the "End of the Week" there will be other events of national importance to the Jews, that will precede the setting up of the Millennial Kingdom.

DANIEL'S GLORIOUS LOT

VERSE 12:13—"But go thou thy way till the end be: for thou shall rest, and stand in **THY LOT** at the **END OF THE DAYS."**

Daniel was over ninety years of age. He had lived in Babylon, away from his beloved Land and City, for over seventy years. His life had not been an idle one. He had been active in the public affairs of two Empires. His religion had received the severest tests. God had honored him by taking him into His confidence, and revealing to him the history of the "Times of the Gentiles." In his last Vision he had the blessed privilege of seeing and hearing the voice of his Lord. But his work was done. The time for rest had come. So he was told to "go his way," depart to his home. and rest there until the summons came for him to make his "Exodus" from Babylon to the Heavenly Land. Then when the "Times of the Gentiles" have run their course, Daniel will stand in **HIS LOT.** What that **"Lot"** is to be we are not told. But if the Apostles are to be raised and sit on "Twelve Thrones," judging the "Twelve Tribes" of Israel (Matt. 19:28), what may not Daniel's lot be, who participated in the affairs of Empires, and was the trusted adviser of kings.

OTHER BOOKS BY THE SAME AUTHOR

Dispensational Truth

or

God's Plan and Purpose in the Ages

The book contains 34 chapters of descriptive matter and 42 splendid prophetical charts 9x20 inches, 48 one page charts, and 15 cuts. The charts and cuts are interspersed through the descriptive matter. There are 300 columns of reading matter, each column 4½x8½ inches, equivalent to any ordinary book of 450 pages. The charts are unique, simple, clear, uniform in style, and present every phase of "Dispensational Truth." The book is bound in cloth, atlas form, size 11x11 inches, and the large charts spread over two pages.

The book is the result of 30 years' study of "Dispensational Truth." It is **sane.** Not a **"time-setter."**. Contains no **speculative matter.** Is not made up of quotations from other writers, but is based solely on the Scriptures from the **"Futurist"** standpoint. It is of permanent value, and a standard authority on "Dispensational Truth," and is a mine of information on "Prophetic Truth" for the busy pastor, evangelist, Bible teacher, and all lovers of the Word.

This work is not an experiment. Is no longer in its elementary form, but has been revised and enlarged and is now in its fourth edition, is widely circulated over the world, is highly commended by leading prophetical scholars, and is being used in many Bible schools. The author has been a preacher and teacher of "Dispensational Truth" for 35 years, but only recently has put into printed form the result of his studies, with the hope that they may be a blessing to the world.

TITLES OF THE CHAPTERS

The Prophetic Word—Pre-Millennialism—Mountain Peaks of Prophecy—The Second Coming of Christ—Rightly Dividing the Word—The Present Evil World—The Dispensational Work of Christ—The Dispensational Work of the Holy Spirit—The Jews—The Gentiles—The Church—The King—The Kingdom—The Spirit World—Spiritism—The Resurrections—The Judgments—Satan—Antichrist—The Satanic Trinity—The Four Gospels—The Seven Churches—The Tribulation—Babylon the Great—Renovation of the Earth—The Covenants—The Mysteries—Types and Antitypes—The Feasts of the Lord—The Offerings—The Three Trees to Which Israel is Compared in the Scriptures—The Dispensational Teaching of the Great Pyramid—Scripture Numerics—The Signs of the Times.

TITLES OF THE CHARTS

(Only the Prominent Ones Named)

The Ages as Viewed From Different Standpoints—The Mountain Peaks of Prophecy—The Perspective of Prophecy—The Two Comings—7000 Years of Human History—Rightly Dividing the Word—Relation of Jew, Gentile and Church to Each Other—The Times and Seasons—The Creation of the Earth—Six Days of Re-Creation—7 Cosmic Phases of the Earth—Book of Genesis—The World's 7 Great Crises—The Prophetic Days of Scripture—Greater Life and Work of Christ—The Jews—Book of Exodus—The Royal Grant to Abraham—Book of Daniel—Prophetical Chronology—Daniel's Seventy Weeks—Map of Old Roman Empire—The Gentile Nations—The Church—Failure of Christianity—The King—Kingdom of God Versus Kingdom of Heaven—The Kingdom—The Church Versus the Kingdom—Kingdom of Heaven Parables—Book of Matthew—The Millennial Land—Book of Ezekiel—The Spirit World—Threefold Nature of Man—The Resurrections and Judgments—Judgment of Reward—Satan—Antichrist and "Times of the Gentiles"—The Four Gospels—When the New Testament Books Were Written—Book of Revelation—Messages to the 7 Churches—Daniel's Seventieth Week—Daniel and Revelation Compared—The Covenants—The Mysteries—Types and Antitypes—The Feasts of the Lord—The Tabernacle—Book of Leviticus—The Great Pyramid—Christ and the Saints Compared to the Heavenly Bodies—The Weeks of Scripture—The Signs of the Times.

The Book of Revelation

This book is the result of 25 years' study of the Book of Revelation. The Book is interpreted from the Futurist Standpoint The writer's purpose is to show that the Book is to be taken literally, and that it is written in chronological order. The text of the Old Version is used, and is printed at the top of each subject. The text and descriptive matter is emphasized by the use of capitals and black type.

The book is illustrated with over 30 charts, maps, and diagrams. There are also numerous cuts of the symbols, beasts, etc., spoken of in the Book of Revelation, distributed through the book. These help to elucidate the text and add to the value of the book, and save much explanatory matter. The make-up and printing of the book is unique. The divisons and headings of the subjects are all printed in heavy black type. This adds to the cost of the book, but makes the subject matter of the book stand out in bold relief. While there are but 225 pages in the book, the size of the tvpe, and the enlarged page, 6 x 9 inches, make it equivalent to an ordinary book of 400 pages.

The book is sane, contains no speculative matter, nor opinions of the writer. The book is not a commentary made up of quotations from other writers. The writer is neither a copyist nor compiler. The only **Author** the writer has sought to follow is the Author of the Book, the **LORD JESUS CHRIST.** He has simply sought to interpret the **"MIND OF CHRIST"** as revealed in the Book of Revelation. The writer's aim has been to prepare a standard work on the Book of Revelation, from the Futurist Standpoint, that can be used as a text-book in Theological Seminaries and Bible Schools, and a help to Ministers, Missionaries, and Bible Students, generally. Its appearance at this time is timely, when the prophetic utterances of the Book of Revelation are rapidly approaching their fulfilment.

Rightly Dividing The Word

THIS BOOK COMPARES IN VALUE WITH THE BOOK ON "DISPENSATIONAL TRUTH." ITS PURPOSE IS TO "RIGHTLY DIVIDE THE FUNDAMENTAL DOCTRINES" IN A SERIES OF "CONTRASTS," AS "LAW AND GRACE," "FAITH AND WORKS," ETC.

The author has made it the work of his ministry to preach the "Fundamentals." This volume contains the cream and meat of his sermons and Bible lectures. The book contains twenty-nine chapters and fifty-five charts. The charts are one page charts, clear and simple, and suitable for lantern slides, or biopticon, in Bible class work. The book contains 330 pages, and is bound in cloth.

CHAPTERS

Rightly Dividing the Word—Ages and Dispensations—Jew and Gentile—Church and Kingdom—The Four Gospels—The Two Advents—The Spirit World—Satan—The Satanic Trinity—"The Mystery of Godliness" and "The Mystery of Iniquity"—Resurrection of Jesus—The Resurrection—The Judgments—The Two Adams—Atonement and Redemption—Sin and Salvation—Law and Grace—Faith and Works—The Two Natures—Standing and State—Regeneration and Baptism—Election and Free-will—The Reciprocal Indwelling of Christ and the Believer—The Threefold work of Christ—Christ Our Passover—Heaven and Hell—Judaism and Christianity—The Circles of the Christian Life—Palace Beautiful.

CHARTS

The Prophetic Days of Scripture—The Times and Seasons—Ages and Dispensations—The Three Stages of the Earth—The Prophetic Earth—First and Second Re-creative Days—Third and Fourth Re-creative Days—Fifth and Sixth Re-creative Days—The Dispensation of Judgment—The Jews—The Five Great World-Wide Kingdoms—The Gentiles—The Church—The Church Versus the Kingdom—Kingdom of God—Kingdom of Heaven—The Church—The Four Gospels—The Two Comings—The Mountain Peaks of **Fourth Re-creative Days—Fifth and Sixth Re-creative Days—The Dispensation of Judgment—The Jews—The Five Great World-Wide Kingdoms—The Gentiles—The Church—The Church Versus the Kingdom—Kingdom of God—Kingdom of Heaven—The Church—The Four Gospels—The Two Comings—The Mountain Peaks of**